T0419812

Becoming couture

Manchester University Press

To buy or to find out more about the books currently available in this series, please go to: https://manchesteruniversitypress.co.uk/series/studies-in-design-and-material-culture/general editors

general editors

SALLY-ANNE HUXTABLE

ELIZABETH CURRIE

LIVIA LAZZARO REZENDE

WESSIE LING

founding editor

PAUL GREENHALGH

Becoming couture
The Italian fashion industry after the Second World War

Chiara Faggella

Manchester University Press

Published by Manchester University Press
Oxford Road, Manchester, M13 9PL

www.manchesteruniversitypress.co.uk

British Library Cataloguing-in-Publication Data
A catalogue record for this book is available from the British Library

ISBN 978 1 5261 5524 5 hardback

First published 2024

The publisher has no responsibility for the persistence or accuracy of URLs for any external or third-party internet websites referred to in this book, and does not guarantee that any content on such websites is, or will remain, accurate or appropriate.

Typeset by Newgen Publishing UK

Per Corrado, Emil e Gianluca

Contents

List of figures   viii
Acknowledgements   x

Introduction   1

1   Rome: new standards of fashion   11

2   New York: from handicrafts to fashion   37

3   Florence: old culture and new commerce   67

4   Across the United States: *Italy at Work*   96

5   Fashion councils of Turin, Milan, and Rome   128

6   Florence: a new experience of couture   162

Conclusion   199

Bibliography   212
Index   223

List of figures

1.1	Italian footwear	23
1.2	Mita Corti photographed by Genevieve Naylor	31
2.1	Advertisement for Barra gloves	49
2.2	Shopping tips recommending Barra gloves	50
2.3	Handbags from the House of Italian Handicrafts	55
2.4	Fornasetti screens from the House of Italian Handicrafts	56
2.5	Fornasetti screen photographed by CADMA, spring of 1948	57
2.6	Fornasetti screen photographed by CADMA, spring of 1948	58
3.1	Mario Vannini Parenti with New York Mayor Fiorello La Guardia and Italian Consul-General Gaetano Vecchiotti, ca. 1937	69
3.2	Gucci bag	73
3.3	Three Ferragamo shoes	74
3.4	Ferragamo advertisement by Saks Fifth Avenue	75
3.5	From the invitation to the 1947 Neiman Marcus Award for Distinguished Service in the Field of Fashion: description of the event	76
3.6	From the invitation to the 1947 Neiman Marcus Award for Distinguished Service in the Field of Fashion: list of honorees	77
3.7	From the invitation to the 1947 Neiman Marcus Award for Distinguished Service in the Field of Fashion: cover reproducing the symbols of the honorees' home countries	78
3.8	Advertisement for Terragni of Como textile manufacturer and its New York agent Domenico Orsi	90
4.1	Skirt by Irene Kowaliska, from the exhibition catalogue of *Italy at Work: Her Renaissance in Design Today*, 1950	102
4.2	Ingrid Bergman wearing a Kowaliska skirt	104

4.3   Short article and photographs on Maria Chiara Gallotti,
      Tessitrice dell'Isola   105
4.4   Full shot of a woman modelling a Tessitrice dell'Isola
      shawl. From the press pack of *Italy at Work: Her
      Renaissance in Design Today*, 1950   106
4.5   Alternate styling of a Tessitrice dell'Isola shawl. From
      the press pack of *Italy at Work: Her Renaissance in Design
      Today*, 1950   107
4.6   'Mediterranean fashion accessories' at the M.H. De Young
      Memorial Museum of San Francisco display of the *Italy at
      Work: Her Renaissance in Design Today* exhibition,
      18 June–31 July 1951   109
4.7   Ferragamo advertisement for The White House department
      store   110
4.8   Installation view of *Italy at Work: Her Renaissance in Design
      Today* at the Brooklyn Museum with Giuliana Camerino
      bucket bag 'Apache', 1950   111
4.9   Giuliana Camerino, 'Apache' bucket bag. *Bellezza*, April 1950   112
4.10 Meyric R. Rogers wearing a straw jacket   117
4.11 Advertisement for the *Italian Artisans Exposition* at Watson
      & Boaler   120
5.1   Images from *Mostra Nazionale Arte Moda* in Turin   135
5.2   Images from *Mostra Nazionale Arte Moda* in Turin   136
5.3   Carosa cocktail dress shown during the Venice Film Festival   141
5.4   Cynthia Cochrane Dunn wearing Sorelle Fontana, by
      Federico Pallavicini   146
5.5   Advertisement for the J.L. Hudson Italian couture collection   150
5.6   *Women's Wear Daily*'s report of the Italian couture
      collection at J.L. Hudson, Detroit   151
5.7   Cover of *Harper's Bazaar*, May 1950   155
5.8   Italian knitwear by Mirsa   156
6.1   Andrew Goodman of Bergdorf Goodman at the Second
      Italian High Fashion Show, July 1951   169
6.2   Evening gown by Simonetta Visconti   174
6.3   French 'boutique' fashions   177
6.4   'Marvelous' Italian leather handbags   180
6.5   Boboli garden fashion shoot   183
6.6   Mario Vannini Parenti, First Lady of Italy Donna Carla
      Gronchi, and Giovanni Battista Giorgini. Thirteenth Italian
      High Fashion Show, 23 January 1957   191
7.1   Inscription from the 1956 *Calendario Giorgini*   201
7.2   Ambassador of the United States to Italy James C. Dunn
      and his wife photographed at the Venice Film Festival   203
7.3   ENIT advertisement promoting the 'new exciting'
      Italian couture   207

Acknowledgements

As often happens with academic projects, this book has been several years in the making and therefore the list of people who contributed in one way or another goes way back in time. From the outset, this research project was generously funded by the section for Fashion Studies at the Department of Media Studies, Stockholm University and by the Erling-Persson Family Foundation in Stockholm, Sweden. I am grateful to the Robert Schuman Centre for Advanced Studies and the History and Civilization Department at the European University Institute in Florence for hosting me as a visiting fellow in 2019–20. The opportunity to experience their interdisciplinary community greatly helped me step outside the 'fashion bubble' and ground my project within a more heterogeneous context of interconnected references. My participation in the FARB 2021 research project 'VO Project | Voices of Objects. The Italian Design from Museum to Home', financed by the Department of Design at Politecnico di Milano, Italy, was the logical position for me to conclude a book with so much to say about the impact of the travelling exhibition *Italy at Work: Her Renaissance in Design Today* on Italian fashion.

In its final stretch, the book suffered the unexpected strains caused by a global pandemic, which made it seem for a while that the pleasures and perils of archival research were over for good. Luckily they were not, so I could expand further the list of people that I wish to thank for their support and for facilitating my visits to archives and libraries: Roberto Fuda at Archivio di Stato in Florence; Stefania Ricci, Ludovica Barabino, Chiara Fucci, and Eleonora Geppi at Fondazione Ferragamo; Elizabeth St George and Monica Park at the Brooklyn Museum Libraries and Archives in New York; Rebecca Perry and Marci Morimoto at The Costume Institute, The Metropolitan Museum of Art; Francesca Pozzi and Sara Meoni at Fondazione Licia e Carlo Ludovico Ragghianti in

Lucca; Pandelis Nastos at the Historical Archives of the European Union in Florence; Claudia Urbanelli at Liceo Artistico Statale di Porta Romana in Florence; Charles Doran and AnnaLee Pauls at the Special Collections division of Princeton University Library; Christine S. Windheuser at the Archives Center of the National Museum of American History, Smithsonian Institution; Brooke Guthrie at the David M. Rubenstein Rare Book & Manuscript Library at Duke University in Durham, North Carolina; and the staff at Archivio Centrale dello Stato, Rome.

A fashion history book could not be published without illustrations and thus I am very grateful for the support provided by many in this crucial matter: Viviana Damiano at Biblioteca '*Fiamma Lanzara*', Accademia Costume & Moda, Rome; Erin Harris at The Richard Avedon Foundation; Leigh Grissom at the Center for Creative Photography, Arizona Board of Regents; Wendy Israel at Hearst Magazines; Debbie Paitchel, Jina Park, and Bridget Schelzi at PMC Archive for Fairchild/*Women's Wear Daily*; Cole Hill and Jasmine Kennedy at Condé Nast; Vittorio Pavan at Archivio Cameraphoto Epoche; Roberto Gollo and Tiziana Porro at Biblioteca Nazionale Braidense in Milan; Luca Mulazzi at Biblioteca Centrale del Campus di Rimini, Alma Mater Studiorum – Università di Bologna; Raffaella Pipitone at ENIT Spa; and Hugh Chatterton, Chris Cotton, and Noah Tjijenda at ProQuest/ Clarivate. My deepest gratitude goes to the Pasold Research Fund for the Publication Grant I received to fund the inclusion of images.

I am indebted to those who shared with me their invaluable first-hand knowledge and memories: Roberto Capucci, who welcomed me into his house to talk about the splendours of fashion past; Clelia Bruno Marzili, to whom I owe my deepest gratitude for letting me share her professional experience as a fashion buyer in the golden years of the Florentine Shows; Giovanni Battista Giorgini, Giovanni Battista Fadigati, and Neri Fadigati, for their precious family memories; and Letizia Pagliai, who generously eased me into a research path that started where hers had ended.

This book could not have been made without the patience and support of Emma Brennan and Alun Richards at Manchester University Press, for which I am thankful. Through the years people have read the book's manuscript at various stages of its development, giving their insights and suggestions: I am extremely grateful to Vittoria Caterina Caratozzolo, Lauren Downing Peters, Caroline Evans, Andrea Kollnitz, Maaret Koskinen, Ulrika Kyaga, Klas Nyberg, and Marco Pecorari. The generosity of David W. Ellwood, Stephen Gundle, and Véronique Pouillard in their feedback and their support of my ideas deserves a special mention. My gratitude goes also to Giorgio Riello, at the History and Civilization Department of the European University Institute, who helped me conceive the overall shape of this book and set boundaries to limit the scope of my many digressions over the topic of fashion intermediaries. At Politecnico di Milano, Paola Cordera gave me the possibility to exit the 'Giorgini' tunnel, connect the final dots with the monumental *Italy at Work: Her Renaissance in Design Today* exhibition, and share a mutual love for archival anecdotes in an exciting research project.

Since the beginning of my scholarly path, Alessandra Vaccari has been my voice of reason, a model of integrity, and a source of inspiration that today I am happy to call my friend. My dear friends and colleagues Elizabeth Castaldo Lundén and Sara Skillen held my hand along the way, providing technical and academic advice, and, most importantly, their precious friendship. A heartfelt mention goes to my parents, who have been supportive of my career whatever turn it might take and wherever it might take me. My sons kept my spirits high and my heart full, while they were incredibly patient with me and with the demands of academia. Last but not least, to Gianluca, who bears with me since 1997 and has been my most encouraging supporter: I am and will always be, just like always/still your passenger.

Introduction

It was a bright spring morning in 2017 when I entered a sunny rooftop apartment in downtown Rome and, in a vibrantly colourful drawing room decorated by old pictures and works of art, I was introduced to fashion designer and artist Roberto Capucci. I consciously took that short trip to Rome and visited the last living legend of the Italian fashion history of the twentieth century because, at the time, the preliminary steps of my research were enmeshed in a seemingly immobile discourse that I kept on reading in the press and many academic works alike. It appeared that the man who had 'invented' Italian fashion was a certain Giovanni Battista Giorgini, who, in 1951, had the clever intuition of setting up the first fashion show exclusively organized for American clients in Florence. Giorgini, a commissionaire with a background in the trade of handicrafts, antiques, and home- and giftware, had developed a network of contacts with department stores, decorators, and retailers operating in the United States.[1] The same contacts helped him organize the First Italian High Fashion Show in Florence on 12 and 14 February 1951, a two-day presentation of all-Italian models and accessories for American buyers and manufacturers. As interests in international trade grew, the Shows established themselves as biannual events, becoming larger and their press coverage growing more prominent each year. Eventually, ensuing the developments of the ready-to-wear industry and the shift towards Milan as a relevant site of cultural and industrial production of fashion, the Shows slowly morphed into what is now Pitti Immagine.[2] That was, by and large, the extent of the history of fashion Made in Italy in the postwar years and its launch. The trip to Rome made me extremely excited about the possibility of discussing the 'behind the scenes' of the founding myth of Italian fashion, since Capucci, who first opened his dressmaking shop in 1950, was one of the few Italian designers invited to participate in the First Italian High Fashion

Show of 1951. During our talk, Capucci fondly remembered the beginning of his career and the role that Giorgini played in it:

> I just opened my dressmaking shop, and my managing director went to Florence, with all my drawings. Giorgini ... came to meet me in Rome the following day. Then he told me: 'You are still nobody, so I cannot put you in [the Shows] with the other ones.' Yet in the end, he gave me a much bigger privilege because he asked me to design [gowns] for his family, his daughters and wife, for the gala evening at the end of the fashion show. Then he had an idea: 'Make me five tableaux: five *tailleur*, five coats, five cocktail [dresses], five evening [dresses], as you want, so that during the party ... I will present this new designer'[3] ... This caused incredible jealousy because all the other dressmakers ... banned me from showing my five tableaux. I was devastated because I prepared all those dresses! So Giorgini, who was really a brilliant man, told me: 'Look, we will fix everything. Just come [and sit] at my table during the party, with your *directrice*, and we will fix it.' And indeed, as [it happens with] all things prohibited, it aroused curiosity in the press: everyone came to interview me ... so, I came out of it like a boom![4]

Thus, concluded the designer, it was Giorgini who triggered his remarkable career path. From that moment on, the designer's fame grew considerably, including a parenthesis in Paris during the early 1960s, a fashion brand still active today, and a foundation in his name. I was indeed familiar with this narrative since I had read Capucci's story before in newspapers, magazines, and exhibition catalogues. Yet, while hearing it directly from Capucci felt like an immense privilege, when I left the meeting I could not help but think how the almost legendary qualities of Giorgini's intuition had crystallized even into Capucci's own story and had established a mythologized place in the history of Italian fashion. I soon realized I was not alone in this feeling: when I finally got hold of an exhibition catalogue from 1985, I realized that even art historian Arturo Carlo Quintavalle had stumbled upon the same methodological halt and observed how, for those 'who played leading roles on the fashion scene, the reconstruction of events is tainted with mythology', further encouraging me to realize that the emergence of an Italian fashion scene of the postwar period 'as if conjured up by the magic wand of Giorgini in 1951' was covered by thick rhetorical tropes and a series of well-circulated promotional discourses that had trickled down into academic works.[5]

In April 1951 the Italian fashion magazine *Bellezza* published an editorial by Florentine journalist Margherita Cattaneo, describing how Italian fashion was finding its way to America through the city of Florence. Cattaneo described how commissionaire Giovanni Battista Giorgini had just recently caught the attention of Florence's high society by organizing an extremely exclusive fashion show in his home the previous February. During this First Italian High Fashion Show, a small group of Italian dressmakers presented innovative and original fashion designs, bearing no reference whatsoever to current Parisian styles and trends. The audience, a small number of US and Canadian buyers and a handful of Italian journalists, avowed the success of the event. Giorgini's Show had indeed responded to the complaints of those who, especially through the pages of *Women's Wear Daily*, lamented difficulties in selecting Italian export goods: dressmakers were distributed in far too many locations across the country, and the quality of fashion merchandise was often reported as uneven. The intuition of Giorgini was celebrated by Cattaneo, who argued that it all had been possible thanks to his long-standing experience with Made in Italy exports to America.[6] As the popularity of the Italian High Fashion Shows grew through the years, journalists in Italy and abroad chimed in to confirm the confidence and willpower of Giorgini in devising such an innovative platform for Italian fashion. Misia Armani, one of the few journalists invited that evening, wrote in the magazine *Omnibus* that 'for the first time, and it must be said immediately, thanks to that magician that Giorgini is, the most important American buyers, many of them coming from Paris, were brought together in the presence of the leading Italian dressmakers'.[7] Vera Rossi Lodomez chimed in:

> As is always the case when an honest, intelligent, and proactive person sets out to do something he has never done before, Mr. Giorgini has dedicated himself to the fulfilment of this project with that freshness and naivety (we mean the word naïve in the best sense) that are excellent cards in the hands of those who know how to play them ... The enthusiasm, confidence and determination of this smiling Florentine gentleman attracted everyone.[8]

The attractive novelty that the Fashion Shows represented quickly circulated in the discourses of the Italian press, finally celebrating the alleged supremacy of Italian fashion against Paris and its dominance. This flattering narrative, found in newspapers, weeklies, and fashion magazines of the 1950s, was the result of a careful public relations strategy. As such, it was repeated in early historical accounts that sought to identify the beginnings of Italy's participation in the international fashion circuit and was thus institutionalized. The earliest works documenting the impact of Giorgini in the history of Italian fashion combined fragmented oral histories, collected from fashion professionals, within the framework of the official narrative provided by Giorgini's daughter Matilde.[9] Following the sudden death of Giorgini in 1971, the influence of his daughter Matilde's memories, her reluctance to open the archive to the public, and the desire to protect her father from posthumous criticism heavily shaped portrayals of Giorgini in fashion literature.[10] Indeed, for quite some time popular culture and academic contributions alike displayed an almost hagiographic quality to their narratives, in which the Italian High Fashion Shows were described as a sudden, absolute success, and in which authors offered convoluted praise to the genius of Giorgini, such as the creation of an atmosphere that 'titillated the snobbish weaknesses of the American guests'.[11] As the field of fashion studies became more institutionalized in academic settings, studies in Italian fashion history enjoyed increasing scientific thoroughness and further comparisons with international research, resulting in the development of contributions that are more objective and multidisciplinary. The impact of Giorgini was re-evaluated, in this sense, by studies that eschew the nation-state paradigm, emphasize the transatlantic exchange that he was part of, and contextualize the network of intermediaries with whom he shared similar goals.[12]

This book originates as an attempt to closely read the celebratory narrative destined for Giorgini until the early 2000s through the lens of the historical perspective outlined in *The Historian's Craft*, the posthumous book written by French historian Marc Bloch. The preoccupation with origins is what Bloch calls the obsession of historians. To him, 'the word origin is disturbing because it is ambiguous'[13] and its ambiguity derives from two aspects: the first is the difficulty of singling out a phenomenon's beginnings, since the definition of a starting point is, for its nature, arbitrary; the second aspect originates from the assimilation of meaning that 'origins' and 'explanation' share in popular usage: 'an origin is a beginning which explains. Worse still, a beginning which is a complete explanation'.[14] The tendency to magnify the extraordinary momentum gained in 1951 attributed the sudden success of the Italian High Fashion Shows to a limited number of fixed causes: the ingenuity of Giorgini in the organization, the simplicity of designs, and their competitive prices. Focusing on the First Show as a predetermined origin, the attention was lost on the conditions that had allowed for its establishment. The book thus discards the notion of an 'origin' of Italian fashion as non-productive in general, and in particular with the Italian High Fashion Shows, since the identification of Giorgini with the absolute beginnings of Italian fashion has fallen into the 'fetish of the single cause', which for Bloch resolved in 'the search for the responsible person – hence a value judgement'.[15] Drawing upon Bloch's paradigm and reconnecting with the many valuable scholarships that have discussed the impact of Fascism on the developments of Italian fashion, the book argues that the historiography of Italian fashion is not so simple and linear as it has appeared so far. There never was a clear watershed dividing the accomplishments of the Italian fashion industry from its recent Fascist past, therefore the book sets out to contextualize the appearance of the Florentine Shows with preceding and parallel events. In this perspective, the book performs an analysis of the antecedents that constituted both causation and context for Giorgini's affirmation in the transatlantic circuit of fashion promotions.[16]

Many historical studies have now reassessed the period of Fascism in Italy as a considerable background to the postwar developments of Italian couture and fashion merchandise. While this book does not directly address the period coinciding with the Fascist *ventennio*, it acknowledges some of the actors that were active in that period to find continuities between pre- and postwar times within the 'microhistories' of the intermediaries and tastemakers mapped out.[17] The national fashion council Ente Nazionale della Moda and its fashion magazine, *Bellezza*, both especially crucial in the development of a discourse revolving around the necessity of a national fashion industry, remained key references in the historical narratives tackling the 'origins' of Italian fashion. In the early 2000s three seminal texts by Sofia Gnoli, Eugenia Paulicelli, and Mario Lupano and Alessandra Vaccari challenged traditional historiography and the historical resistance to deem the cultural politics of Fascism as worth taking into consideration. They transformed a concept, the origins of the distinctiveness of Italian fashion, by pushing it backwards and rooting part of its foundations in this controversial period of Italy's political and cultural history.[18] Although with different approaches, these texts reveal how the intention to structure the Italian fashion system was already developed in the Fascist period in a multidimensional manner, rejecting the idea of interwar fashion as negligible because of its being simply Fascist and revising the standpoint according to which the postwar years represented the clear watershed for the stylistic independence of Italian designers. According to Paulicelli in particular, 'Italian fashion was not born in the period of reconstruction … The great strides forward that the Italian fashion industry took in the years following 1945 … were posited on what the industry had already achieved in the prewar period'.[19] In this book's assessment of the intermediaries contributing to developing the postwar Italian fashion exports, the Fascist period provides a framework both for biographical issues concerning several intermediaries involved with the Italian fashion industry, but also for retracing the use of certain themes that would build up a steady national identity in fashion, among which the Renaissance as a historical backdrop to the value of Italian craftsmanship in fashion was a key component and will be discussed further in Chapter 6.

This book outlines the conditions that prepared the establishment of Italy in the transatlantic trade of fashion and investigates the earliest promotions and publicity instances involving Italian fashion in the American press. It maps out the circulation of discourses constructed by American and Italian intermediaries around Italian fashion exports. It explores primary sources relating to their activities and business efforts in the cultural and commercial aspects of the Italian fashion industry: production, retail, promotion, and publicity. The work of intermediaries is seen through their business documents and the accounts of the press, guided by the definition given by Regina Lee Blaszczyk, according to which there is a need to understand the historical and social realities of fashion through an in-depth study of activities 'behind the scenes', interposed between production and consumption.[20] The analysis is centred around the actions of six main intermediaries, whose programmes are addressed in different chapters of the book: the cluster comprising of Handicraft Development, Inc., the House of Italian Handicrafts, the Florentine office of CADMA, and Compagna Nazionale Artigiana; the G.B. Giorgini buying office of Florence; Ente

Italiano della Moda of Turin; and Centro Italiano della Moda di Milano. The perspective adopted in this book looks at Italy through the lens of several of its fashion representatives, actively incorporating the adaptations requested by their customers into elements that resonated in the press and contributed to establishing the legitimization of Italian fashion merchandise first and couture later in the transatlantic fashion market.

The title of this book encapsulates the postwar journey of recognition of Italy as a country capable of exporting fashion ideas and merchandise by chronicling how the actions of professional intermediaries eventually led to the recognition of Italy as a source of original designs for ready-to-wear and high-end dressmaking. It fleshes out the transition through which Italy's export of handcrafted fashion merchandise started to slowly include samples of luxury ready-to-wear to finally become synonymous with couture. It identifies the Italian *moda boutique* export as one of the elements that facilitated the transition, and it locates examples of it in different promotional efforts, one of which was represented by the travelling US exhibition *Italy at Work: Her Renaissance in Design Today* (1950–53). Stemming from the French tradition, Italian couture boutiques were shops inside the couture house, where customers could find accessories, ready-made pieces and simplified, cheaper versions of models presented in the main collection.[21] Following a chronological and geographically situated structure, the book explains how Italy would gradually become a destination for informed American buyers seeking not only accessories and textiles but also looking for a certain Italian distinctiveness in design. The recognition eventually attributed to Italian fashion designers from the late 1940s onwards, which is clearly marked in the American press by the use of the phrasing 'Italian couture', materialized into an original dressmaking industry whose skills historically derived from the technical abilities required to copy and adapt Parisian couture.

Additionally, this book seeks to address the critical interpretation of primary sources from the archive of Giovanni Battista Giorgini and his import–export firm, G.B. Giorgini.[22] The book compares the documents preserved in the Giorgini archive with other primary sources of the time, such as business records of external firms or organizations, magazines, newspapers, trade journals, and memoirs. The significance of the Florentine Shows is charted within their historical context and reassesses the multiple cultural and commercial relationships that occurred between Italy and the United States after the Second World War. Along this line of reasoning, the book contributes to an understanding of the role of Italy as an active participant in the postwar transatlantic fashion scene. Demonstration of commercial interest from the United States represented an opportunity for the emancipation of the Italian fashion industry, which emerged from the 1943 armistice looking for a stylistic distinctiveness that would help its designers to break with the Fascist past of the country and establish a new, modern identity. As the United States was considered the most powerful buyer (in terms of volume of purchases) in the international couture and fashion circuit, the need to supply their local market with novel designs and merchandise was among the reasons for introducing Italian exports. The book contextualizes the export initiatives set off by scholar and philanthropist Max Ascoli first and Giorgini later within the political scenario of the Allied Military Government and the later Allied Controlled Commission, the early Cold War years, and the United States' fear of the spread of Communism in Southern Europe.

This polyphony of disciplines concurring with the advancement of historical research in fashion is an expression of the type of history advocated by Bloch and fellow historian Lucien Febvre through the *Annales* tradition.[23] By apparently complicating the scenario that it sets out to investigate, the book combines diverse sources and methodologies to demonstrate that previous research on the Florentine Shows has largely relied on simplifications and, to some extent, romanticizations of the causes and the contingencies that allowed for their establishment.[24] As if using a methodological compass of sorts, the book draws an imaginary circle whose centre is set in 1951 and then proceeds to move along its chronological surroundings to investigate the material evidence left by journalists, entrepreneurs, non-profit organizations, governmental agencies and private individuals. In this way, the book retraces the earliest characterizations of Italy as a country with an independent, non-derivative fashion market for United States buyers and manufacturers within the cultural and political context of the immediate and later postwar years.

In addition, this book wishes to contribute to the field of transnational history, as it represents an attempt to write *a* history of postwar Italy and its cultural and commercial interactions with North America within the larger configuration of the international fashion market. Historian Pierre-Yves Saunier outlines how transnational history is a useful approach for those researchers who wish to investigate the 'relations and formations, circulations and connections, between, across and through' the units that characterize the collective life of those human groups that organized themselves into nations.[25] The book thus historicizes the interchange between Italy and America in the definition of a new cultural identity of postwar Italy in the field of fashion; it evaluates the mutual influences and contributions between the two countries in the circulation of fashion merchandise and ideas; and lastly, it outlines trends and patterns that emerged from professional groups, individuals, and cities involved with the earliest promotions of the Italian fashion exports. Paraphrasing film historian Andrew Higson, the book draws the parameters of Italian fashion at the site of its production, Italy, as much as at the site of its intended recipient, the United States, as it focuses on the personalities and events that aimed directly at that specific market.[26] The term 'transnational' is conceptually characterized by a specific porousness that recognizes a certain level of agency to the countries involved, without implying an a priori parity between the two and, at the same time, acknowledges their 'relations of unevenness and mobility'.[27] The unevenness of the two countries involved is particularly evident in the rehabilitation efforts of the non-profit agencies sponsored by Max Ascoli within the connection between fashion and handicraft production. Until the diffusion of ready-to-wear garments during the 1960s, most fashion-related businesses in Italy were linked to the handicraft industry. According to Italian commercial law, the work of dressmakers belonged to the field of handicraft industry, as their firms were being catalogued as *ditte artigiane* (artisan firms) by law. In connection to this, the book explores how fashion was positioned within the Italian handicraft industry and how the evident political undertone towards the support of Italian artistic craft tradition, formerly enhanced by Fascism and later inextricably linked to the European Recovery Program (ERP) funds and ExIm bank loans discussed in Chapters 2 and 4, affected the language used and the discourses circulating for its promotion in the United States.

The book relies on the analysis of American and Italian specialized press and their communication styles relating to the promotion of postwar Italian fashion, heavily focusing on the information provided by the trade newspaper *Women's Wear Daily*. Elizabeth Castaldo Lundén discusses the unexplored area of study of fashion journalism and communication, pointing out the need to 'move away from semiotic interpretations and into the many cultural, social, and economic factors that directly or indirectly influence fashion as a cultural product and as an industry' and the often-overlooked fact that fashion media is inevitably intertwined with commercial demands.[28] The book's use of fashion and feminine press as a primary source responds to what Castaldo Lundén identifies as the need for a new fashion media history, where the hagiographic and celebratory perspectives are problematized and questioned. In the first comprehensive academic essay to pan over the earliest instances of US press articles devoted to Italian fashion designs, fashion historian Valerie Steele writes:

> [t]he discourse on Italian fashion in the American press provides important insights into the development of what came to be known as 'the Italian look'. Fashion journalists at that time were often justifiably enthusiastic about the work of Italian designers, but they also perceived Italian fashion through a veil of stereotypes.[29]

This seminal media analysis was written in connection with the exhibition *The Italian Metamorphosis 1943/1968*, whose fashion section derived from the 1992 exhibition *La Sala Bianca*, celebrating the fiftieth anniversary of the First Italian High Fashion Show held in the Sala Bianca of Palazzo Pitti. It charted the most celebratory media appearances of Italian fashion in the American press, providing the original nucleus of this book's analysis.

Finally, the book's reading of the press is contextualized with the archival sources of many Italian and American professional organizations and individuals, adopting a multi-methodological and transnational approach to the history of intermediaries, grounded in the new business history of fashion studies, developed since the early 2000s and proposed by Regina Lee Blaszczyk, Pierre-Yves Donzé, Ben Hubs, Elisabetta Merlo, Francesca Polese, and Véronique Pouillard. Pouillard highlights the value of the social and entrepreneurial histories of that 'new type of intermediaries [who] appeared to complement the classical commercial activity of fashion retailing',[30] while Regina Lee Blaszczyk's model of fashion history combines a study of the cultural dimension of fashion with the economic history of the professionals and the business actors that populated it,[31] contributing to a thorough analysis of the 'behind-the-scenes' processes that lie between the design and sale of fashion.[32] The following chapters implement such perspectives in the Italian postwar context.

Notes

1 A commissionaire is a trade agent who acts as an intermediary between manufacturers and buyers. This professional profile will be further discussed in Chapter 3.

2 Pitti Immagine is the organization that manages the fashion industry events taking place annually in Florence, such as Pitti Uomo for menswear or Pitti Bimbo for children's apparel.

3 A prodrome of the fashion catwalk, the late nineteenth-century practice of *tableaux vivants* consisted of a staged performance accompanied by music, during which mannequins acted as living statues parading models: see C. Evans, *The Mechanical Smile: Modernism and the First Fashion Shows in France and America, 1900–1929* (New Haven: Yale University Press, 2013), p. 13. In this case, Giorgini was commissioning Capucci to produce what today would be perhaps called a small 'capsule' collection.

4 Roberto Capucci to the author. Rome, 5 April 2017.

5 G. Bianchino, Grazietta Butazzi, Alessandra Mottola Molfino, and Arturo Carlo Quintavalle, eds. *Italian Fashion; the Origins of High Fashion and Knitwear* (Milan: Electa, 1985), pp. 49–50.

6 M. Cattaneo, 'Da Firenze la moda italiana trova la via dell'America'. *Bellezza* April 1951, p. 49.

7 M. Armani, 'A Firenze la moda italiana per gli americani'. *Omnibus* 4 March 1951, p. 33.

8 V. Rossi Lodomez, 'Donne allo Specchio'. *Bis* 3 March 1951.

9 G. Chesne Dauphiné Griffo, 'G.B. Giorgini: The Rise of Italian Fashion'. In *Italian Fashion: The Origins of High Fashion and Knitwear*, edited by Gloria Bianchino, Grazietta Butazzi, Alessandra Mottola Molfino, and Arturo Carlo Quintavalle (Milan: Electa, 1985), pp. 66–71; G. Vergani, 'The Sala Bianca: The Birth of Italian Fashion'. In *The Sala Bianca: The Birth of Italian Fashion*, edited by Giannino Malossi (Milan: Electa, 1992), pp. 23–87.

10 N. Fadigati, 'Giovanni Battista Giorgini, La Famiglia, Il Contributo Alla Nascita Del Made in Italy, Le Fonti Archivistiche'. *ZoneModa Journal* 8(1), 2018, pp. 1–15, 13.

11 G. Vergani, 'February 1951. Italian Fashion Is Born. Not Even Mussolini Succeeded in Accomplishing as Much'. In *1951–2001: Made in Italy?*, edited by Luigi Settembrini (Milan: Skira, 2001), p. 130.

12 L. Pagliai, *La Firenze Di Giovanni Battista Giorgini. Artigianato e Moda Fra Italia e Stati Uniti – Florence at the Time of Giovanni Battista Giorgini / Arts, Crafts and Fashion in Italy and the United States* (Firenze: Edifir, 2011); S. Stanfill, 'Anonymous

Tastemakers: The Role of American Buyers in Establishing an Italian Fashion Industry, 1950–55'. In *European Fashion. The Creation of a Global Industry*, edited by Regina Lee Blaszczyk and Veronique Pouillard (Manchester: Manchester University Press, 2018), pp. 146–69; C. Faggella, '"Not So Simple": Reassessing 1951, G.B. Giorgini and the Launch of Italian Fashion' (PhD Dissertation, Stockholm University, 2019); S. Stanfill, 'G.B. Giorgini: Fashion, Florence and Diplomacy, 1950–55'. *ZoneModa Journal* 11(15), 2021, pp. 29–40; L. Savi, *A New History of 'Made in Italy'. Fashion and Textiles in Post-War Italy* (London: Bloomsbury Publishing, 2023).

13 M. Bloch, *The Historian's Craft* (Manchester: Manchester University Press, 1992).
14 Bloch, *The Historian's Craft*, 25.
15 Bloch, *The Historian's Craft*, 160.
16 J.L. Gaddis, 'Causation, Contingency, and Counterfactuals'. In *Landscape of History* (Oxford: Oxford University Press, 2002), pp. 70–80, 73.
17 All my gratefulness goes to Elizabeth Castaldo Lundén for introducing me to the work of Carlo Ginzburg.
18 S. Gnoli, *La donna, l'eleganza, il fascismo: la moda italiana dalle origini all'Ente Nazionale della Moda* (Catania: Edizioni del Prisma, 2000); E. Paulicelli, *Fashion Under Fascism: Beyond the Black Shirt. Dress, Body, Culture* (Oxford: Berg, 2004); M. Lupano and A. Vaccari, *Fashion at the Time of Fascism: Italian Modernist Lifestyle 1922–1943* (Bologna: Damiani Editore, 2009).
19 E. Paulicelli, 'Fashion, the Politics of Style and National Identity in Pre-Fascist and Fascist Italy'. *Gender & History* 14(3), 2002, pp. 537–59, 546.
20 R.L. Blaszczyk, *Imagining Consumers: Design and Innovation from Wegwood to Corning* (Baltimore: JHU Press, 2000), p. 12.
21 A. Palmer, *Couture & Commerce: The Transatlantic Fashion Trade in the 1950s* (Vancouver: UBC Press, 2001), pp. 183–87.
22 For clarity and consistency throughout the text, whenever I refer to Giovanni Battista Giorgini (1898–1971) I will indicate his surname only (e.g. 'Giorgini reprised his travels to the United States in the autumn of 1946'.). Whenever I refer to the activities of his commissionaire firm, the text will address the subject as 'G.B. Giorgini'. The only exception to this nomenclature will be applied when referencing primary sources in footnotes, such as correspondence between individuals. In these cases, the use of 'G.B. Giorgini' will indicate the person, Giovanni Battista Giorgini (1898–1971).
23 J. Tosh, *The Pursuit of History* (London: Routledge, 2013).
24 The idea of a 'not so simple' representation offered by the traditional historiography of the Florentine Shows is also connected to a discourse on the simplicity of Italian designs that circulated in the US fashion press of the time and has, in turn, permeated the existent literature on the matter until today (see Chapters 1 and 5).
25 P. Saunier, *Transnational History* (London: Palgrave Macmillan, 2013), p. 2.
26 A. Higson, 'The Concept of National Cinema'. *Screen* 30(4), 1989, pp. 36–47, 36.
27 N. Durovicová and K.E. Newman, eds. *World Cinemas, Transnational Perspectives* (New York: Routledge, 2009), p. ix.
28 E. Castaldo Lundén, 'Exploring Fashion as Communication: The Search for a new fashion history against the grain'. *Popular Communication* 18(4), 2020, pp. 249–58, 250–51.
29 V. Steele, 'Italian Fashion and America'. In *The Italian Metamorphosis, 1943–1968*, edited by Germano Celant (New York: Guggenheim Museum Publications, 1994), pp. 484–97.
30 V. Pouillard, 'From Dressmakers to Fashion Consulting: Intermediaries in the Fashion Business (1920–1960)'. EBHA Conference, Barcelona, 16–18 September 2004.
31 Blaszczyk, *Imagining Consumers*, 345; R.L. Blaszczyk, *The Color Revolution* (Cambridge: MIT Press, 2012).
32 R.L. Blaszczyk, 'The Hidden Spaces of Fashion Production'. In *The Handbook of Fashion Studies*, edited by Sandy Black, Amy de la Haye, Joanne Entwistle, Agnès Rocamora, Regina A. Root and Helen Thomas (London: Bloomsbury, 2013), pp. 181–97, 183.

1

Rome: new standards of fashion

The emergence of Italy as a source of fashion ideas and merchandise in the immediate postwar years needs to be contextualized according to the status of Paris at the time. Fashion historians have explored the paths through which French couture resuscitated itself once the German Occupation ended, for instance adopting marketing strategies such as the touring exhibition *Théâtre de la mode* or resisting the challenges posed by both the US ready-to-wear industry model and the copyright issues linked to the reproduction of couture models.[1] During wartime, many *haute couture* establishments in Paris remained operational.[2] Thus, after the war ended the Chambre Syndicale de la Couture Parisienne worked hard to thrust aside the accusations of collaborationism and lure American buyers back to France.[3] It was only by the beginning of 1946 that transatlantic trade resumed, and French designs became exportable once again, successfully.[4]

The immediate postwar months were, however, characterized by the general feeling that the extravagance of Parisian couture at the time soundly clashed with the average taste of US women. By fostering such opinions, US journalists and commentators prepared the ground for opening a favourable spot in the international trade of fashion for Italian novelties. The international circulation of the first Parisian fashion designs after the Liberation of Paris in August 1944 had brought a widespread feeling of dismay in the United States towards French couture models and their Occupation style, as was reported by many in the Allied fashion press.[5] Autumn/Winter 1944–45 Parisian couture collections reportedly featured large quantities of fabric, in either billowy or dolman sleeves, pleated full skirts, or close-to-the-throat necklines.[6] Valerie Steele and Dominique Veillon provide some rationalizations for the existence of such extravagant styles. On one hand, Steele notes how some couturiers asserted that the extravagance was an attempt to make German clients look absurd. Others, she suggests, might have concentrated the allowed yardage of fabrics on smaller quantities of models. It could also have been, she argues, that 'Parisians at the time really liked their "exaggerated" wartime modes', but also that 'the more material a garment used, the less the Germans would get'.[7] On the other hand, Veillon maintains that Parisian fashion creators justified the exaggerated Occupation styles with the need to employ their workers despite the perils of war, thus contributing to keeping the traditional manufacturing processes of Parisian couture alive and functioning.[8] In any case, American journalists were shocked by the fact that those designs were not even remotely influenced by the rationing policies on textiles and decoration, as had been the case in the United States. Consequently, the lavish styles and the excessive usage of fabrics were seen, in the eye of France's once loyal customers in the United States, as a complete absence of patriotism and utter coalescence with the Vichy government.[9] The scandal caused the following Parisian collections to pursue a more modest and restrictive silhouette, conforming to the restrained wartime styles approved in the rest of Europe and North America. Nevertheless, the shocking designs that accompanied the first reports of fashion correspondents in 1944 somehow haunted the reputation of Paris, and the future of Parisian couture remained uncertain until 1946.

With some exceptions, as pointed out by recent scholarships, the majority of fashion manufacturers in the Western world were prevented from accessing Parisian influences during the Second World War.[10] The same happened in the United States, where, as a result of the isolation, the fashion industry developed a nationalistic attitude towards its creativity and a preference for simplicity in design, mostly due to rationing guidelines and the modest styles that came out of their application. Jennifer M. Mower explains that, after the attack on Pearl Harbor, in 1942 the War Production Board of the US Government introduced the L-85, which consisted of a series of restriction orders on the manufacture of women's apparel.[11] The limitations imposed by L-85 resulted in an attempt to freeze the silhouette as it was in 1942, eliminating fabric-rich details such as pleats and cuffs, and enforcing authorized measurements of features like skirts' sweeps, hems, and lengths. The government found its emissary for L-85 in Stanley Marcus, of the department store Neiman Marcus, who was appointed head of the women's and children's section of the War Production Board's clothing division. Since the outbreak of the Second World War Marcus had been an advocate for the independence of American designers, whose seclusion effects on the fashion industry, he argued, had to be considered an opportunity for 'enforced emancipation'.[12] The majority of US fashion professionals would have agreed with this vision: Hollywood studios tried to promote the expertise of their designers and commentators so that California could become a new centre of fashion ideas, while the city of New York was actively trying the same route backed by Seventh Avenue manufacturing businesses and championed by Mayor Fiorello La Guardia.[13]

Nevertheless, as pointed out by Pouillard, in 1945 the Office Art et Création, the governmental agency that supervised the activity of Parisian couture houses under the war, concluded that surely 'Paris fashion would be successful when it re-entered the US market'.[14] Among many influential personalities in the American fashion industry, *Harper's Bazaar* editor-in-chief Carmel Snow appeared to be the one who most wholeheartedly supported the French cause. Her insights into the Parisian couture industry derived from close and long-standing relationships with designers and manufacturers, so much so that in later years she would recount that, after the Occupation of France, she felt 'no more willing to concede the permanent fall of Paris than was General de Gaulle'.[15] She would later obtain permission from the Immigration and Naturalization Services of the United States to travel to Europe as a war correspondent, aiming to be the first to report on the recently liberated Paris. Once back in the United States in the spring of 1945, Snow held a lecture for her fellow members of the Fashion Group, during which she praised the efforts of Chambre Syndicale's then-president Lucien Lelong in maintaining the Parisian fashion system almost intact despite the war.[16] A strong supporter of the cause of French couture, Snow wrote in *Harper's Bazaar* in May 1946:

> One can no longer say, 'French fashions for the French and American fashions for the Americans.' Fashion is fashion. In spite of the fact that they have been cut off for six years and that very few American films are playing in France today, the French designers have got the feel of America. The young French girl is very much her American contemporary – she's even wearing those Norwegian-patterned sweaters that swept America last fall. Frenchwomen fling themselves on the American fashion magazines; they are fascinated by the work of American fashion designers, eager to pick up new ideas from across the water. It seems inevitable that we, on our side, will again feel a strong French influence in our American fashions.[17]

As Snow actively contributed to promote the popularity of French designs in the United States, at the same time she acknowledged the end of Paris' monopoly of ideas on the transatlantic fashion trade, nodding to increased American influences in Europe. The German Occupation of Paris had haltered the flux of both goods and ideas from couture houses for six years. The many countries that relied on French inspiration for their fashion markets had to make do in some other way. The seasonal buying appropriations of US stores, which translated into budgets that individual buyers could dispose of for their purchases abroad, would soon expand to include more quantities of fashion merchandise from countries other than France, and their country of origin would soon start to appear and be recognized.

Stanley Marcus was at the time frequently presented in *Women's Wear Daily* as favouring further openings to foreign markets and downplaying the French momentum. Giving a lecture to the Fashion Group of New York in 1946, the former L-85 spokesperson lamented that US fashion magazines were going 'overboard on the renewed significance of French couture' and that it was their responsibility not to overpower consumers with distorted reports.[18] For Marcus, those journalists enamoured with anything French made it impossible to report to American women objectively, as they failed to see the bad instances of French design and give credit to good American ideas. Marcus' words supported the interests of American manufacturers and designers, who had considered wartime a period to acquire a creative, and therefore economical, independence from Parisian trends. Aside from the yoke of creativity, this dependency meant constantly dealing with tariffs, custom legislation, and international agreements, plus currency fluctuation and deflation. Furthermore, Marcus' speech contained an opening towards the possibility of exploring other countries, noting that 'in the field of ideas there will always be inspiration from any country which is mainly a handcraft nation'. In that early summer of 1946, Marcus had just returned from a long trip to England, France, Switzerland, and Italy, an experience that arguably inspired him to deliver such a speech to his audience. Among those in the audience sat Dorothy Shaver, president at Lord & Taylor and board member of the House of Italian Handicrafts; Ethel Frankau, director of the Couture Salon at Bergdorf Goodman; and James A. Keillor, vice-president at B. Altman. All these characters would become, in one way or another, crucial to the developments of the Italian fashion scene in the years to come.

A city 'dressed for inaction'

Not much was done by Italian fashion professionals to attract rich North American customers until the last stages of the Second World War. Exports had been limited and mainly directed to ally and neighbouring countries such as Switzerland, as was the case for the autumn/winter collections of 1943.[19] However, by 1944 the international configuration of political alliances and the progress of the Allied Forces throughout the Italian peninsula made it evident that the United States was soon to become a profitable and receptive export market for Italian apparel. A fresh appearance of Italian fashion in American fashion magazines, subjected to the latest developments of the war, started in 1944 when a discourse concerning fashions from Rome began to circulate.

Liberated in June 1944, Rome became the first Italian city whose fashion scene was worth mentioning. The attractiveness of its women was anticipated by the trade newspaper *Women's Wear Daily*, which announced their 'pretty freshness' welcoming the Allied soldiers entering the Italian capital on its Liberation. The article constructs a striking contrast between the women's handsome appearance, the 'biggest beauty parade the American Army has seen in the war', and the towns of Southern Italy that the Army had just left behind, described as 'dirty' and 'slumlike'. Rome, instead, provided a breath of fresh air with its people 'well-dressed and clean. Its girls wear cosmetics, skillfully applied, sharply contrasting to the lipstick smeared on the southern Italian girls'.[20] On a similar note and only a couple of months later, *Vogue* published a feature concentrating on Roman fashion and lifestyle in which the fictitious correspondent Anis Mead chronicled her experience under the title 'In Rome – Dressed for Inaction'. 'Today Rome is virtually undamaged by war', Mead wrote, unravelling what the title of the article anticipated and pointing out how, despite the Occupation, the nobility in Rome seemed to live undisturbed, its members constantly hungry for new fashions. Arriving from impoverished and derelict Southern Italy, Mead was shocked to set foot in Rome and see clean streets, well-clothed kids, and shops filled with goods. The women, in particular, sported some very interesting and locally made tailored outfits. She commented: '[t]he women are beautifully dressed. I never thought that prints could be so seductive, but made into simple, low-necked dresses, worn with bare brown legs, and Tripolitanean sandals, they lose all that stuffy, town-y look that prints too often have'.[21] Despite not being accompanied by drawings or pictures, the vivid description of the garments helps locate similar styles in the Italian fashion press of the time.

Similar trends concerning fabric prints and informal dresses were often shown in contemporary Italian fashion magazines at least since the spring of 1943, in anticipation of the summer season. In particular, these informal styles had a partial correlation to the appearance of *sfollati*, or evacuees. The progression of the Italian Allied campaign, the routing and displacement of the German troops, and the frequent air raids forced most of the Italian population to flee their homes in search of shelter. The dynamics of how *sfollati* moved across Italy affected the whole population even though the wealthiest were privileged in their arrangements, evacuating from the main cities and relocating to the countryside and resort areas. The social reporting found in the Italian glossy magazine *Bellezza* in these years, along with the suggestions for packing the most efficient trousseau and for adapting to the simpler life outside of the bustle of the city centres, mainly catered to the rich Italians who repopulated the lake district's second homes in the North and enjoyed a comfortable life to escape the bombings that had been damaging Milan since August 1943. Articles had a belittling undertone in advising their affluent readership on how to dress and care for one's self, commenting that 'to play the part of the beautiful farmer, one must be able to change one's clothes: the morning must see us all well washed and ironed: this fresh look is de rigueur in the open air, even for these modest home-made or mass-produced clothes', whether in the countryside, in a villa, at the lakes. It is not unusual, then, to find there several editorials on the most appropriate apparel for the new destinations, often consisting of informal ensembles, blouses and skirts, and apron-like day dresses.

Bellezza demonstrated that, if leaving the city meant leaving aside formal suits and evening gowns, a new normal could be found in simpler, practical designs. The pinafore, reinterpreted by Milanese dressmaker

Tizzoni, could be made with autarkic, man-made *fiocco* printed fabric that had the additional benefit of being crease-proof; the freshness of the cloth and the gaiety of the motif paired well with the flower pattern where the dominant burgundy red was found also in the colour-block pockets, belt, and shoulder straps. A short jacket completed the otherwise informal appearance of the dress bodice.[22] In the accompanying photo, a model stands atop a rowing boat and her slender figure is framed in the background by an unspecified lake scenario: it was probably Lake Como since the firm Tizzoni had moved there from Milan's via della Spiga because of the war. Contextualized in this scenario, the garments presented could easily demonstrate how '[g]etting used to country life makes one discover not only new pleasures but also new elegances'.[23] The trend persisted the following summer and fashion editors rhetorically asked if the city day costume indeed still existed, since it was largely neglected in favour of 'dresses that do not require efforts and that relieve from [wearing] stockings and hats'.[24] The same was happening in Rome: no woman would cover their legs with stockings, affirmed Mead, and no one was wearing hats.

In this book's journey to assess the transition of Italian dressmakers from being mostly copyist to becoming capable of independent couture design, we can consider Mead's article as the first American recognition of a glimpse, albeit faint, of independent creativity found in Italy as a source of fashion ideas. The common opinion in the United States about Italian dressmakers, in fact, was that their business was entirely dependent on producing and adapting Parisian copies: if they had any, their potential creativity was invalidated by such strong stylistic dependence. While several excerpts from the trade newspaper *Women's Wear Daily* show how this opinion would affect some American fashion professionals until the 1950s, this and the following chapters will demonstrate how the international market opened up, slowly but steadily, to the possibility of heralding independent Italian fashion creations. The cause had been dear to Fascism, as demonstrated amply by Eugenia Paulicelli and Sofia Gnoli: yet even when some dressmakers did reach the other side of the Atlantic, the abundant propaganda of the period never matched the actual exports.[25] The course of the war and the Occupation of France imposed an effective turn of events in business for the majority of Italian dressmaking establishments, who were relying on Parisian inspiration for their collections. From its establishment in 1941, the fashion magazine *Bellezza* devoted pages and pages to announcing the upcoming independence of Italian dressmakers, unavoidably fostered by the limited circulation of Parisian models and toiles. A sense of this self-declared and quite recent campaign for the independence of Italian dressmaking was not lost in Anis Mead's article in *Vogue*. She reported how her acquaintances in Rome asked if she saw the latest dress collection at local dressmaker Gabriellasport, apparently 'so good, they said, and with no help from Paris'. In this surreal setting of international socialites, Mead's narrative focused on the latest news in fashion as a vital subject of conversation among those who, thanks to their status and privilege, had survived the war and were waiting for everyday life to get back to its old routine.

At the same time in which Mead was writing from Rome, *Vogue*'s former Paris correspondent and future fashion editor Bettina Ballard was on 'war leave' as staff coordinator for the American Red Cross. The owner of fashion house Gabriellasport, the noblewoman Gabriella di Giardinelli, remembered the presence of Ballard in Rome during the summer of 1944 in her memoir and how the American journalist frequently participated in the bubbly, gossipy social atmosphere run by local aristocrats.[26] During her deployment, Ballard occasionally sent reports from overseas that *Vogue* would publish, generally signed with her real name, which at the time was Bettina Wilson. When she penned her 1960 memoir *In My Fashion*, Ballard recalled her experiences during the passage through Italy in a writing style that strongly resembled the impressions recorded in Anis Mead's article.[27] Besides, Ballard confirmed in the memoir that, during her brief time in Italy, she did write about Rome and took photographs there that were published by *Vogue* in December 1944.[28] The similarity of language, the level of detail, and the linguistic expressions used suggest that *Vogue* correspondent Anis Mead was really Ballard herself; the fact that no one named Anis Mead ever wrote again for *Vogue* adds further substance to this hypothesis. What is of particular interest to the history of Italian fashion abroad is how Ballard noted that 'when [she] arrived in Rome the summer of its Liberation and saw the lovely, warm-skinned Roman women in their gay pretty print dresses, their long, aristocratic feet smartly clad in Roman sandals, the contents of [her] foot locker lost their glamour'.[29] Such an experience of 'fashion blooming around' Rome prompted her to visit a dressmaker's shop and have clothes made out of dyed parachute silk, in accordance with what she deemed the new 'standards of Roman fashion'. Both the article and Ballard's memoir focus on the same details with strikingly similar language, demonstrating a distinctive interest in the styles seen in Rome. The outstanding simplicity of printed fabrics used in dresses, the summery look of the Roman women's warm-toned skin, and the popularity of barefoot sandals, considered quintessentially elegant in their minimalism, soon became journalistic tropes used by American fashion correspondents. This group of features will become increasingly present from here on in US reports of trends from Italy and will constitute an early characterization of the discursive features attributed to the Italian fashion merchandise and couture of the postwar years.

The glimpses of reality that a contemporary reader catches in the article 'In Rome Now' undoubtedly contrast with the depictions of the Second World War to which popular culture has accustomed us to today. In 1944 Rome, everyday life for the wealthiest kept on going almost undisturbed, which appeared to foster the creativity and the impulses later found in the Italian fashion industry. Ballard's memoir emphasized how it was 'all too easy to forget the war that summer in Rome, where the life in the palazzos, the gossipy frivolity of the Romans, made everything seem so gay and splendid'.[30] These atypical impressions clash with the harshness of warfare, but somehow provide explanations as to why several Roman fashion houses found international fame and circulation after the end of the war. In general, the recovery of fashion businesses in postwar Europe has been by and large explained as a reaction to war, fuelled by a newly found vanity in women, so long subjected to the harshness of the conflict. Fashion journalist Elsa Robiola laid claim to the right for Italian women to be frivolous again, to display elegance, and to show a proud new femininity now toughened by all the concerns and mourning they had to endure.[31] Roman dressmaker Roberto Capucci still recalls today that, after experiencing harsh living conditions, in the postwar years women wanted to properly get dressed again, to shake off the misery of combat and destruction, and to live again at the fullest after the demise of a dictatorship that interfered with their individual interpretations of femininity.[32] This narrative trickled down in many texts that document those momentous years. In 1951, dressmaker Simonetta Visconti produced a biography of her earliest business activities that the G.B. Giorgini office included in the press pack of the Second Italian High Fashion Show, expressing the same point of view:

> One must go back to that epoch, to Rome just liberated from German occupation and still lacking the smallest necessity, to have some idea of what it meant to open a house of Haute Couture and to present 14 models! The most unthought of and humble materials were employed for the extraordinary collection: kitchen cloths, garden overalls, maid uniforms and the few cords and ribbons which [sic] one could find on the market. A pathetic effort but produced with such ability and good will that the result was brilliant and full of promise.[33]

Despite this romantic portrayal of postwar revitalization provided by the Italians, at the time the pages of *Vogue* and *Harper's Bazaar* contributed to the popularization of an opposite image in the United States. In Rome there indeed existed wealthy, affluent people who were able to escape the brutality of war; the city was never meant to endure that war, and it seemed that it never did. A few years later, this same opinion would be shared by Frances Keene, a correspondent for *Harper's Bazaar*, who asserted how 'untouched, is the word for Rome. After five years of this war, and as many again since Fascist Italy, pushed and bullied by the lure of empire, Rome is still serene, unruffled, a lotus land'.[34] The fact that several high-level fashion houses and dressmaking shops in Rome were run by members of the aristocracy was consistent with the fact that many of them kept their businesses open during the war. Concerning this, Anis Mead did have a comment on how

> [m]any people here seem to have no conception of war ... Within the city, there is a remoteness in spirit and a remoteness in actuality. The people are troubled because they have no cars, because they can't go to the golf, because their swimming pools aren't filled, because their electric lights go off.[35]

The depicted scenario seems to suggest to the reader that a relative remoteness from the harshness of combat might have allowed for a renewed creativity in arts and crafts. Yet these articles represent also early examples of the sympathetic US press reports that would contribute, in the long run, to the rehabilitation of Italians in the eye of international observers.

Despite the aloofness of the aristocracy, what emerges in the articles examined so far is a sense of industrious activity that worked towards reconstruction. A dressmaker frequently mentioned, for instance, was Gabriella di Giardinelli's fashion and couture business Gabriellasport.[36] She originally started her career in Venice, then established the Gabriellasport boutique in Milan, and in 1942 moved to Rome where she bought the local branch of Milanese dressmaker Ventura. Gabriellasport is an interesting case study of business differentiation during wartime: while its original specialty was separates and sportswear, the move to Rome was planned to take over Ventura's couture house with its prestige and core business in custom-made adaptations and reproductions of French models. This was made possible by the fact that Ventura's original *directrice*, Madame Anna, remained at Gabriellasport and with her all the precious clientele who had appreciated and trusted her expertise for decades, as previously observed by Sofia Gnoli.[37] On one hand, it is relevant to point out that this business transaction occurred at a time in which Italy was already heavily involved in the war, implying that a certain request for luxury still existed despite the conflict. On the other hand, excerpts from di Giardinelli's later memoir paint a very subjective picture of how Gabriellasport operated during the Occupation of Rome:

> Gabriellasport was our only means [of survival] and so we kept on working, with caution and without making too much noise. The nine windows facing Piazza di Spagna were barred to give an impression of abandonment. Clients would exit, one at a time, from a backdoor leading on a side alley. Since there was no electricity, we would use oil lamps and keep the curtains lowered.[38]

Describing her experience of the Occupation, di Giardinelli amalgamated memories of frivolity and harshness to emphasize how 'at Gabriellasport life was not easy. Fabrics were lacking and the dresses that we managed to make were certainly not very lavish. Yet they satisfied the moment's needs. A new dress, a useless but whimsical hat, could sometimes lift the spirits'.[39] After the Liberation of Rome, business seemed to prosper considerably at Gabriellasport and many of her competitors, since the social occasions needing appropriate outfits rapidly multiplied: distinguished local socialites set out to entertain the higher ranks of the Allied Forces and the long-lost American friends who were in Rome deployed with the US Army. Occasions for dressing up increased, and so did business in fashion and apparel. In its highly romanticized tone, *Vogue* noted how the 'pretty dresses' of Gabriellasport, the new dressmaking firm of Russian-born aristocrat Irene Galitzine, and the inventiveness of Baroness de Reutern's costume jewellery signalled the start of a new Renaissance in a town that had never lost its beauty. The liberal aristocrats, who happened to either own or run several of those ingenuous fashion houses, were praised for finding a moral scope in their industriousness, and so were the countless anonymous artisans, responsible for the whimsical playfulness of handcrafted fashion merchandise contributing to the postwar narrative of Italian fashion, slowly regenerating from the ashes of totalitarianism.

The barefoot Roman sandal

The naked sandal, a stylistic feature that characterized several early fashion commentaries, is an item that powerfully conveys the relationship between the emergent Italian fashion scene and the export possibilities of its artisanal market. Elizabeth Semmelhack notes how the limited raw materials available to Italian manufacturers inspired them to revive the style of ancient Roman sandals, with results praised by American journalists who saw them worn by local women across the different echelons of society.[40] Even if their appearance in the fashion press was tightly anchored to the scarcity of a war that had not ended yet, which caused the necessity of making shoes that could be worn without stockings,[41] the barely there or barefoot sandals were also embedding a notion of anti-fashion, found in the work of Austrian architect and designer Bernard Rudofsky and his conceptualization of the 'inhumanity of fashion' as first discussed by Mario Lupano and Alessandra Vaccari.[42] The focus of these early press reports points to the body features of the wearer and the performativity of the newly found Roman fashions, describing not so much a temporary fade but rather a manner of carrying oneself, aided by fashion accessories. Ballard herself mentioned the 'long, aristocratic feet smartly clad in Roman sandals' that she saw in Rome, matching the stocking-free legs and tanned skin sported by local women. The experience struck her in a way that reportedly impressed her significantly. Seeing the fashion scene in Rome transforming before her eyes, she reprised her journalistic habits and reported to the New York offices of Condé Nast all 'about the way the Romans lived and dressed and entertained'.[43] Enticing her readers with descriptions of the elegant feet of Italian women in Rome, she wrote as Anis Mead:

> These women have the loveliest feet – long and thin and brown. They rarely cover them with shoes – never with stockings. They wear completely flat Tripolitanean sandals, with bright coloured leather thongs between the toes, attached to a band up the instep, which loops onto an ankle strap.

Those same sandals were featured in December 1944 in *Vogue*, and Ballard would later admit in her memoir that she photographed them herself showing 'the beautiful small feet of the Princess Galitzine in her Roman sandals and the long, aristocratic, sandal-clad feet of the Contessa Marta Matarazzo'.[44] Embedded in a *Vogue* issue dedicated to beachwear and 'Southern Fashion', the descriptions accompanying these carefully placed pictures reminded readers that such previously unheard-of Italian trends were wholly compatible with fashions already popular in the United States. The skillful artisans who made them had envisioned beautiful and resistant structures, worn by Roman women 'perforce, all day long', but perfectly suitable for American feet to wear 'for resort or evening'.[45]

The constant reference to Italian women's feet in postwar American fashion reports is somehow puzzling for first-time readers. Upon a more careful investigation, however, the references link quite clearly with another trend that involved barefoot sandals in the United States. In 1944 the Museum of Modern Art in New York organized the exhibition *Are Clothes Modern?* and created an interesting buzz around it and its curator Bernard Rudofsky, an Austro-Hungarian architect who had recently moved to the United States.[46] In particular, Rudofsky dedicated a section of the exhibition to footwear, where he explained that the sandal represented the perfect coverage to keep the foot naturally flexible and unrestrained. Praising the introduction of barefoot sandals, Rudofsky affirmed the necessity to apply a loose fit to footwear, to preserve the foot's 'tactile sense, perfect shape and unhindered movability'.[47] The striking resemblance between the shapes of footwear advocated by Rudofsky and those praised in the pages of *Vogue* suggests a strong contamination of influences. On this specific issue, Gabriele Monti has emphasized the connection between the rational aesthetic advocated for by Rudosfky and the rediscovery of the southern atmospheres dear to glossy magazine photographers in the 1950s, perfectly embodied by the barefoot sandal and the exotic scenery that it conjured up as a symbol of Mediterranean charm.[48] At the roots of Rudofsky's 'juxtaposition of primitive and modern', as defined by Monti, was a collaboration with Italian architect and designer Gio Ponti and his magazine *Domus* in a series of architectural projects in the south of Italy during the 1930s.[49] Here, around Naples and the resort towns along the coast, it is arguable that Rudofsky had become familiar with the so-called Capri sandals, which *Vogue* claimed to 'cost as little as a dollar'.[50] In particular, photographs of sandals designed by Rudofsky himself had appeared on the pages of Italian design magazine *Domus* already in 1938.[51] The ideal shoe, according to Rudofsky, was basically the same beach footwear introduced in the United States from European resort places years before.[52] Rudofsky's proposals for rational, exposed footwear would later materialize in a commercially successful shoe line. In the spring of 1946 Florentine leather goods manufacturer Aldo Bruzzichelli produced a collection of six models designed by Rudofsky, called 'Bernardo sandals'.[53] Rudofsky reportedly stressed that they '[we]re neither beach wear nor evening nor sportswear; they [we]re all this and more – they [we]re elementary foot coverings'. This first Bernardo collection capitalized on the nude sandal trend that had been hinted at by Ballard in 1944, and that had inflated with the publicity generated by the 1944 exhibition at MoMA and Rudofsky's controversial anti-fashion positions.[54] Even *Women's Wear Daily*, presenting a collection of Julianelli sandals for Saks Fifth Avenue in March 1945, specifically quoted the influence of Rudofsky's exhibition and the fact that 'this naked foot fashion is a novelty derived from sandals of antiquity', noting that '[t]he more exposed the shoe, the better the sales this summer'.[55] Consequently, other US firms reportedly presented their collections of sandals adopting the same nude look that would be noticed in fashion columns for years to come.[56]

It could be argued that the promotion of sandals might have been motivated by the scarcity of raw materials, as argued by Semmelhack.[57] On one hand, while both silk and leather were scarce at the time, the lack of means to produce shoes that would fully cover the feet might have contributed to this fashionable fad. On the other hand, the persistence of barefoot sandal models in US fashion magazines throughout the postwar years, well until the 1950s, can also be interpreted as the first marker of an 'Italian Look', establishing its presence in the fashion segment of resort wear. The reported abundance of nude sandals in the streets of Rome started to indicate how the new fashion trends emerging there were compatible with both the taste of the American market and the capability of Italian artisans to come up with fashionable items of respectable quality. In 1947, *Harper's Bazaar* repeated that 'everyone in Rome wears sandals, morning, noon and night, and they are usually made to order, for the seemingly casual intertwining of thongs is, in fact, a studied art'.[58] The press highlighted how the simplicity of a barefoot sandal, in its minimalist aesthetic, paired well with the perceived skilfulness of Italian artisans, whose imagination could yield endless combinations of colours and materials.

The publicity generated by Rudofsky's statements in 1944 and his 1946 footwear collection translated into an abundance of sandals featured in the pages of *Vogue* and *Harper's Bazaar*. Frances Keene, writing for *Harper's Bazaar* from Rome, noted that even if foreigners loved to shop for shoes at Ferragamo, a name already known in the United States, 'for sandals many Romans like to shop in the little back alleys, where skilful artisans, like Corallo, present a half dozen models for your choice or sketch special designs adapted to your foot' (Figure 1.1).[59] The popularity of nude sandals in the US fashion press became an occasion for discussing Italian artisans and their offer in fashion merchandise, and an opportunity to revamp the Italian handicraft industry, seriously impaired by the war. Quoting Italian Minister of Foreign Affairs Carlo Sforza, Keene observed that Italians were 'a people at home in adversity, and [their] periods of greatest fertility prove this again and again'.[60] Sforza, an Italian diplomat, formerly self-exiled in New York, and long-standing anti-fascist, is quoted here not unintentionally.

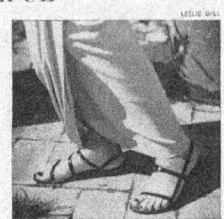
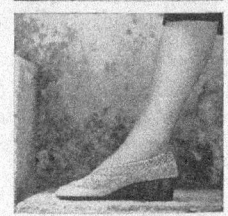
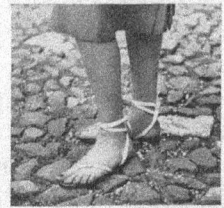

ROMAN ARTISANS ARE SKILLFUL

• To Europeans accustomed to the meager displays of London or Paris, the Roman vitrines are a revelation. Italy's economists have discovered that their country's big chance for revival lies in the encouragement of the luxury trades, and especially in those fields of production in which the Italian artisan reigns supreme. Many new enterprises have sprung up during the past year; fledgling ventures often started in the corner of a living room, converted to showroom, have become flourishing businesses, absorbing new talent and increased staffs. In Rome, all along the Via Condotti, the leather shops display their wares. Franceschini, Gucchi, and—tucked away in an enchanting courtyard—Siro, all turn out marvelous classic handbags, elegant travel things, and long, patrician umbrellas with beautiful handles of Malacca or bamboo. Luciana de Reutern, long with Chanel in Paris, has opened a shop and workroom for her fantastic costume jewelry; she even shows shaped bands of silver for long-toed, slender feet. Everyone in Rome wears sandals, morning, noon and night, and they are usually made to order, for the seemingly casual intertwining of thongs is, in fact, a studied art. Ferragamo is still Italy's leading shoe designer, with Frattegiani a close second. Both have showrooms in Rome, but for sandals many Romans like to shop in the little back alleys, where skillful artisans, like Corallo, present a half dozen models for your choice or sketch special designs adapted to your foot. Romans like the EMEF scents put out by half-Russian Moussia Marchesina Fumasoni-Biondi, the classic suits in English wool hand-loomed in Italy, tailored by Caraceni (about $90 by current exchange). And at Gabriellasport, on the Piazza di Spagna, Contessa Gabriella di Robilant is dressing the smartest women in Rome in fashions as Italian as California clothes are American, or Paris clothes French, and in silks, exquisite in color and design and texture, from Italian looms. (For these fashions turn the next page.)

TOP, SANDALS FROM CAPRI CENTER, A SHOE BY FERRAGAMO. BOTTOM, BARONESSA DE REUTERN'S SANDALS (NOTE THE TOE RING) BY FRANCESCHINI

1.1 Italian footwear. *Harper's Bazaar*, July 1947. Courtesy of *Harper's Bazaar*, Hearst Magazine Media, Inc. Image published with permission of ProQuest LLC. Further reproduction is prohibited without permission

Described in 1943 by *Vogue* as 'that somewhat lone figure in European politics, an aristocratic democrat', Sforza's point of view serves as a political seal of approval towards the emerging renaissance of Italian artisanal exports.[61] Consequently, asserted Keenes, Italian economists were guessing that the best chances for a revival of the nation's balance of payments could be provided by a significant development in the transatlantic trade of luxury goods: in this field the artisans could shine at their best with vast opportunities.[62]

'Italy Revives': the rehabilitation of artisans

Printed pretty dresses, long tanned legs, simple leather sandals with almost bare feet: it seemed like Roman smart women invented their own postwar uniform, an attire that would capture the attention of the US fashion editors who would come, one by one, to visit the country after the transatlantic travel barriers reopened. After *Vogue*'s articles on the fashion scene of

Rome, the most considerable bulk of reports concerning Italy was published in that magazine between 1946 and 1947 and was authored by the same correspondent, American journalist Marya Mannes (1904–90). Mannes was familiar with Italy, because in early 1936 she had left her job as fashion editor at *Vogue* and had followed her artist beau Richard Blow to Florence, Tuscany, where he set out to revive the traditional Florentine handicraft of hard stone inlay, the *mosaico fiorentino*.[63] Mannes would recount later that, during the three years she spent in Italy, she felt ostracized by the *gente per bene* of Florence, who reportedly did not approve of the fact that her and Blow were not married. 'I did not brood too much on this', she noted in her autobiography, 'but for a gregarious American it was strange, incredible'.[64] After the Second World War and a brief parenthesis in the US wartime intelligence department, the Office of Strategic Services (OSS), Mannes went back to the United States and resumed her work in journalism.[65]

In 1946 Condé Nast Publication Inc. sent Mannes and British photographer Clifford Coffin to Italy, on an assignment to cover the most notable personalities of its culture. In particular, Mannes' stories were set to ask 'what had happened to the writers and painters and sculptors and actors now freed from Fascism'.[66] The expedition produced a total of five articles, published in three different Condé Nast magazines between September 1946 and June 1947.[67] Among these, 'The Fine Italian Hand', countlessly cited by fashion historians, was published in the September 1946 issue of British *Vogue* and reappeared in the US edition of *Vogue* under the title 'Italian Fashion', in January 1947, consisting mainly of an overview of major fashion houses. The six-page long spread, photographed by Coffin, showed the noteworthy clothes and accessories one could shop for in Rome, Florence and Milan, highlighting both strengths and let-downs. Though Mannes considered the Italian clothes that she saw to be 'seldom highly imaginative or arresting', she nevertheless admitted that 'Italian design as a whole excels in [playsuits] and in bathing-suits, which seem to do wonderful things for the figure' anticipating the practical separates and knitwear sets typical of Italian *moda boutique* that will be discussed in Chapters 4 and 5.[68] The most distinctive characteristics that Italians seemed to have in common were a taste for prints and a talent for casual, easy clothing.

Just as Ballard, Mannes noticed how the nobility in Rome had survived the war, even relatively thriving during its course, their *palazzi* virtually left untouched by the bombings and sporting 'a style unknown to even rich Americans'.[69] Mannes would recount how 'those beautiful noble ladies in their ravishing clothes came clammering [sic] to be photographed for *Vogue*. It gave me a childish pleasure to tell one in particular, who had snubbed me in Florence, that our assignment covered only working artists'.[70] Indeed, while it mainly centred on artists of the time, Mannes' 'Italy Revives' depicts some carefully selected members of the Roman nobility.[71] There are no discussions of the emergent, striking fashion scene that captured Ballard's imagination only a couple of years before, but Clifford Coffin's photographs speak of the same characters.[72] Even though the disenchanted and stern writing style of Mannes refrains from mentioning the 'sophisticated Italian women' that she had previously resented, the article visually falls into the whirl of socialites' names that would be increasingly popular in the following years.

Yet, while repeating the ever-present adagio according to which 'everyone wears sandals', Mannes included in the picture 'the poor' as well, who wore them but made of canvas and wood. Mannes' and Ballard's Roman reportages were written with different sentiments towards how Rome was reprising its ordinary life. Mannes included a critique of the nobility who, prophesizing the end of beauty and culture, failed to remember that beauty and culture were created by people coming from below, and not from the upper ranks of society. Her being sympathetic to the lower social classes emphasized the population's efforts to rebuild the country, whose special kind of vitality made 'one believe, rightly or wrongly, that if Italy is allowed a period of peace and freedom, she may contribute to Europe and to us an extraordinary creative vitality'.[73] Yet, despite a few jabs at the old aristocracy, Mannes remarked that 'yet, the Italians – north and south, right and left – are pulling themselves together into a sort of defiant unity'.[74] Everyone, she continued, was busy restoring a torn country, especially the numerous anonymous artisan talents 'to whom the creation of things of beauty is the normal birthright'. The following November, *Vogue* published photographs of a Gucci leather satchel and Ferragamo shoes that spoke of the beauty and supposed centuries-old perfection of Italian leather accessories, further discussed in Chapter 3. The short half-page article accompanying Coffin's four photographs was almost certainly written by Marya Mannes, since the same photographs and similar wordings were used in Mannes' earlier article, 'The Fine Italian Hand'. As the commentary observed, this was what Italian women, with their 'beautiful legs and feet [that] are possibly the best in Europe', would buy: the accessories were now promoted for American women, and made by 'the same celebrated school of shoemaking that gave us the wedge sole, the thong-sandal' and by the experienced artisan masters who executed their 'perfections in leather'.[75] It was not so strange, after all, that there was such a bustle concerning high-end fashion in Italy at the time, echoed *Bellezza* in the December issue of 1946. Nor was it so strange that 'Englishmen and Americans, surprised, find beautiful things in our shops'.[76] The characteristic that was soon to be discovered by these markets, remarked *Bellezza*, was that the Italian people had been accustomed for centuries to patiently working on accessories of adornment, only for the sake of creating something beautiful.

There is an overall implication that permeates Mannes' articles, which is in line with the mainstream sentiment of the United States towards the political situation of Europe after the war. Because of the cultural vacuum originated during Fascism, concluded Mannes, artisans were hungry for connections with the United States in searching for an exchange of ideas, and not merely, she argued, for the commercial opportunities offered by such an extensive market. Besides the potentials of the handicraft industry, Mannes expressed her assumption that this mixture of efforts and creativity would eventually originate 'a new fresh culture, which may very possibly take the lead in Europe as well as in the new world'.[77] In Mannes' perspective, the possibility of opening its market to the artisanal products of Italy would have provided the United States with a further possibility to help Italy through the country's own means and capabilities, eschewing mere philanthropy. The idea was that Italy should have been able to help itself by employing its artisanal talents, whose outputs seemed to be living a favourable moment in the eyes of US consumers. It was not a coincidence that, in this same period, Italian émigré and scholar Max Ascoli was establishing the operative foundations, in Italy and New York, for a non-profit organization to support the regeneration of trade between Italian artisans and American buyers, in line with his political view on new liberalism and anti-communism. Consistent with the standpoint advocated for by Mannes' articles, in his 1949 book *The Power of Freedom* Ascoli would argue that the right to work was a pre-political right, especially in the postwar configuration of the Western world where it was 'coming to be recognized as the unquestionable foundation of whatever legal and political order men can give themselves'.[78] Mannes would later join the journalistic team of Max Ascoli's *The Reporter*, 'a magazine of causes' and a platform for Ascoli to convey his point of view on international policies, liberalism, and anti-communism through the names of his correspondents.[79] This detail adds an additional layer of perspective in considering Marya Mannes' 'Italy Revives' as an early, deliberate attempt to re-establish trust in a country that had once been on the other side of the war fence. An article as such is instrumental in the analysis of the promotional strategies that paved the way for an effective introduction of Italian fashion merchandise in the United States. It represents one of the earliest postwar instances in which features of the Italian people and workers are described to appeal to potential US consumers. Mannes' articles represent an initial attempt to stress the importance of the handicraft industry of Italy, the hard-working character of its artisans, and the ingenuity that could come out of their skills, even at a moment in time in which the harshness of the war had deprived them of raw materials and the instruments of their work. In connection to this, and to Marya Mannes' future relationship with Max Ascoli, the fact that many of the ideas expressed in her articles would correspond to the principles articulated by Ascoli's ventures (Handicraft Development, Inc., CADMA and the exhibition *Italy at Work*) are an interesting springboard to the analysis that will be presented in the next chapter.

'The sophisticated Italian woman'

In 1949, *Vogue* published 'In Rome Now', an article dedicated to the Roman socialite season and some of its most fashionable protagonists. Reinstating what had been claimed of Italian noblewomen since Mannes reported during the Occupation, the article affirmed that Italian women displayed 'contradictory casualness and inimitable authority' in their clothing.[80] Representations of casual elegance, in combination with their 'easy grace' and the 'nonchalance' of their 'art of distinction', merged to define a distinctive style modelled on the resort clothes seen by the correspondent in Rome. The simplicity of discreet and sturdy fabrics like raw silk, poplin, and linen was paired with the use of prints and omnipresent sandals. The article grouped these features into defining 'a fresh part of what Italy has begun to call its "*mode nationale*" – its fashion which grows out of the life of Italy itself and takes on a special quality from its surroundings'. This effortlessness in style reflected what American journalists observed while reporting predominantly on the most elegant ladies of the Roman aristocracy, so that the features of their distinctiveness became a reflection of that milieu. The pictures that accompanied the article, once again shot by Clifford Coffin, displayed the best entertaining outfits of either noblewomen or the wives and daughters of illustrious men, as, 'among marble stairways, vast ceilings, historically painted walls and *gallerias*, the evening dresses move in an air of ceremony'. It was not unusual for postwar issues of *Vogue* and *Harper's Bazaar* to feature Italian socialites and noblewomen, especially considering that these publications had always catered to the upper-middle classes and thus devoted space on their pages to report on fashionable social engagements. Many of these women had some international connections, due to marriage or family heritage. Marya Mannes' epytomization of their Italianness, anyway, added a further layer.

According to Stephen Gundle the appeal of the European aristocracy within American mass culture was undoubtedly declining, as the world experienced an upheaval in its traditional structures of class and power. Nevertheless, blue-blooded Italian women were interesting subjects for the US fashion press, who slowly turned them into ancillary 'heroines of consumption'.[81] Aristocrats featured in fashion magazines were interesting because of their looks and fashionable presence, and not anymore because of their noble descent or wealthy marriages into society, argues Gundle. In many instances, these same women had already appeared in US magazines' fashion columns, photoshoots, or society news in previous years. At this point, their resurfacing had more to do with whether their moral integrity could still be appealing to the new reconfiguration of international politics, meaning to anti-fascist, anti-communist Americans, and less with their fashionable allure. The question of assessing collaborationism was a hot topic, something that plagued the relationships between Italian officials and Allied Forces during the Reconstruction: even the so-called epuration committees would eventually have a limited impact, and the collective efforts would instead focus on containing Communist influences over the liberated population.[82] Consequently, the socialites portrayed yielded the ideal mix of proven political morals and interesting cultural allure needed for a glossy feature. Besides, it became evident that a significant number of dressmaking shops and accessory firms in Rome were run by aristocrats, many of which were women.

Taking, for instance, the case of Gabriellasport, one notices how both the firm and its owner were frequently mentioned in the earliest fashion reports of American correspondents. Yet owner di Giardinelli was not completely unknown to international and American readers of fashion publications: her brand had received some credit from the American press in previous years. In 1936 she had been involved with the American launch of man-made casein fabric Lanital, presenting a collection of hand-knitted pieces at Bergdorf Goodman, sponsored by Italian textile company SNIA Viscosa and showing 'the decisive stamp of Italian chic'.[83] She would later participate in the Italian Pavilion at the 1939 New York World's Fair, again in collaboration with SNIA Viscosa. Her thick network of social connections greatly aided her publicity in the postwar years: well acquainted with glamorous characters such as Gabrielle Chanel, Elsa Maxwell, Cole Porter, the Agnelli family and so forth,[84] di Giardinelli had long been a 'sophisticated Italian woman', as Mannes would call socialites like her.[85] Contributing to the emergence of Italy in the transatlantic fashion market as a reputable source of fashion inspiration and merchandise, the ways in which these women were presented by the US press embodied the aloofness of a detached, effortless style that would be consistently used in years to come to define a supposed unifying, quintessential nature of Italian fashion.

The bustle experienced by American journalists was indeed happening. Mannes had written that, by the end of the Second World War, Italy possessed 'everything necessary to a vital and original fashion industry: talent, fabric, and beautiful women. With the postwar easing of materials and labour, and more expert direction, Italian clothes should command a distinguished audience'.[86] At that time, Ascoli's non-profit firm Handicraft Development, Inc. had started its activities to promote the exports of Italian handicraft goods in the United States. Among other councils, Ente Italiano della Moda, linked to the former governmental agency for the promotion of the Italian fashion industry, had organized its first fashion exhibition in Turin. Notable Italian fashion magazines, such as *Bellezza*, started to be published again. Prefiguring the later mass debut of Italian designers in the United States, Mannes suggested the importance of using local beauties as models for the promotion of Italian merchandise. Therefore, following the traditional use of debutantes and socialites in fashion magazine spreads, the presence of Italian socialite women in US magazines became a vehicle to promote the sophisticated sense of style subsequently embodied in the 'Italian Look'. While initially the presence of Italian well-to-do women was not necessarily linked to Italian fashion merchandise or couture *per se*, it eventually served to visually convey the stylishness and refinement linked to their being Italian. As Italian designers were not yet known, their names accustomed the magazine's readership to Italian sounds and appearances, proving that elegance and taste could be found in the well-off Italian society.[87]

It was pointed out earlier in this chapter how Mannes, whose standpoint at the time largely conformed to anti-communism and liberalism, wrote an interesting account of the state of liberated Italy in 1946. Echoing the 1944 piece 'In Rome Now', 'Italy Revives' documents how it was quite fascinating to see that the nobility in Italy managed to endure its privileged existence after the end of the Second World War. In particular, Mannes wrote:

> Rome is a city of palaces ... inside them the life of an old régime still goes on. It is hard, in fact, to decide which survival in Italy is the more extraordinary: that of the humble ... or that of the landed nobles-a mere handful of fifty thousand who have managed to survive, complete with treasure and charm, through the wars and upheavals of centuries.[88]

As pointed out earlier, the difficulties of war seemed to have left the Roman nobility unscathed, and the appearance of beautifully dressed noblewomen in fashion magazines confirmed it: the Italian-born or Italian-by-marriage beauties joined the ranks of Babe Paley, Gloria Guinness, and the Duchess of Windsor on the pages of glossy magazines, sporting the latest trends from Paris, Italy, and the United States.

Promotion and publicity instances for the emergent Italian styles were thus modelled against sophisticated Italian women who were already recognizable to international readers of fashion and society magazines. Countess Sandra Spalletti, born in the ancient Florentine family Della Gherardesca, was reportedly one of the most beautiful women of Italy in her youth, according to local and US press alike: Cholly Knickerboker considered her a 'perennial best-dressed' lady.[89] Her refined taste was possibly the reason why, following the end of the Second World War, she held jobs at Hattie Carnegie and Bergdorf Goodman in New York. Indeed Spalletti was featured multiple times in the articles written by Mannes following her Italian trip, with photographs showing the countess wearing two different gowns made by ever-celebrated dressmaking atelier Gabriellasport. In one of these descriptions Spalletti wears a long, silk dress, whose floor-length skirt slits in the front and drapes on the hips: the caption recites the rule for her outfit being a characteristic example of new Italian fashion featuring 'rich silk, rich colour, straight, calm lines'. Made in a yellow nuance, the dress reportedly was the ideal companion to Italian women's apricot skin tones.[90] Later, she was featured in a *Vogue* style column featuring impeccably dressed women, who had 'found: the right lines, the right colours, the right fashion roles for themselves'.[91] These women's skills and tastes were meant to be taken by *Vogue*'s readers as successful examples of how women should model fashion's whims on their own personality, social requirements, and appearance. The key was a fruitful combination of understatement, suitability, and balance, characteristics embodied in their own ways by different women, who nevertheless shared 'taste and a knowing eye for their own best possibilities'.[92] Spalletti's presence in this exclusive circle of fashionable society women was confirmed by her attendance at a Fashion Group luncheon in New York, where a presentation of thirty original Parisian models illustrated the latest trends of autumn/winter 1950.[93] The authority attributed to Spalletti's taste both at home and abroad made her the perfect candidate for modelling in the earliest fashion spreads featuring the postwar resurgence of Italian designers.

Similar recognition was granted to Mita Corti. Born in Rome to a family merging Russian and Sicilian nobilities, in 1947 Corti lived in New York with her husband Uberto, Count of Santo Stefano Belbo.[94] Although she was the sibling of Roman fashion designer Simonetta Visconti, when featured in magazines Corti did not always sport garments made by her creative sister. Instead, when she first appeared in *Vogue* in 1947, photographed by John Rawlings, Corti wore an American-made woollen coat available at Bergdorf Goodman. In 1948, Corti was again featured in US magazines three times, sporting either American or French designs, and joined by other notable women of the time (Figure 1.2).[95] Yet her first photoshoot wearing Italian creations appeared in the already cited 'In Rome Now', where Corti, her mother, and her sister wore evening gowns by Simonetta Visconti.[96] In the same article, Corti exchanged the eveningwear in favour of a Caraceni suit.[97] The suit, explained the caption, was to be considered the uniform of 'the smart Roman women', who would wear such a practical and comfortable garment from morning until five in the afternoon, to then change into a more appropriate and elaborate gown for the evening. Corti here portrays the distinctive appearance of Italian smart women, as *Vogue* condensed it in a sentence. 'The keynote of the smart Italian women's look is "*raffinata e elegante*" [refined and elegant]', the magazine would affirm:

> They are famous for their superb figures, long legs, their easy grace, and lovely, sun-warmed complexions. They wear clothes with contradictory casualness and inimitable authority. The art of distinction to them is nonchalance, always to be in the minor key by day, flowering into superb magnificence for evening.[98]

The Visconti evening gown and the black, woollen suit that Corti wore for the 'In Rome Now' photoshoot exemplified the bookends of the Italian fashion spectrum as interpreted by the American perspective of *Vogue*. Several Roman and Milanese socialites, photographed wearing creations

1.2 Mita Corti photographed by Genevieve Naylor. Reproduced by the kind permission of Peter Reznikoff. *Harper's Bazaar*, April 1948. Courtesy of *Harper's Bazaar*, Hearst Magazine Media, Inc. Image published with permission of ProQuest LLC. Further reproduction is prohibited without permission

by still anonymous Italian dressmakers, abound in the article. In some cases, the captions point out the Italian fabrics with which the 'nameless' garments were made: '[t]he materials from which their clothes are made are among the best in the world', the article explained, 'woven by native craftsmen and printed by hand by artisans whose parents and grandparents were artisans'. Praising the artisanal nature of the local fashion scene, the article links back to the emphasis on the cultural and economic value of Italian handicraft.

Fostering the earliest presentations of Italy as having an independent, non-derivative fashion scene, *Vogue* initiated the popularization of a set of characteristics that would accompany the promotion of Italian fashion merchandise for years to come: in its discourse, simplicity appeared key. Through the constant depiction of international socialites and noblewomen, the image that US glossy magazines such as *Vogue* and *Harper's Bazaar* projected of Italian fashion in its early postwar appearances referred directly to the simple elegance of Italian noblewomen, highlighting the effortless and understated looks of women such as Mita Corti, Alessandra Spalletti, or Gabriella di Giardinelli, who would additionally put her good taste to use at her fashion atelier Gabriellasport. The aloof elegance of the nobility represented one of the main cultural and historical references that the American press referred to when describing the emergent Italian fashion scene, adding a backdrop of 'ruins and antique draperies scattered through the city constructed for the consumption of American readers' and offering 'a fantasy of a fresh, new style based in myth, intrepidly thrusting itself upon the international garment market while offering a glance at a remote past, by no means irremediably lost' as keenly observed by Vittoria Caterina Caratozzolo.[99] Adding their social commentary, both *Vogue* and *Harper's Bazaar* made sure to celebrate and encourage the efforts spent by the creativity and the vigour demonstrated by the Italians in the aftermath of the war. As observed by Frances Keene, '[t]he fierce burst of creative vitality which has caught the imagination of the entire Western world can keep on going after its euphoric impulses start to flag, only if a world public can turn its attention and its buying power to the Italian scene'.[100] Here Roman artists were 'vigorous', their talent was 'pyrotechnic', and the artisans were 'skillful', while Roman women were indeed 'beautiful' and almost all of them preferred the couture models made at Gabriellasport.[101] Moreover, the nobility's anti-fascist stances and family connections to the United States portrayed in the articles were dutifully noted, contributing to reinforcing a sense of renewal in both morals and costume. Overall, these articles introduced their international readership to a nobility in great need of political rehabilitation; the exposure, in turn, translated into a vigorous publicity boost, both for the aristocrats' business activities in fashion and for an emergent market that could complement, and perhaps hope to challenge, the Parisian one.

Notes

1 A. Palmer, *Couture & Commerce: The Transatlantic Fashion Trade in the 1950s* (Vancouver: UBC Press, 2001), p. 15.
2 V. Pouillard, *Paris to New York. The Transatlantic Fashion Industry in the Twentieth Century* (Cambridge: Harvard University Press, 2021), pp. 126–27.
3 L. Taylor, 'Paris Couture, 1940–1944'. In *Chic Thrills: A Fashion Reader*, edited by Juliet Ash and Elizabeth Wilson (Berkeley: University of California Press, 1993), pp. 127–44, 131.
4 S. Stansbery Buckland, 'The Fashion worlds of Paris and the USA during World War Two: Competition, Contact and Business, 1939–45'. In *Paris Fashion and World War*

Two, edited by Lou Taylor and Marie McLoughlin (London: Bloomsbury Publishing, 2020), p. 156.

5 L. Taylor and M. McLoughlin, 'The liberation of Paris and the state of the haute couture industry: late August 1944–1946'. In *Paris Fashion and World War Two*, edited by Lou Taylor and Marie McLoughlin (London: Bloomsbury Publishing, 2020), pp. 303–317.

6 'Paris Collections Not Adjusted to New Status', *Women's Wear Daily* (10 October 1944), p. 3.

7 V. Steele, *Paris Fashion: A Cultural History* (Oxford: Oxford University Press, 1988), p. 267.

8 D. Veillon, 'The Impact of Shortages on Couture Fashion Accessories in Paris, 1940–44'. In *Paris Fashion and World War Two*, edited by Lou Taylor and Marie McLoughlin (London: Bloomsbury Publishing, 2020), pp. 76–95.

9 Taylor, 'Paris Couture', 135.

10 L. Taylor and M. McLoughlin, eds., *Paris Fashion and World War Two* (London: Bloomsbury Publishing, 2020).

11 J.M. Mower, '"Pretty and Patriotic": Women's Consumption of Apparel During World War II' (PhD Dissertation, Oregon State University, 2011).

12 G. Votolato, 'Nice Threads: Identity and Utility in American Fashion'. In *The Fashion History Reader*, edited by Giorgio Riello and Peter McNeil (Abingdon: Routledge, 2010), pp. 478–91, 479.

13 For a thorough discussion on the attempts of Hollywood to gain a foot in the international fashion market, see Elizabeth Castaldo Lundén, *Fashion on the Red Carpet. A History of the Oscars®, Fashion and Globalisation* (Edinburgh: Edinburgh University Press, 2021).

14 V. Pouillard, 'Keeping Designs and Brands Authentic: The Resurgence of the Post-War French Fashion Business Under the Challenge of US Mass Production'. *European Review of History: Revue européenne d'histoire* 20(5), 2013, pp. 815–35, 819.

15 C. Snow and M.L. Aswell, *The World of Carmel Snow: Editor-in-Chief of Harper's Bazaar* (New York: McGraw Hill Book Company, 1962), p. 145.

16 Palmer, *Couture & Commerce*, 20; P. Rowlands, *A Dash of Daring: Carmel Snow and Her Life In Fashion, Art, and Letters* (New York: Atria Books, 2008), p. 327.

17 C. Snow, 'Notes from Paris: Paris Collections Spring 1946'. *Harper's Bazaar* May 1946, p. 190.

18 'Marcus Blames Forces Here for Overplaying Paris Styles'. *Women's Wear Daily* (21 June 1946), p. 7.

19 'Nascita dei Modelli'. *Bellezza* September–October 1943, p. 9.

20 'Well-Dressed Girls Welcome "G-I Joe" Entering Rome'. *Women's Wear Daily* (6 June 1944), p. 2.

21 A. Mead, 'In Rome – "Dressed for Inaction"'. *Vogue* 1 September 1944, p. 196.

22 'Tele Fiorate'. *Bellezza* July 1943, p. 6.

23 E. Celani, 'Intermezzo Rustico'. *Bellezza* July 1943, p. 5.

24 'L'Abito per la Città', *Bellezza* June 1944, p. 19.

25 S. Gnoli, *La donna, l'eleganza, il fascismo: la moda italiana dalle origini all'Ente Nazionale della Moda* (Catania: Edizioni del Prisma, 2000); E. Paulicelli, *Fashion Under Fascism: Beyond the Black Shirt. Dress, Body, Culture* (Oxford: Berg, 2004)

26 G. di Giardinelli, *Una gran bella vita* (Milan: Mondadori, 1988), p. 85.

27 Sara Skillen has pointed out how it was common practice for journalists (and couturiers as well) to use old press cuttings from one's career to put together their memoirs, extremely popular in the 1950s. S. Skillen, '"Dior without Dior". Tradition and Succession in a Paris Couture House, 1957–2015' (PhD Dissertation, Stockholm University, 2019), p. 57.

28 'Barefoot sandals', *Vogue* 1 December 1944, p. 87.

29 B. Ballard, *In My Fashion* (London: Secker & Warburg, 1960), p. 187.

30 Ballard, *In My Fashion*.

31 E. Robiola, 'Ritorno alla Femminilità'. *Bellezza* November 1945, p. 3.

32 R. Capucci to the author. Rome, 5 April 2017.

33 Archivio di Stato di Firenze, Archivio della Moda Italiana di Giovanni Battista Giorgini (hereafter ASF-AMIGBG), Album 3. Promotional biography for fashion house Simonetta Visconti, undated (prob. 1951). Originally in English. Similar remarks can be found in Simonetta Visconti's own biography, confirming the observation made by Skillen that memoirs often made use of press clippings and old promotional materials: see S. Colonna di Cesarò, *Una vita al Limite* (Venice: Marsilio, 2008), p. 42.

34 F. Keene, 'Italy: The Clean Wind from the North'. *Harper's Bazaar* September 1945, p. 128.

35 Mead, 'In Rome – "Dressed for Inaction"', p. 142.

36 Born Gabriella de Bosdari; following the dissolution of her marriage to Count Andrea Nicolis di Robilant, she married Prince Francesco Starrabba di Giardinelli in 1948.

37 S. Gnoli, *The Origins of Italian Fashion 1900–1945* (London: V&A Publishing, 2014), p. 67.

38 Di Giardinelli, *Una gran bella vita*, 82.

39 Di Giardinelli, *Una gran bella vita*, 82.

40 E. Semmelhack, *Shoes: The Meaning of Style* (London: Reaktion Books, 2017), p. 57.

41 Semmelhack, *Shoes: The Meaning of Style*, 60.

42 M. Lupano and A. Vaccari, *Fashion at the Time of Fascism: Italian Modernist Lifestyle 1922–1943* (Bologna: Damiani Editore, 2009), p. 19.

43 Ballard, *In My Fashion*, 187.

44 Ballard, *In My Fashion*, 185.

45 'Barefoot Sandals', 87.

46 The exhibition lasted from 28 November 1944 to 4 March 1945.

47 B. Rudofsky, *Are Clothes Modern? An Essay on Contemporary Apparel* (Chicago: Paul Theobald, 1947), p. 205.

48 G. Monti, 'Are Clothes Modern? La moda secondo Bernard Rudofsky'. In *Il corpo umano sulla scena del design*, edited by Massimiliano Ciammaichella (Padova: Il Poligrafo, 2015), pp. 94–117, 100–01.

49 T. Beyerle and K. Hirschberger, eds. *A Century of Austrian Design 1900–2005* (Basel: Birkhäuser, 2006), p. 120.

50 'Barefoot Sandals', 87.

51 Lupano and Vaccari, *Fashion at the Time of Fascism*, 254.

52 '"Symmetrical Foot", Thong Sandal Ideas Give Lively Inspiration Mood to New Exhibit at Modern Museum', *Women's Wear Daily* (1 December 1944), p. 8.

53 'Flexibility and Freedom of Movement Stressed in Sandal', *Women's Wear Daily* (30 April 1946), p. 14.

54 Monti, 'Are Clothes Modern?,' 96.

55 'Exposed to High Style … Nudity', *Women's Wear Daily* (30 March 1945), section II, p. 4.

56 'Roman Sandal Theme Developed in Raffia and Leather for Shoes and Handbags on West Coast', *Women's Wear Daily* (30 November 1945), section II, p. 12.

57 Semmelhack, *Shoes: The Meaning of Style*, 57.

58 F. Keene, 'The New Italy', *Harper's Bazaar* July 1947, p. 36.

59 Keene, 'The New Italy', 36.

60 Keene, 'The New Italy', 31.

61 A. Tamley, 'Prophet with Honour'. *Vogue* December 1943, p. 77.

62 Keene, 'The New Italy', 36.

63 Richard Blow's firm Montici would participate in the exhibition *Italy at Work: Her Renaissance in Design Today* (1950–1953).

64 M. Mannes, *Out of My Time* (Garden City: Doubleday and Company, 1971), p. 165.

65 During her time with the OSS, Mannes officially presented herself as a reporter for *The New Yorker*; E. Pace, 'Marya Mannes, the Writer, Dies; Social Critic and Satirist Was 85', *New York Times* (15 September 1990), p. 29.

66 Mannes, *Out of My Time*, p. 198.

67 'The Fine Italian Hand'. British *Vogue* September 1946, pp. 44–49; M. Mannes, 'Italy Revives'. *Vogue* 15 September 1946, pp. 196–203, 324–27; 'The Italian School'. *Vogue* 15 November 1946, pp. 166–67; 'Italian Fashion'. *Vogue* 1 January 1947, pp. 118–21, 155–56; 'Italy Looks Ahead'. *House & Garden* June 1947, pp. 92–101, 140–41.

68 Mannes, 'Italian Fashion', 119.

69 Mannes, *Out of My Time*, 198.

70 Mannes, *Out of My Time*, 199.

71 Mannes, 'Italy Revives'.

72 Which are instead present in both 'The Fine Italian Hand' and 'Italian Fashion'.

73 Mannes, 'Italy Revives', 198.

74 Mannes, 'Italy Revives', 197.

75 Mannes, 'The Italian School', 166.

76 Original in Italian: 'No, non è strano che si parli di 'alta moda' in Italia, oggi. Come non è strano che inglesi e americani trovino con stupore nei nostri negozi cose bellissime; sono l'espressione di un lavoro che nasce dalla fantasia e dall'esperienza di una gente che da secoli conosce l'arte di attendere con paziente cura alla creazione di un bell'oggetto, di un ninnolo. Per il solo gusto, a volte, di creare una "bella cosa".' M. Testa, 'Forse', *Bellezza* December 1946, p. 3.

77 Mannes, 'Italy Revives', 199–200.

78 M. Ascoli, *The Power of Freedom* (New York: Farrar, Straus and Company, 1949), p. 148.

79 E. Van Cassel, 'A Cold War Magazine of Causes: A Critical History of The Reporter, 1949–1968' (PhD Dissertation, Radboud University, Nijmegen, 2007), pp. 153, 169.

80 'In Rome Now'. *Vogue* 1 March 1949, p. 218.

81 S. Gundle, *Glamour: A History* (Oxford: Oxford University Press, 2008), p. 218.

82 D.W. Ellwood, *L'alleato nemico. La politica dell'occupazione anglo-americana in Italia 1943/1946* (Milan: Feltrinelli, 1977), pp. 252–58.

83 'Italian Sponsor of Lanital Fashions Shows Models Today at Bergdorf Goodman', *Women's Wear Daily* (14 December 1936), p. 104; 'Shop-hound, the sleuth'. *Vogue* 1 February 1937, p. 104.

84 S. Gnoli, *Eleganza Fascista: La Moda Dagli Anni Venti Alla Fine Della Guerra* (Rome: Carocci Editore, 2017), pp. 62–63.

85 Mannes, 'Italian Fashion'.

86 Mannes, 'Italian Fashion'.

87 By the end of the 1950s, when *Women's Wear Daily* approached the editorial shift that transformed it from pure trade journal into a gossipier publication, additional reports on these ladies' fashion preferences confirmed their status as 'femmes-pilotes' of the Italian couture: 'Italy's Fashion "Femmes Pilotes"', *Women's Wear Daily* (6 January 1959), p. 15.

88 Mannes, 'Italy Revives', 196.

89 'Cholly Gives His Own Choices Of Best Dresssed', *San Francisco Examiner* (1 January 1950), p. 4.

90 Mannes, 'Italian Fashion', 120.

91 'The Way She Wears It'. *Vogue* 1 March 1950, p. 110.

92 'The Way She Wears It', 109.

93 'Paris Models Shown at Fashion Group', *Women's Wear Daily* (20 September 1950), p. 3.

94 S. Colonna di Cesarò, *Una Vita al Limite* (Venice: Marsilio, 2008), p. 43; V.C. Caratozzolo, J. Clark, and M. Luisa Frisa eds. *Simonetta, La Prima Donna Della Moda Italiana* (Venice: Marsilio, 2008), p. 157.

95 She was photographed by Cecil Beaton with her husband, wearing: 'a small jewel of an evening coat' by Monte-sano, in 'People and Ideas: Count and Countess Corti'. *Vogue* 1 March 1948; wearing a Henri Bendel silk lace evening dress, a 'The New York Dressmakers'. *Harper's Bazaar* April 1948; and modeling a Jacques Fath cape of grey satin, trimmed with fur around the cuffs, in 'They Chose in Paris ...'. *Vogue* 1 November 1948.

96 'In Rome Now', 168.

97 Caraceni, the renowned men's tailor in Rome, and later in Milan, catered also to a female clientele.

98 'In Rome Now', 170.

99 V.C. Caratozzolo, 'Enchanted Sandals. Italian Shoes and the Post-World War II International Scene'. In *Accessorizing the Body: Habits of Being I*, edited by Cristina Giorcelli and Paula Rabinowitz (Minneapolis: University of Minnesota Press, 2011), pp. 220–36, 225.

100 Keene, 'The New Italy', 94.

101 Keene, 'The New Italy', 35, 36, 38.

2

New York: from handicrafts to fashion

> When the American buyer vanished from Italy, hard days fell on the artisan class. Skilled workers lost their customers and the country's export trade suffered. Two years ago, Dr. Max Ascoli … started the non-profit organization known as Handicrafts, Inc. [sic] Its aim was to help the Italian artisan by letting him help himself. Small factories were rehabilitated. The best products were exported to America where outlets were found for them.[1]

In the immediate postwar period, Italian handicrafts – including fashion merchandise – could not reach the largest export market possible, the United States. Demand for Italian goods was suffering limitations that were more keenly felt for four main reasons. First, Italy's past alliance with Germany, its Fascist dictatorship, and the demise of war had all contributed to undermining the country's reputation, now in dire need of rehabilitation in the international political landscape. Second, Italian craft makers were not accustomed to the tastes of overseas customers and needed to learn how to adapt their local aesthetics to consumers more used to mass-produced goods. Furthermore, prices of goods had to be reasonable to compete within the transatlantic market and face competing French, British, Scandinavian, and Spanish exporters. Finally, the perceived quality of Italian merchandise destined for the United States was generally deemed to be poor, which impacted negatively on their potential volume of luxury exports. Acting as one of the first and most effective intermediaries of the postwar period, Handicraft Development, Inc. helped to solve these issues and to partially surpass the anonymity that had, until this period, characterized most Italian fashion handicrafts.

The political setting

After the Liberation of Italy in 1945, the United States expressed concerns about the Italian political situation. Troubled by the highly favourable reputation that the Communist Party enjoyed in Italy, the US Government considered the first Italian elections of the postwar period as a crucial event in the establishment of a stable political atmosphere in Europe. The active role played by Communist and Socialist partisans in the local Comitati di Liberazione Nazionale or National Liberation Committees (CLN) increased the popularity of their parties.[2] Despite this, both the Communist (PCI) and Socialist (PSI) parties were excluded from participating in the new national government. The appointment of former partisan Ferruccio Parri in 1945 as head of the Government acknowledged the role of the resistance in the Liberation, even though Parri was a member of Partito d'Azione, a more moderate wave of socialist-liberal politicians. In the general elections of April 1948, Alcide De Gasperi's Christian Democracy party (DC) won with a majority of votes, defeating the Socialists and Communists, who had united to form the Popular Democratic Front. The Communist coup in Prague in February 1948 was considered a precursor of what could happen in either Italy or France, where the Communist parties were strongly favoured by voters. Because of this, the US Government tailored its interference in Italian national politics to support the Christian Democrats. Covert funding supplied financial means to both the Christian Democrats and right-wing socialists of the Italian Democratic Socialist Party (PSDI), and the only strategy was based on 'explanation, terror and reassurance'.[3] As the elections approached, the ultimate warning was announced in March 1948: if the Italian electorate decided to elect a Communist government, the aid promised by the United States through the newly approved European Recovery Program (ERP) would not be administered to Italy.[4] The victory of the Christian Democrats thus secured future support from the United States. A report commissioned by the Economic Cooperation Administration (ECA), the government agency that administered the ERP aid locally, stated in 1949 that:

> Politically, the present Italian Government is considered to be stable, moderate, and oriented both economically and ideologically toward the West. The Christian Democratic Party of Prime Minister De Gasperi is considerably more powerful than any other in Italy, and its alignment with minor political groups to the right and left of its own central position gives it a broadly representative character.[5]

Nevertheless, the threat of a Communist coup lingered for years afterwards. A 1952 report from the Joint Intelligence Committee of the United Kingdom assessed that Italy and France were still the most problematic countries in Europe in terms of political sympathies. Their strong support of Communism was preoccupying, being second only to the countries in the Soviet Union.[6]

Fear of an imminent revolt in Italy was a widespread feeling in the United States during the earliest postwar years. As highlighted by David W. Ellwood, the US Government assessed that Italy had 'pre-revolutionary' conditions, meaning that it could easily surrender to Communist power by either legal or extra-legal means.[7] Thus, to project the 'American Way' as the most favourable alternative as opposed to Bolshevism, both state officials and private individuals enrolled the civil society through 'popular', or 'public' diplomacy.[8] Early efforts included the 1947 'Friendship Train', originated by journalist Drew Pearson and initially financed by Hollywood producer Harry Warner, followed by the 'Letters to Italy' campaign, urging relatives in Italy to vote against Communism and prevent Italy from becoming a godless Soviet colony.[9] The publicity of such efforts constituted an important marker of the US attitude towards Italy, which would soon materialize in rehabilitative initiatives as the one envisioned by Max Ascoli.

Handicrafts against Communism

Before the establishment of the ERP in 1948 and the systematization of ECA's reconstruction efforts, a few non-governmental initiatives in the United States appeared to promote the economic rehabilitation of Italy. Given the urgency of the situation, the first wave of organizations aimed to provide immediate assistance through large-scale donations of goods and supplies, operating with a perspective that considered the population as passive recipients of aid.[10] For instance, American Relief for Italy was headed by Myron C. Taylor, the personal representative of President Roosevelt to Pope Pius XII. Other types of independent agencies soon appeared, designed to allow individuals and companies to reprise their active participation in society. Sensing the urgency of the issue, in 1945 Italian scholar Max Ascoli (1898–1978) decided to establish Handicraft Development, Inc. (HDI), a non-profit agency that would 'apply the hard-headed principles of American philanthropy to the rehabilitation of Italian handicraft production', a moral code that would end up characterizing much of Ascoli's literary production.[11] By designing a system of support that would boost productivity and jump-start exports in an otherwise traditionally national market, HDI sought to 'help a devastated and impoverished country to help itself'.[12] The aim was to bridge the traditional artisanal production of crafts with modern taste and make it a palatable export for the United States market, which perfectly aligned with the reconciliation of postwar liberalism and the defence of individual liberties outlined by Serge Guilbaut in his reconstruction of 'the politics of freedom' that affected the New York cultural scene of the late 1940s.[13] Within the context of handicraft production, most of the Italian fashion industry workers at the time were undoubtedly in need of help to relaunch their businesses. This aspect was quickly understood by Ascoli and his staff, who disseminated information on the work and the developments of HDI and its Italian subsidiary agency, CADMA, in the trade publication *Women's Wear Daily*.

The business records of HDI's operations and, most importantly, those of CADMA in Florence, show how the two organizations knew from the beginning that fashion accessories and textiles would constitute a large part of their business concerns and that promotions should go accordingly. Fashion industry workers, scattered across the Italian peninsula, would soon start to benefit from promotional activities in the American fashion press that HDI largely invested in.

The placement of fashionable merchandise within the category of handicrafts might evoke the aesthetics of traditional costume and folk accessories, which Lou Taylor identifies as a form of commodified national dress.[14] The strong link between tourism and fashion in Italy certainly played a role in the characterization of those early exports as 'items destined to resort fashion, characterized by a peculiar echo and reference to local "culture" and to the historical identity of the places', as pointed out by Ornella Cirillo in her studies of Campania as a creative centre key to the developments of Made in Italy fashion.[15] However, finding news about the Italian handicraft industry in the most relevant fashion trade newspaper of the time highlights three characteristics of Italian fashion merchandise exports of the time. The first is a legitimization of fashion as part of the handicraft export market in Italy. The heterogeneous nature of the Italian fashion system at the time included a significant number of *imprese artigiane*, handicraft companies producing various types of goods: small batches of clothing, leather accessories, hand-woven textiles, costume jewellery, and so forth. The second characteristic is that Italian fashion handicrafts became worthy of discussion and news circulation in *Women's Wear Daily* since the beginning of HDI's operations. The third characteristic, which was consequent to the second one, was that HDI invested significant efforts in promoting Italian textiles and fashion accessories as worthy of being exported to the United States. Handicraft workers faced structural issues that had only been worsened by the war. Their development was inherently impaired by a weak business structure, often consisting of one individual or a small group of family members. Furthermore, the scarcity of sources such as leather, metal, raw fibres, and finished textiles made the actual manufacturing slow, if not impossible, in certain cases. Additionally, buying offices were forced to significantly slow down or halt their businesses, as national and international transportation suffered the trade embargo's lack of available transport and shipping services. The role of intermediary networks, crucial to the international circulation of exported goods, needed to be reactivated.

The purpose of HDI, in Max Ascoli's original idea, was to be the non-profit alternative to commissionaire firms and intervene in a moment of historical crisis to make Italian artisans regain creative and economic independence. Ascoli, born in Ferrara into a Jewish family in 1898, emigrated to the United States in September 1931 as his religion and anti-fascism prevented him from obtaining a tenured position at Italian universities.[16]

Two years after his arrival in New York, thanks to a fellowship from the Rockefeller Foundation, he became a professor of political and social sciences at the New School and, in 1939, an American citizen.[17] A fervent proponent of liberalism, during the years preceding the Second World War Ascoli opposed Fascism and Communism alike. He advocated for private capitalism to be tempered by the strenuous defence of democratic rights, among which the right to work constituted the foundation of political freedom. His scholarly works often expressed the necessity to establish private and public agencies to regulate the job market. Their role in supporting and training labourers represented to Ascoli the main guarantee of the right to work and to an economically stable society – the only alternative to falling prey to totalitarian ideologies. The evolution of this thought was discussed at length in his 1949 book *The Power of Freedom*. Firmly planted in early Cold War political struggles, the book argued that the United States, conceived as democracy's exemplary embodiment, needed to rebuild its inner strength and restate the concept of freedom it emblematized for the benefit of the 'partisans of America all over the world'.[18] Even if America was not a political and social pattern for universal adoption, continued Ascoli, it could offer a 'frame of mind' and an example of the means through which its allies could become 'self-supporting partners and not parasitical satellites, and … create conditions of national or continental independence that might check the recklessness of the major powers – including the United States'.[19] In his vision, the United States could gain as much freedom as Europe from mutually beneficial rehabilitative initiatives, a goal that he would later personally pursue with HDI and the projects interconnected with it.

The political responsibility that HDI invested in the rehabilitation of the handicraft industry resembled and, according to Raffaele Bedarida, prepared the resurgence of Italian art in the United States.[20] As demonstrated further by Bedarida's study of the 1949 exhibition *Twentieth Century Italian Art* at MoMA, the diplomatic value of Italian culture was acknowledged and actively promoted in the fight against Communism, to demonstrate that those creative forces thriving in the newly appointed democratic government had only been dormant under the totalitarian oppression.[21] This portrayal of Italian workers and their morals would become particularly evident in the discourses employed to promote the travelling exhibition *Italy at Work: Her Renaissance in Design Today*, discussed in detail in Chapter 4. In particular, the use of the Renaissance as a narrative theme to describe the rebirth of the arts in the postwar context of the early Cold War years created a rhetorical continuity with the artistry of the old masters that politically aligned with Benedetto Croce's conceptualization of Fascism as a parenthesis in the history of Italy, a trope beneficial to the fight against Communism advocated by American patronage in the arts.[22] Within this perspective, the empowerment granted by having a job was a key aspect in the establishment of HDI in New York. The self-help principles outlined in *The Power of Freedom* found a concrete application in the support of handicraft production in

Italy. The self-proclaimed non-profit organization HDI essentially operated to advise American intermediaries interested in importing goods from Italy. By improving the material conditions of Italian artisans, HDI aimed at the same time to create interesting products for American retailers, importers, and manufacturers combining affordability, exotic distinctiveness, and a philanthropic goal. In pursuing these aims, Ascoli was firmly convinced that HDI's main role was to contribute to the eradication of Communism in Italy by providing a stable economy to a relevant portion of the labour force.

The board of directors of HDI comprised a vast array of people including socialites, industrialists, publicists, and scholars, a group who supported Ascoli's vision in theory and in practice. It included Paolino Gerli, silk industrialist; Almerindo Portfolio, clothing manufacturer and politician; Enrico Pavia, consultant and member of the Mazzini Society; Mrs Max Ascoli, daughter of Julius Rosenwald of department stores Sears, Roebuck & Co; Anna Rosenberg Hoffman, HDI's own publicist and PR consultant; René d'Harnoncourt, vice-president in charge of foreign activities and later director at MoMA; economist Bruno Foà, executive director; and Hélène Walker, executive assistant.[23] The board initially appointed Freda Diamond, a home furnishing designer and a successful consultant to the design industry, as the leading artistic director of HDI. HDI expected Diamond to steer the production of Italian artisans by means of practical guidance. Her reputation as an authority on taste in home furnishing and décor was intended to inspire the creation of a new wave of modern, artistic objects that would break free from traditionally stale designs of the past and establish Italian handicrafts as a luxury export to the United States for the long-term. Her competence was immediately put to work during HDI's first research trip to Italy in August 1945, when Ascoli, Diamond, and the economist Frank M. Tamagna travelled by car through Tuscany, Lombardy, Naples, and Rome to inspect craft workshops and investigate the possibility of an operational subsidiary of HDI in Italy. Tamagna reported that, during the trip, he

> spent about half of the time in Rome and, in addition, visited Naples and surroundings in Southern Italy, the Umbria and Tuscany regions in Central Italy, and the Liguria, Lombardy and Emilia regions in Northern Italy. Travelling by car and speaking the Italian language, he had the opportunity of making direct contacts with and obtaining first hand information from people in various parts of the country, not only in urban centers, but also in rural areas.[24]

Their interest was directed to those 'branches of production where devastation is not too hopeless, where adequate help can bring about immediate employment and where the goods produced are most exportable to the United States'.[25]

In Florence, Ascoli set up the first Italian subsidiary to HDI, an agency named Comitato Assistenza Distribuzione Materiali Artigianato (Committee for Assistance to the Distribution of Materials to Artisans, or CADMA).

Ascoli had more than one reason for setting up CADMA in Florence, and one of those was undoubtedly the city's identity, rooted in the handicraft industry. In her reconstruction of the political and cultural events that led the city of Florence to consciously adopt an artisanal identity, Anna Pellegrino identifies the Unification of Italy as the founding moment of a process that, during Fascism and especially because of Florentine *gerarca* Alessandro Pavolini, set up a reorganization of the handicraft sector that responded to a specific cultural project that would have made Florence the most artisan city in Italy.[26] For this and other reasons further explored in Chapter 3, CADMA was formally established in November 1945 and had headquarters at the Istituto d'Arte (Art Institute) di Porta Romana and Palazzo Strozzi.[27] Its president was Carlo Ludovico Ragghianti (1910–87), a prominent art historian, art critic, member of the Italian Resistance, and former president of Tuscany's Comitato di Liberazione Nazionale (CTLN). In short, the politically apt choice for CADMA. Ragghianti's role in CADMA represented a guarantee of sorts that the initiative did not have a commercial scope behind its philanthropic goals.[28] On the other hand, vice-president Mario Vannini Parenti was a controversial character, whose uninterrupted career, between Fascism and Liberation, in the Florentine public administration involved the promotion of tourism, handicrafts, and, later, fashion. Ascoli's decision to entrust Vannini Parenti with the practical matters of CADMA's activities was motivated by his ambition, dynamism, and well-established connections.[29]

Nevertheless, despite the good intentions, the coordination between the two organizations proved to be challenging. The physical distance between their offices seemed less problematic than the personal, bureaucratic, and operational differences experienced by their staff.[30] Additionally, neither the technical guidance from Freda Diamond nor her highly anticipated sketches, bulletins, and informational pamphlets ever reached Florence. While her presence was highly advertised in the first press releases, the famous industrial designer failed to respect her contract and was dismissed after a year. Ascoli was loud in declaring his disapproval of Diamond's conduct, to the point of calling her a 'phoney' in private communications.[31] Because of this initial *faux-pas*, Ascoli would later stress the importance of cooperating with CADMA's technical committee in purchasing the samples and of having Gertrude Dinsmore, Diamond's replacement, inform them about the latest trends in the American market:

> You are absolutely right: the technical advice, drawings, papers, etc. that we promised to send were not sent to you. The fault lies with that phoney Miss Diamond who was put in charge for the service and did absolutely nothing. Unfortunately, she had a year's contract with us, which, as honest people, we had to honour. But now the year is over and off goes Miss Diamond. This service has now been put into better hands. You will then see another American female [sic] come to Italy, whose functions are strictly demarcated: to cooperate with the technical committee in the purchase of samples and to offer ideas on trends in the American market to the members of the technical committee.[32]

The following section will show how the year 1946 served as a testing period for the two Italian-American agencies, during which decisions were taken to change the nature of the assistance provided to Italian artisans and the artistic vision imposed by some of the intermediaries.

Helping exporters help themselves

The main purpose of CADMA, as its Italian name suggested, was to be a temporary aiding committee by distributing starter kits of equipment and raw materials to Italian artisans. After submitting an application, the artisans' requests were screened and evaluated. If accepted, they became eligible to receive the supplies, sent by HDI from the United States to CADMA in Florence and shipped through a confidential agreement with an officer of the United Nations Relief and Rehabilitation Administration (UNRRA). The *liaison man* was Vincent Checchi, employed with the Allied Military Government in Italy and then transferred to UNRRA in the economic management of operations.[33] Thanks to the intermediation of Checchi, at the beginning of September 1946 CADMA received thirty-four boxes with items destined to students at the Istituto d'Arte di Porta Romana of Florence and to several local artisans. A further 100 boxes were expected in the same period to be distributed among various art institutes in Italy and an unspecified number of artisans. Among the artisans selected was Salvatore Ferragamo, whose firm benefited from the mediation of CADMA's Mario Vannini Parenti and was helped to relaunch its shoe collection in New York department store Saks Fifth Avenue. This case study will be further discussed in Chapter 3, focusing on the intermediary network of CADMA and the influence of Vannini Parenti in Florence. The first shipments remained isolated events and after a year of activities HDI had to rethink the aim of its Italian counterpart. Shipping raw materials from the United States was unfeasible: many of these, especially leather, were now scarce in the United States since normal, peacetime levels of production had resumed.[34] Furthermore, any raw material that artisans wanted to import to Italy needed to be approved by means of a license submitted to the Ministry of Industry and Commerce first, and to the Ministry of Finance later. Such a lengthy bureaucratic process was significantly slowing down the procurements, thus it became impossible to follow a similar procedure every time an artisan firm requested new materials.[35] Bruno Foà, HDI's executive director in New York, established three new goals for the upcoming year: '[to] help buyers coming to Italy (see Westinghouse), [to] help Italian [artisans ready to export] ... and [to] properly organize the exhibition of Italian artistic objects in New York'.[36]

The first goal echoed Ascoli's statement according to which the role of HDI was to be an 'unpaid broker' between the two countries, an intermediary creating the conditions for trade to be possible and profitable on both sides.[37] The expertise of the American staff, together with the knowledge of local markets provided by their Italian colleagues, provided much-needed assistance to buyers by reducing the length of tours to manufacturing sites and thus speeding up their trips to Italy. The perfect occasion for testing the skills of HDI came in 1946 when *Women's Wear Daily* reported about large US heavy industry firms deviating from their traditional business to enter the import of Italian weaved silks, exchanging them with machinery on a barter basis.[38] Archival sources pertaining to HDI and CADMA document a deal with the import division of the Westinghouse Electric Corporation that ran at the same time as the *Women's Wear Daily* article, although they do not disclose the nature of the contract or specify a barter agreement. The import division of Westinghouse was formed in 1945 to officially support the economy of foreign countries interested in buying the company's products. Imports to the United States included four categories of items, of which 'merchandise as tooled Florentine leather, alabaster and other novelty goods of the gift shop type' constituted one.[39]

The deal with Westinghouse, an unprecedented occasion, became a test for CADMA's vice-president Vannini Parenti and had the potential of 'organizing production, orders and deliveries according to [HDI's] own principles ... influencing quality, quantity and prices of certain items in a wholesome way ... demonstrating to an American company (whose spending power is basically unlimited) that we are able to deliver the goods'.[40] The agreement with Westinghouse comprised purchasing miscellaneous handicrafts (alabaster, ceramics, linen, leather, glassware, silverware and holloware) and custom-made silk textiles. A representative of Westinghouse International travelled to Florence, where Vannini Parent personally helped him buy artistic handicrafts for a considerable amount of money.[41] Additionally, HDI's representative Ann Roberts helped Westinghouse select Italian silk mills to which the company could commission the weaving of personalized silks.[42] Providing a further example of the tastemaking role of HDI, Roberts located mills in Milan and Como that would be apt to receive instructions for creating custom designs, and supplied the Italian manufacturers with styles and motifs suitable for the US market.[43] Westinghouse publicly disclosed its purchases as a way to help the Italian economy and to 'gauge potentialities of Italian silk', although the company would later have to defend its purchases by accusations of having established a barter arrangement.[44]

The problematic nature of such an agreement, based on barter exchange and not on regular purchases involving credit or monetary transactions, emerges clearly by analysing the specialized press of the time. News of the Westinghouse barter exchange sparked severe reactions from the United States, with local manufacturers opposing the circulation of textiles that would result from the agreement.[45] The ECA later confirmed that Italian silk exports had enjoyed the emergence of a temporary market with United States importers, 'hungry for a commodity which had been excluded during the war', and in agreeing to pay up to $9 for a pound of

Italian raw silk, ending up buying 2 million pounds of it.[46] Once Japanese silk re-entered the US market, Italian exports dropped and the perception of their quality declined accordingly. Indeed, only a year later, Westinghouse restricted the original agreement, limiting the quantities of exported silk textiles to just a few designs, which were still developed under the stylistic direction of Roberts.[47] This case of intermediation is of particular interest for two reasons. First, it further supports previous research on the same topic, recently highlighted by Lucia Savi in her reconstruction of the developments of fashion Made in Italy, according to which the reputation of quality that Italian textiles enjoyed far preceded that of Italian fashion design.[48] Silk, in particular, was appreciated by exporters for its qualities as a raw material and for its exquisite finishing when woven since the eighteenth century.[49] The Westinghouse case highlights how Italian raw silk was readily available in the summer of 1946, as most silk mills, concentrated in the north of the country, had been spared by the war ravaging and the bombings.[50] The large quantities exported demonstrated an appreciation for Italian silk, proving that this segment of the textile industry was back on its feet soon after the war. Additionally, it describes an instance of what HDI and CADMA considered a successful brokerage, despite the controversies it stirred up in the US press. The competencies of staff members such as Roberts and Vannini Parenti directed the interest of the buyer towards multiple lines of product, demonstrating to American retailers the wide variety of goods available on the Italian handicraft market at that point.

The second goal proposed by Bruno Foà to advance the role of HDI as an intermediary in the export of Italian handicrafts was finding a solution to the prewar stocks of outmoded finished items that many artisans had accumulated in their storage spaces, preventing them from producing new items under commission or stylistic advice.[51] New samples required new supplies, now scarcely available because of high prices and shortages even in the United States. For this reason, HDI quickly embarked on a different route to assist Italian exporters, in line with Ascoli's founding principle of self-help. The most valuable assistance that HDI could provide would then be to find suitable buyers in the United States for the unsold prewar goods.[52] The expertise of Diamond before and Dinsmore later served exactly the purpose of evaluating and selecting the merchandise suitable for export, even if not necessarily produced with a foreign customer in mind, without affecting the reputation of Italian handicrafts in the United States with unsuitable styles.

To be able to do so, HDI needed a long-term plan to produce high levels of quality and consistency in the export goods it styled over time. These were key issues to Ascoli, who constantly expressed his deep concern towards the opinions that Americans had of Italian goods. In his view, shared by his Italian collaborators, too many low-quality goods in US department stores had ruined Italy's reputation:

We want to help Italian exports, but not in today's abnormal conditions. Today the American market is absorbing everything and Italian products are frantically exported: it's only a form of capital drain in disguise. Once this sort of feverish demand has passed, the market for Italian handicrafts in America will be ruined and discredited. Our function must be to prepare [another] Noah's Ark, because the great flood is about to come.[53]

The House of Italian Handicrafts (HIH) became the ark of Italian artisans, in Ascoli's vision, and served the purpose of achieving the third goal advocated for by Foà: setting up a showroom for high-quality, luxury exports and artistic handicrafts Made in Italy. The three-storey building purchased by Ascoli at 217 East 49th Street, New York and inaugurated on Thursday, 10 April 1947, became a permanent showcase for approved samples. A month earlier, Ascoli had warned Ragghianti that the work for CADMA would soon take off and that each of the incoming shipments of samples to New York would be discussed and analyzed with an intense exchange of letters between HDI and CADMA. Furthermore, he finally announced a regular flow of informative bulletins containing stylistic direction keyed to US customers, to be distributed to Italian producers: 'Mrs. Dinsmore is not Miss Diamond', commented Ascoli on the failed attempt incurred with industrial consultant Freda Diamond.[54] HIH's newly appointed board of trustees included key names from the retail industry and experts in the fashion trade, among which were Adam Gimbel, president of Saks Fifth Avenue, and Dorothy Shaver, president of department store Lord & Taylor and founding member of the Fashion Group. Shaver in particular, contacted by HDI's publicist Anna Rosenberg and asked to deliver a speech at the inauguration, stressed both the novelty of a non-profit organization venturing for the first time in the commissionaire business and the beneficial effects it would have on a market that, plagued by 'the dislocations of the postwar period', was extremely confusing to buyers.[55] The inauguration reportedly excited the press and the retailers invited, who commented on the elegance of the interiors and how they provided a sophisticated setting for the Italian luxury goods shown. Almost 600 visitors visited the showroom in the first six days since the opening, half of which were either buyers or store representatives.[56]

The opening put on display handcrafted fashion merchandise such as 'handbags in lightweight, polished leather', lingerie, blouses, baby clothes, 'garments of wool, linen and organdy all exquisitely embroidered', beside housewares and furniture.[57] The descriptions of the goods found in the press of the time detail luxury items rather than garments for everyday wear, such as bridal sets and high-end loungewear.[58] Pure silk lingerie stood out particularly, as it combined traditional embroidery techniques with unique stylings, successfully conveying a modern image of Italian craftsmanship tuned to contemporary international customers. Artisans were informed through a pamphlet that the only criteria adopted to select the items on show at HIH was a clear demonstration of superior quality and fit, in answering the needs of the American market.[59] All showcased objects had to be compulsorily marked with the lettering Made in Italy, as requested of manufacturers by CADMA's staff.[60] HIH would eventually demonstrate how philanthropic efforts could produce attractive and sophisticated objects, and that Italian crafts were now aspiring to become a new luxury segment of imports in the United States. Envisioned as an experimental shop of sorts, HIH and its results in terms of sales and diffusion of goods and styles could assess whether the artistic direction exerted by CADMA's technical committee, Dinsmore, and her collaborators would seep through the makers' efforts.

Price and quality issues

Thanks to the intermediation of HDI and CADMA, the creation of artistic handicrafts of high value specifically styled for foreign retail changed the perspective of American buyers towards the available options in the Italian market. In an epistolary exchange coordinating the earliest activities of CADMA, vice-president Vannini Parenti remarked to HDI's Foà that American buyers needed 'to convince themselves that Italian handcrafted goods cannot be bought any longer at ridiculous prices, like those asked before the war, [prices] that contributed to destroying this magnificent industry'.[61] The price of newly crafted samples, according to Vannini Parenti, was twenty to thirty times higher than those to which buyers were accustomed before the war. Among the reasons for the lower prices of prewar Italian merchandise was that its country of origin often did not convey any positive significance, and thus something translatable into economic value, for the average consumer in the United States. Here Simona Segre Reinach's considerations on the making of the Italian fashion identity are useful to understand why. In prewar times, Made in Italy lacked the ideological backbone that would later 'transform the manufacturing industry into a cultural industry' to become a collective brand of sorts.[62] Yet it also had a negative connotation, partly caused by the low status of the many Italian immigrants in the United States. Made in Italy fashion merchandise was thus either re-labelled by the importer or used as a component of more complex items. The item markings that could identify the country of origin were often eliminated after purchasing and before reselling, since the retail market in the United States displayed little if no interest in ordering Italian goods that consumers could identify as such.[63] In the immediate postwar years Italy was thus identified as a cheap source of provision of accessories that, at the time, were indispensable to the female wardrobe, such as gloves. This tendency to buy in Italy increased due to convenient prices and the range of items available, but the quality of goods reportedly declined in the eyes of both retailers and journalists, exactly as Ascoli had worried.

Armando Barra of Barra of Italy (Figures 2.1 and 2.2), a New York retailer of Italian fashion merchandise, was directly affected by the issue and relayed his concerns to *Women's Wear Daily*.[64] The problem, he affirmed, needed solutions on both sides of the ocean. On one hand, Italian

2.1 Advertisement for Barra gloves. *Harper's Bazaar*, September 1947. Courtesy of *Harper's Bazaar*, Hearst Magazine Media, Inc. Image published with permission of ProQuest LLC. Further reproduction is prohibited without permission

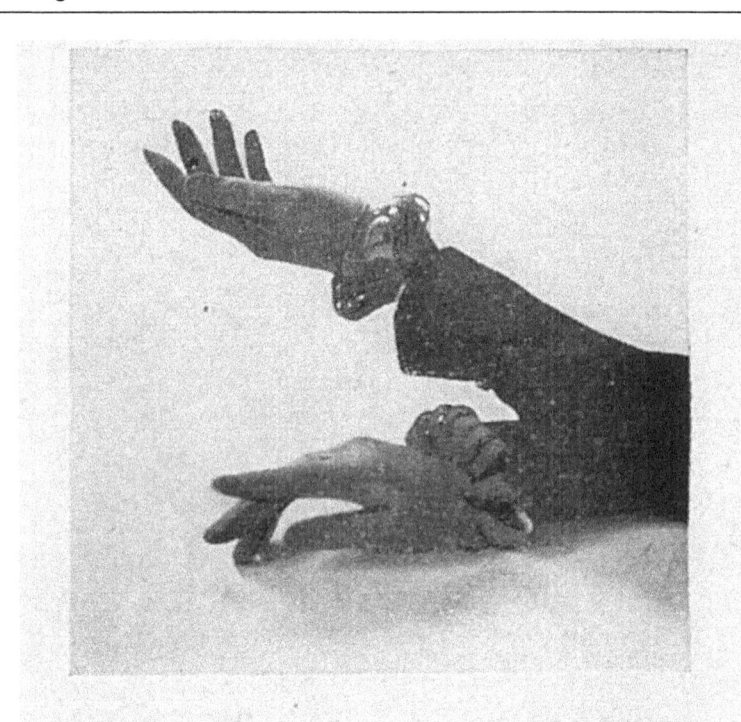

Fringed Gloves that flare out in the manner of a courtier's cuff— neat looking and fitted closely with an elastic at the wrist. They are imported from Italy, and may be ordered in black, brown, or royal blue suede, with the cutout fringe lined in white, beige, or gray. $8.50. Barra Gloves, 519 Madison Avenue.

2.2 Shopping tips recommending Barra gloves. *Harper's Bazaar*, April 1948. Courtesy of *Harper's Bazaar*, Hearst Magazine Media, Inc. Image published with permission of ProQuest LLC. Further reproduction is prohibited without permission

manufacturers ought to use only the best materials and not be tempted to use cheap leather. Yet the vicissitudes experienced by CADMA at its inception demonstrated that the availability of raw materials was fluctuating and the market frequently unfavourable. Only those artisans who could afford high costs or had strong connections with suppliers managed to secure decent or superior leather for their products. On the other hand, many American buyers were unaccustomed to the variety of options available from Italian manufacturers, and thus tended to buy cheap goods in large quantities, creating discontent among the retailers who would later sell the gloves in the United States. Barra remarked that, apparently, when 'the gloves reach America, the stores are disappointed in them and the result is a prejudice against the Italian product, with the retailers thinking that Italian gloves are inferior. That prejudice is so great that buyers go over and make the same mistake all over again'.[65] A further Barra of Italy employee echoed the concern, again in *Women's Wear Daily*.[66] He advocated that gloves Made in Italy should have been recognized as premium quality goods, considering that the fine reputation enjoyed by American and French gloves was linked to their use of Italian kid leather. Thus American retailers, he continued, diminished the value of Italian gloves by not advertising their country of origin. Buyers confronted with Barra's complaint agreed on the 'tremendous potential' of Italian gloves, mostly given their cheap prices compared to French ones. Still, the buyers complained about the discrepancies often recorded between samples and the final deliveries, as

> more adequate supervision and inspection of the product on both sides of the ocean is necessary for an improvement of the Italian glove on the American market. If such inspection and supervision were maintained, buyers say that they would be willing to count on delivery and quality which they have not felt they could do.[67]

These were the premises on which HDI was striving to find its place in the complicated market of Italian exports. The concern of US buyers was directed at the quality of samples, which reportedly did not match the orders that followed, a concern frequently voiced by Ascoli. HDI placed itself at the core of the issue highlighted by Barra: it helped American buyers supervise and select manufacturers, and it aided manufacturers in delivering high-quality goods in pre-approved forms and designs. The presence of HIH introduced new artistic qualities in the market for Italian goods, with the press noting a consequent change in prices, particularly in relation to furniture pieces. The exhibition of larger décor items was usually accompanied by a scattering of smaller, attractive apparel goods, such as the handmade leather sandals that had proven to be very popular with United States fashion journalists.[68] The revival of Italian decorative arts became a mainstream narrative trope used by specialized and generalist commentators alike, as is evident from a 1948 shopping column in *The New Yorker* detailing the merchandise available at HIH that winter. HIH helped draw attention to the fact that the US market, at least on the East Coast, was now offered stylish alternatives to 'those marvellously executed but artistically atrocious souvenirs that cluttered up the luggage of at least three generations of touring Americans'.[69] The article explained that, finally, the numerous Italian 'hereditary craftsmen … have been guided away from their gimcracks into works of the most original and delightful sort', and goods of real aesthetic value were now produced in Italy, even if at a rather high price.[70] Ironically, it was noted that HIH's prices were so high that one could think 'that the concern was trying to settle the Italian national debt by the sale of one chair'. Still, the distinctive look of the pieces carried by HIH was undoubtedly convincing to New York customers, because some of its imports started to be sold in other shops as well.

At the same time, though, the media circulation discussing the influence of HIH was key in promoting new sources of trends from Italy and, with them, powerful all-round professionals. Those trendy pieces seemed to combine traditional materials with modern aesthetics and undoubtedly contributed to a more contemporary image of Italian decorative arts, industrial design, and crafts. The influence exerted on the reception of fashion merchandise represented a step forward in the establishment of what Vittoria Caratozzolo defines as 'the cultural terrain for fashion' and the 'interweaving of old and new'.[71] Forerunning what the 1950–53 travelling exhibition of industrial design and crafts *Italy at Work* would promote, the aesthetic spectrum represented by HIH comprised 'the different faces of Italian material culture': namely modern industrial design, 'folkloric' items, and daring, experimental 'art-craft' objects.[72]

The House of Italian Handicrafts in the press

The opening of HIH was crucial to establishing the earliest wave of prominence for postwar Italian fashion in New York. An informative bulletin on the opening of HIH, sent by CADMA to Italian artisans, clearly specified that the showroom aimed to promote Italian handicrafts through substantial and specific exposure in the media; magazines, newspapers, trade newspapers, and radio shows were considered primary outlets.[73] The appearance of HIH in fashion-related media is imputable to two different strategies: the circulation of news about Italian fashion merchandise, and the legitimization of HIH and the cultural capital it would come to represent as a reputable source of fashionable exports. Regarding the former, the showroom on East 49th Street showcased textiles, accessories, and leather goods from its inception. Business records pertaining to the organization of HIH's first large exhibition in June 1947, *Handicraft as a Fine Art in Italy*, list several works commissioned by CADMA for various samples of fabrics either panted or hand-printed.[74] Some of the artists included were Fabrizio Clerici, Enrico Bordoni, Piero Fornasetti, and Renato Guttuso: the fabrics included motifs such as watermelons, wicker-covered bottles or *fiaschi*, and amphoras, highly suggestive of the Southern European charm within which the Italian Look would become so representative in the following years.[75] By echoing and amplifying the overlapping between Mediterranean and Made in Italy outlined by Elena Dellapiana, fashion merchandise would often employ constant reminders not so much to the lifestyle of Italians, but rather to the romanticized gaze of the privileged, wealthy tourists.[76] In regards to the second strategy mentioned earlier, it was always a top priority for HIH to create a polished and sophisticated appearance for its space. The building's interiors featured smart and modern décor, striking murals created by Sardinian artist Costantino Nivola, and an overall sophisticated atmosphere, put together under the supervision of Marion Ascoli. Nothing in the showroom appeared as stereotypically Italian: instead, the sleek and fashionable interior decoration combined the modernity of its design and the tradition of its manufacturing process. HIH functioned as a flagship store to what would constitute the basis for Italy's new 'consciousness of design's economic and social role'.[77] As a result, the rooms of HIH were often used as a backdrop for fashion shoots because of their characteristic aesthetics.

The *New York Times* granted extensive coverage to HIH, frequently reporting on its exhibitions and the selection of items carried. The reports regularly stressed the items' adherence to American taste and the fact that they did not pose threats of competition to national manufacturers. This editorial choice was dictated by the managing team and disseminated trough the press by HDI's publicist Anna Rosenberg. It was paramount to promptly reassure columnists that the Italian exports on display at HIH were non-competitive with domestic production and had been selected especially for their ability to fill particular needs within the US market.[78] The same aspect of non-competitiveness will be highlighted a few years later with the exhibition *Italy at Work*, as repeated throughout the press releases commissioned by the Brooklyn Museum and the exhibition catalogue. While the objects represented in the pages of the *New York Times* included mostly home décor accessories and giftware, the selection of 'fashion accessories' carried by the store expanded when HIH differentiated its activities into wholesale and retail.[79] Until then, the export potential and suitability of Italian-made fashion accessories and textiles on show at HIH had yet to be fully communicated. The only fashion exhibition organized and documented by surviving official records was held there in the autumn of 1947. It consisted of a small selection of garments and fashion accessories, but there is no further information on the items on view, especially because these were not provided by CADMA, but rather outsourced from the stock already available in department stores and to buying offices in New York. Since HDI was not directly representing these exporters, the press was not invited, there had been no inauguration, and it was decided to invite only about fifty guests among buyers and retailers.[80] Aside from this only event, there was a somehow steady presence of textiles and accessories on view during the years of HIH's activity, as HDI sponsored famed shoemakers Frattegiani and Ferragamo from Florence, textile creatives Fede Cheti and Piero Fornasetti of Milan, and Roman costume jewellery makers Eva Carocci Vedres and Luciana Aloisi.

On the one hand, fashion columns did show some interest in the apparel merchandise showcased. *Women's Wear Daily* devoted articles to the precious handmade lingerie, the ingenuous textiles often decorated by famous artists, and the straw bags and hats on display. On the other hand, the same journal favoured news on the business structure and activities of the two organizations over reports on the available merchandise. News on the most recently appointed members of the board of HDI, changes in management at HIH and so forth were quickly reported, while not so much information can be found on HIH's exhibitions from 1947 to 1949. Similarly, *Vogue* and *Harper's Bazaar* published a few articles marking the opening of HIH and did in fact publish some photographs of the fashion accessories on display. Yet the presence of Italian goods in the two magazines was often limited to furniture pieces, drapery fabrics, and homeware, used either as props in fashion shoots or promoted in dedicated advertisements.

The first mention of HIH in a major US fashion magazine is found in the June 1947 *Harper's Bazaar* issue where, against the backdrop of Pennsylvania Station in New York, Italian leather bags are paired with three fashionable outfits in the two-page spread 'Make It From A Pattern'. The capture describing the photograph reads briefly 'Other bags, House of Italian Handicrafts'.[81] In the photograph, taken by Richard Avedon in bold Kodachrome hues (Figure 2.3), a model on the right holds two leather bags in contrasting colours: a smaller frame purse in black and a large, chestnut brown tote-like bag. This is the first instance in which HIH was featured in a leading fashion magazine, in a colour photograph, just two months after its inauguration. Ensuing mentions of HIH in *Harper's Bazaar* are articles or fashion shoots in which furniture and home décor objects appear as props, for instance in the case of a silk screen by artist Piero Fornasetti used as a backdrop for a Hattie Carnegie outfit (Figure 2.4). Preparatory photographs of the same three-panel folding screen are still held in the archive of Istituto d'Arte di Porta Romana (now Liceo Artistico Statale di Porta Romana) in Florence, which was once one of the two headquarters of CADMA there. The archive still stores information pertaining to CADMA's activities because of Ferruccio Pasqui, once the director of the school and a member of the CADMA board. There, in a thick photobook labelled 'CADMA', black and white photographs show uncaptioned artistic objects, handicrafts, and furniture. As a catalogue of sorts, the photobook shows the details of the nineteenth-century inspired Fornasetti screen published in *Harper's Bazaar*

2.3 Handbags from the House of Italian Handicrafts. *Harper's Bazaar*, June 1947. Courtesy of *Harper's Bazaar*, Hearst Magazine Media, Inc. Photograph by Richard Avedon. © The Richard Avedon Foundation. Image published with permission of ProQuest LLC. Further reproduction is prohibited without permission

reproducing a five-story building (Figure 2.5) on one side and a series of rosettes and medallions (Figure 2.6) on the other. The aesthetic of these prints was, and still today is, peculiar to Fornasetti's style, in which inspiration comes from classical themes and 'figurative fantasy', but is modern enough to be reproduced on any surface thanks to a special printing process created by Piero Fornasetti himself.[82] Per these photographs, there was more than one screen, and another version featured a portion of a forest in which the trees seemed to open up a passage for the audience.[83] The modern feeling that these props exuded made Italian artisanal export goods attractive to American consumers.

2.4 Fornasetti screens from the House of Italian Handicrafts. *Harper's Bazaar*, March 1948. Courtesy of *Harper's Bazaar*, Hearst Magazine Media, Inc. Photograph by Louise Dahl-Wolfe. © Center for Creative Photography, Arizona Board of Regents. Image published with permission of ProQuest LLC. Further reproduction is prohibited without permission

One of the most beneficial articles for HDI's reputation, partly anticipating the genesis of the touring exhibition *Italy at Work* (1950–53), is a 1947 article written by Marya Mannes for Condé Nast's *House & Garden* magazine. 'Italy Looks Ahead' gives some credit to Ponti in Milan for stimulating the newly found drive in Italian artisanship, but also mentions how 'Handicraft Development, Inc., an organization responsible for the first postwar resumption of Italy's export trade with America, has given great encouragement to artisans working in this field'.[84] In the same issue an advertisement, styled as an editorial, describes and praises HDI and its showroom HIH for being 'not a shop but a reference room for American importers'. The language used by

2.5 Fornasetti screen photographed by CADMA, spring of 1948. Archivio del Liceo Artistico Statale di Porta Romana, Florence

Mannes is highly evocative of what was to later become the main theme around the new wave of Italian national design, in both the handicrafts and, later, the fashion industries. Mentions of the Renaissance linked the newly found creative productivity of artisans and designers to the illustrious pinnacle of Italy's cultural production, but this trope was not new. In fashion, specifically, it had been employed decades earlier by feminist activist and fashion designer Rosa Genoni,[85] while D. Medina Lasansky has keenly captured the Fascist appropriation of the Italian Renaissance heritage, mapping out the highly selective celebration of the past in the

2.6 Fornasetti screen photographed by CADMA, spring of 1948. Archivio del Liceo Artistico Statale di Porta Romana, Florence

discourses circulating to advance Fascism's intertwined political and cultural agendas.[86] Thus the cause for Italy's creative independence and the backdrop of the Renaissance, during which Italy was unanimously recognized as the tastemaker of Europe, re-emerged during Italy's new-found arts and crafts revival, yet this time with a new political connotation aligned with Ascoli's neoliberal view of international trade. The use of such themes in the promotional rhetoric of Italian design will be discussed more fully in the next chapters with the analysis of the exhibition *Italy at Work* and its overlap with Giovanni Battista Giorgini's fashion shows during the 1950s.

Mannes' descriptions of democratic Italy's new-found creativity would soon generate a sort of linguistic corpus used by the US fashion press concerning the emergent Italian fashion trends. Adjectives emphasized novelty and originality, stressing the efforts of a pool of experienced artisans working towards the desires of the US market, often on special-order demand: the language is direct, sentences are short and incisive, details abound but are useful in portraying a vivid image of both handicrafts, their makers, and their surroundings. This is particularly evident in all articles on Italy written by Mannes in this period, in sharp contrast with Bettina Ballard's elaborate and poetic prose analyzed in Chapter 1. By extension, and demonstrating the circulation of such a discourse, that same language can be found in the 1949 four-page advertisement 'Italian Address Book', the first proper appearance of HIH in *Vogue*.[87] The spread followed four introductory pages in which the *Vogue* editors pedagogically pointed out the benefits of quoting *Vogue* when selling fashion-related merchandise. It showcased eight categories of merchandise and listed the addresses of selected Italian makers of apparel and accessories, all of them represented by HIH. The introduction read:

> Italian address book, compiled by the editors of American and French Vogues. Reported here: Italy – important, expanding foreign market; its news in fashion resources (accessories, fabrics, decorative fabrics) from Milan, Florence, Rome. The already recognized and fast-growing handicraft industry is represented in New York by the House of Italian Handicrafts, Inc. This is the coordinating agency for the handicraft field, but its services and knowledge of *all* Italian markets are complete and available to all buyers. For additional information write or visit Vogue's Merchandising Office in New York.[88]

This was the first instance in which HIH promoted its selection of fashion accessories and textiles in a major fashion magazine with a paid advertisement. It is significant that this visibility was paid for, as this particular *Vogue* issue was an 'advanced trade edition'. Business literature of the time explains the function of these special issues, made by both *Vogue* and *Harper's Bazaar*. They were specifically 'designed to help stores tie in selling campaigns with advertising and promotion in current issues of these magazines', with *Vogue* dedicating a prominent part of the magazine to illustrating the most recent news in trends and availabilities. The magazine would additionally send copies of these editions to merchandise managers, buyers, and retailers who had an interest in this trade.[89] The 1949 *Vogue* 'Italian Address Book' thus represents an important legitimization of the good taste of HIH and Italian handicraft makers, granted by the paid approval of the press. The text, bearing a strong resemblance to the language used by Mannes, makes frequent use of adjectives such as important, outstanding, original, supple, and expanding, highlighting the relevance of this newly found export market. Combining traditional skills with modern taste, the advertisement pointed out how '[the] traditional Italian creative art centers

... have received a great new design-stimulus: the work of important architects and interior designers in Italy'.[90] Some of the images in the pages featured backdrops immediately identifiable with Italy. A leather bag by Gucci, for instance, was shown hanging from the arm of a statue of the Roman goddess Minerva, decorating the plinth of Benvenuto Cellini's Perseus under the Loggia della Signoria in Florence. One Ferragamo shoe was shown resting with the heel touching a boundary stone and facing a wrought iron door, while two boots made by Milanese firm Leli Cattaneo were placed over a banister looking over Milan's cathedral in the background. A similar aesthetic, which will be discussed in Chapter 3, had been used in Clifford Coffin's 1946 photographs to display a Gucci bag and three Ferragamo shoe models, as seemingly casually placed objects on the parapets of the river Arno in Florence, with Ponte Vecchio as a blurred but distinguishable background.[91]

Mentions of HIH in the American press accounted for both an increased familiarity towards the East 49th Street showroom and towards Italian handcrafted luxury goods in general. This was in keeping with the many articles in *Women's Wear Daily* reporting on the need to 'boost imports from Italy', discussing 'unparalleled expansion in the volume of shipments' from Italy to the United States, and the 'general acceptance of Italian goods'.[92] Even the *New York Times* spoke of the same trend. In October 1948 the American Chamber of Commerce for Trade with Italy announced that Italian export goods to the United States during the first semester of 1948 totalled nearly $50,000,000 and surpassed those reported for 1947.[93] The news was accompanied by a suggestion to remove American tariffs on this type of merchandise, given their non-competitive nature with the local mass-produced goods, as had been emphatically remarked by HDI and HIH representatives overtime.

The presence of HIH in the *Vogue* special issue marked the final leg of the promotional strategies outlined by HDI and previously identified by Catharine Rossi.[94] In 1948 HDI was merged with CADMA in a new conglomerate, Compagnia Nazionale Artigiana (from now on CNA).[95] Ascoli considered HDI to be a temporary measure that would cease to exist once the American market recognized and accepted its offer. Prophesizing to Carlo Ludovico Ragghianti in 1946, he guessed that the organizations could continue their operations until 1948, and no further than then.[96] Following the creation of CNA, the House of Italian Handicrafts inaugurated its own retail space, the Piazza, in November 1949. After being only available to buyers, storeowners and home decorators, Italian-made goods were now ready to be made available to private customers. The publicity that they received in the printed press contributed to a widespread acquaintance with Italian modern designs among American consumers.[97] This led the way for preparing a final showcase of the results achieved, which consolidated in the touring exhibition *Italy at Work*.

The commercial results obtained by HDI increased interest in Italian fashion items in the United States. The organization actively emphasized the fact that the products imported were different from any other goods found on the American market, while its staff worked behind the scenes to instruct Italian makers in producing objects that would conform to the taste of US retailers and customers. The public discourse, generated by HDI and disseminated through magazines and newspapers, focused on presenting Italian products as non-competitive with American ones, and as original and ingenious artefacts coming from an ancient artistic tradition. Behind the scenes, the most persistent issues circulating in the private discourses among HDI and CADMA officers, found in business records and correspondence, related to the necessity of defending the non-commercial nature of the venture. This was often in contrast with professional buying offices, and the internal disagreements, eventually, excluded the participation of Ragghianti and Vannini Parenti from the transformation of CADMA into CNA and the latter's key role in the organization of *Italy at Work*.

By the end of the Second World War, American private citizens and non-governmental organizations sponsored philanthropic initiatives towards the Italian population, largely within the Italian-American community. As a scholar in the field of philosophy and political sciences, Ascoli advocated for work as a form of empowerment and to escape the political traps of both Communist and Fascist totalitarian regimes. From Ascoli's perspective, America was not a political paradigm for universal adoption, but rather a suggestion for its conceptualization of work; something that could help the newly liberated Italians become self-supporting allies of the United States, and not parasites. The promotional activities linked to Ascoli's envisioned initiatives, from HDI to *Italy at Work*, repeatedly stressed the importance of their philanthropic efforts and the political standpoint of their contributions over the business results of the handicraft trade.

CADMA and HDI considered it crucial to direct the work of Italian artisans and focus their output for export to the United States. HDI frequently stressed the importance of variants in the samples produced to instruct the handicraft workers to be active in their reception of feedback from United States buyers. Yet, to do so, Italian products in the US market had to break free of prejudices relating to their quality and the lack of recognition of their country of origin. In her analysis of the postwar US perception of Italian fashion, Valerie Steele has argued that, even if Italy was not famous for its fashion market, it could indeed count on 'a long tradition of elegant craftsmanship'[98] This was indeed the message that HDI and CADMA so vehemently wanted to convey at the time, especially in connection to the opening of HIH. Considering the breadth of goods available in the Italian handicraft market, quality was undoubtedly inconsistent and unexperienced buyers complicated the situation further: the will to obtain the

cheapest price and their scarce knowledge of this saturated market prevented many from scoring a good deal. The barter agreements stipulated
by Italian manufacturers in the textile business introduced instances of
commissioned weaving which contributed to a further lack of recognition
of Italy as a country of origin. Nevertheless, the flux of buyers that kept
visiting Italian markets and the interest spurred by some affordably elegant
merchandise contributed to rehabilitating the image of some categories
of products. The following chapter will consider the breadth of operations
undertaken by different types of commissionaires in Florence, comparing
the efforts of CADMA and its vice-president, Mario Vannini Parenti with
the establishment of the G.B. Giorgini buying office, and discussing at the
same time the increasing circulation of promotional events that paved the
way to the First Italian High Fashion Show of 1951.

Notes

1   'New Arts and Crafts from Italy', *House & Garden* June 1947, p. 120.
2   S. Guilbaut, *How New York Stole the Idea of Modern Art* (Chicago: University of
    Chicago Press, 1983), pp. 135–36.
3   D.W. Ellwood, *Rebuilding Europe: Western Europe, America and Postwar Recon-
    struction* (London: Longman), pp. 113–14.
4   P. Ginsborg, *A History of Contemporary Italy: Society and Politics, 1943–1988*
    (London: Penguin Books, 1990), p. 115.
5   Economic Cooperation Administration, *European Recovery Program. Italy Country
    Study* (Washington: United States Government Printing Office, 1949), p. 31.
6   The National Archives, United Kingdom, CAB 158/14/24, Ministry of Defence and
    Cabinet Office: Central Intelligence Machinery: Joint Intelligence Sub-Committee
    (later Committee), *Soviet World Communism in 1951*, 21 April 1952. Accessed
    online 28 November 2016. www.secretintelligencefiles.com/Content/swwf.cab
    158/0014/024.
7   Ellwood, *Rebuilding Europe*, 115.
8   W.L. Wall, *Inventing the 'American Way': The Politics of Consensus from the New
    Deal to the Civil Rights Movement* (Oxford: Oxford University Press, 2008), p. 243.
9   E. Martinez and E.A. Suchman, 'Letters From America and the 1948 Elections in
    Italy'. *The Public Opinion Quarterly* 14(1), 1950, pp. 111–25.
10 D. Battisti, 'Italian Americans, Consumerism, and The Cold War in Transnational
    Perspective'. In *Making Italian America: Consumer Culture and the Production of
    Ethnic Identities*, edited by Simone Cinotto (New York: Fordham University Press,
    2014), pp. 148–62, 150–51.
11 Brooklyn Museum Archives, Public Information Department records (hereafter
    BMA, PUB), Press Releases, 1947–1952. 'Statements by Dr. Max Ascoli at the
    Opening of the Exhibition, "Italy at Work" at the Brooklyn Museum, Wednesday
    evening, November 29th, 1950', Document 07–09/1950, p. 109.
12 'Italian Handicrafts', *New York Times* (12 April 1947), p. 16
13 Guilbaut, *How New York Stole the Idea of Modern Art*, 189–93.
14 L. Taylor, *The Study of Dress History* (Manchester: Manchester University Press,
    2002), pp. 223–25.
15 O. Cirillo, 'Fashion and Tourism in Campania in the Middle of the Twentieth
    Century: a Story with Many Protagonists'. *Almatourism. Journal of Tourism, Culture
    and Territorial Development* 9(9), 2018, pp. 23–46, 25.
16 R. Camurri, 'Introduzione. Il Liberale Gentiluomo'. In *Max Ascoli: Antifascista, Intel-
    lettuale, Giornalista*, edited by Renato Camurri (Milan: FrancoAngeli, 2012), pp.
    9–24, 14.

17 J.L. Hess, 'Max Ascoli, Publisher of The Reporter, Dies at 79', *New York Times* (2 January 1978), p. 24.
18 M. Ascoli, *The Power of Freedom* (New York: Farrar, Straus and Company, 1949), p. 49.
19 Ascoli, *The Power of Freedom*, 31.
20 R. Bedarida, 'Export/Import: The Promotion of Contemporary Italian Art in the United States, 1935–1969' (PhD Dissertation, Graduate Center, City University of New York, 2016), p. 111.
21 R. Bedarida, 'Operation Renaissance: Italian Art at MoMa, 1940–1949'. *Oxford Art Journal* 35(2), 2012, pp. 147–69.
22 B. Croce, 'The Fascist Germ Still Lives', *New York Times Magazine* (28 November 1943), p. 9.
23 Fondazione Ragghianti, Archivio Carlo Ludovico Ragghianti, Lucca (hereafter FR, ACLR), CADMA. Fasc. 1, 'Per gli artigiani esportatori', pamphlet, undated [1946]. Document 38/1 1840.
24 F. Tamagna, *Report on Conditions in Italy: A Report on a Trip to Italy Made by Frank M. Tamagna between August 4 and October 14, 1945* (New York: Federal Reserve Bank of New York, Foreign Research division, 1945), p. i.
25 'Mission Going to Italy to Aid Industrial Arts', *New York Herald Tribune* (2 August 1945), p. 22.
26 A. Pellegrino, *La Città Più Artigiana d'Italia. Firenze 1861–1929*. Studi e Ricerche Storiche (Milan: FrancoAngeli, 2012), pp. 79–90.
27 FR, ACLR, CADMA. Fasc. 1, 'Per gli artigiani esportatori,' pamphlet, undated [1946]. Document 38/1 1840, p. 5.
28 G. Coppedè, 'La Promozione Dell'artigianato Artistico Italiano Negli Stati Uniti d'America (1945–1953): Il Contributo Di Max Ascoli e Carlo Ludovico Ragghianti' (Dissertation, Università degli Studi di Pisa, 2009), p. 4.
29 FR, ACLR, Carteggio generale, Ascoli, Max (DOC 83) 1945–1980. Max Ascoli to Carlo Ludovico Ragghianti, 31 May 1946. Document 7 2015a.
30 FR, ACLR, Carteggio generale, Ascoli, Max (DOC 83) 1945–1980. Max Ascoli to Carlo Ludovico Ragghianti, 19 February 1946. Document 802a.
31 FR, ACLR, Carteggio generale, Ascoli, Max (DOC 83) 1945–1980. Max Ascoli to Carlo Ludovico Ragghianti, 18 July 1946. Document 2036b.
32 Original in Italian: 'Un punto della lettera tua e di quella a te di Checchi m'ha fatto andare su tutte le furie, perché avete perfettamente ragione: i consigli tecnici, disegni, giornali ecc. che vi s'era promesso di mandare non vi sono stati mandati. La colpa è di quella ballonara [sic] di Miss Diamond a cui era stata data la responsabilità del servizio e che non ha fatto assolutamente niente. Disgraziatamente aveva con noi un contratto per un anno che da gente onesta abbiamo dovuto mantenere. Ma ora l'anno è finito e exit Miss Diamond. Questo servizio ora è stato messo in mani migliori. Vedrete poi capitare in Italia un'altra femmina americana le cui funzioni sono ben ristrette e definite: cooperare con la commissione tecnica nell'acquisto dei campioni e dare ai membri della commissione tecnica idee sulle tendenze del mercato americano.' FR, ACLR, Carteggio generale, Ascoli, Max (DOC 83) 1945–1980. Max Ascoli to Carlo Ludovico Ragghianti, 18 July 1946. Document 2036b. In December 1946 Dinsmore became director of trade relations and merchandising of HDI. 'Business Notes', *New York Times* (24 December 1946), p. 24.
33 Foreign Affairs Oral History Collection, Association for Diplomatic Studies and Training, Arlington, VA. Transcript of Interview to Vincent Checchi with Melbourne Spector, 11 July 1990. Accessed online 28 November 2016. https://adst.org/OH%20TOCs/Checchi,%20Vincent%20V.TOC.pdf.
34 FR, ACLR, CADMA. Fasc. 3. Max Ascoli to Mario Vannini Parenti, 18 February 1946. Document 1983a.
35 FR, ACLR, CADMA. Fasc. 2. Commissione di presidenza 1945–1948. Riepilogo attività, 5 January 1946. Documents 39/38bis 1945a–b.

36 FR, ACLR, CADMA. Fasc. 2. Commissione tecnica 1946–1947. Verbale commissione tecnica, 6 September 1946. Document 38/28 1871a.

37 'Mission Going to Italy to Aid Industrial Arts', 22.

38 P. Menneg, 'Italian Silk Fabrics Plan Stirs Market', *Women's Wear Daily* (22 July 1946), p. 29.

39 T.H. Conroy, 'Exporter Accepts Imports in Trade', *New York Times* (31 August 1947), section III, p. 1.

40 FR, ACLR, CADMA. Fasc. 3, Bruno Foà to Mario Vannini Parenti, 1 February 1946. Document 39/18 1925e.

41 FR, ACLR, CADMA. Fasc. 2, Commissione di presidenza 1945–1948. Relazione sulle attività della CADMA, June 1946. Document 38/16 1856g.

42 Menneg, 'Italian Silk Fabrics Plan Stirs Market'.

43 B.J. Perkins, 'Furnish Italian Silk Mills With Designs For American Trade', *Women's Wear Daily* (3 September 1946), p. 1.

44 H. Koshetz, 'Imports of silk from Italy begun', *New York Times* (30 June 1946), section III, p. 1; P. Menneg, 'Westinghouse Restricts Italian Silk Fabric Imports', *Women's Wear Daily* (6 March 1947), p. 38.

45 Menneg, 'Italian Silk Fabrics Plan Stir US Market'.

46 Economic Cooperation Administration, *European Recovery Program. Italy country study*, 28.

47 Menneg, 'Westinghouse Restricts Italian Silk Fabric Imports'.

48 L. Savi, *A New History of 'Made in Italy'. Fashion and Textiles in Post-War Italy* (London: Bloomsbury Publishing, 2023), p. 25.

49 C.M. Belfanti, *Storia culturale del Made in Italy* (Bologna: Il Mulino, 2019), pp. 178–79.

50 B.J. Perkins, 'Como's Silk Mills Ready to Start Again', *Women's Wear Daily* (18 June 1945), p. 7.

51 FR, ACLR, CADMA. Fasc. 2, Commissione di presidenza 1945–1948. Verbale commissione di presidenza, 30 December 1945. Document 9/39 1946b.

52 FR, ACLR, Carteggio generale. Ascoli, Max (DOC 83) 1945–1980. Max Ascoli to Carlo Ludovico Ragghianti, 18 July 1946. Document 2036a.

53 FR, ACLR, Carteggio generale. Ascoli, Max (DOC 83) 1945–1980. Max Ascoli to Carlo Ludovico Ragghianti, 13 December 1946. Document 3/1955.

54 FR, ACLR, Carteggio generale. Ascoli, Max (DOC 83) 1945–1980. Max Ascoli to Carlo Ludovico Ragghianti, 13 December 1946. Document 3/1955.

55 National Museum of American History, Archives Center, Dorothy Shaver Papers. Box 7, folder 37, 'Outline of suggestions for a short address to be given by Dorothy Shaver at the opening of the House of Italian Handicrafts on April 10, 1947'.

56 FR, ACLR, CADMA. Fasc. 3, Bruno Foà to the CADMA staff, 17 April 1947. Document 1476.

57 M.M., 'Handicrafts from Italy here again', *Brooklyn Daily Eagle* (11 April 1947), p. 13.

58 'Italian Hand Mades', *Women's Wear Daily* (17 April 1947), p. 43.

59 FR, ACLR, CADMA. Fasc. 1, 'Per gli artigiani esportatori', pamphlet, undated [1946]. Document 38/1 1840.

60 FR, ACLR, CADMA. Fasc. 3, Commissione di presidenza 1945–1948. CADMA commissione di presidenza, circolare interna #2, 31 October 1947. Document 38/40 1897. The same obligation was later requested to artisans by Compagnia Nazionale Artigiana (CNA), the agency that would eventually replace HDI and CADMA in 1948, as recently demonstrated by Paola Cordera and Ali Filippini: P. Cordera, 'L'incantesimo della casa. L'arte e l'industria in vetrina'. In *Storytelling. Esperienze e comunicazione del cultural heritage*, edited by Sandra Costa, Paola Cordera, and Dominique Poulot (Bologna: Bologna University Press, 2022), p. 229; A. Filippini, 'Paolo De Poli e l'America: 1947–1967. Gli Smalti Verso Il "Nuovo Mondo"'. In *L'Italia al Lavoro. Un Lifestyle da Esportazione*, edited by Paola Cordera and Chiara Faggella (Bologna: Bologna University Press, 2023), pp. 133–40, 136.

61 Original in Italian: 'Gli Americani dovranno convincersi che gli articoli artigiani non si possono comprare più ai prezzi di fame e di strozzature che venivano praticati avanti la guerra, e che ad altro non servivano che a rovinare questa magnifica attività.' FR, ACLR, CADMA. Fasc. 3, Mario Vannini Parenti to Bruno Foà, 22 February 1946. Document 39/19 1926a.
62 S. Segre Reinach, 'The Italian Fashion Revolution in Milan'. In *The Glamour of Italian Fashion Since 1945*, edited by Sonnet Stanfill (London: V&A Publishing, 2014), pp. 58–75, 60.
63 B.J. Perkins, 'Glimpses of Paris', *Women's Wear Daily* (21 May 1940), p. 21.
64 'Barra Offic [sic] Here Now Independent', *Women's Wear Daily* (5 April 1940), p. 13; 'Obituary: Armando Barra', *Women's Wear Daily* (11 September 1990), p. 24.
65 'Mutual Education Necessary to Revive Italian Glovers', *Women's Wear Daily* (21 November 1947), p. 28.
66 'Prejudice Against Italian Gloves Called Groundless', *Women's Wear Daily* (30 April 1948), p. 11.
67 'Prejudice Against Italian Gloves Called Groundless'.
68 See Chapter 1.
69 S.H., 'On and Off the Avenue. About the house', *New Yorker* (6 November 1948), p. 100.
70 S.H., 'On and Off the Avenue. About the House'.
71 V.C. Caratozzolo, 'Reorienting Fashion: Italy's Wayfinding after the Second World War'. In *The Glamour of Italian Fashion Since 1945*, edited by Sonnet Stanfill (London: V&A Publishing, 2014), pp. 46–57.
72 P. Sparke, 'The Straw Donkey: Tourist Kitsch or Proto-Design? Craft and Design in Italy, 1945–1960'. *Design History Society* 11(1), 1998, pp. 59–69, 60.
73 FR, ACLR, CADMA. Fasc. 4, 'Casa dell'Artigianato', pamphlet, undated [1947]. Document 39/12 1918.
74 FR, ACLR, CADMA. Fasc. 4, 'Lista Mostra Ottobre 47', undated [1947]. Document 38/35 1991, a–e.
75 Guttuso's fabrics can be seen in 'Guttuso: stoffe e vetrate. Bordoni: stoffe', *Domus* April 1948, p. 25.
76 E. Dellapiana, *Il design e l'invenzione del Made in Italy* (Turin: Einaudi, 2022), p. 87.
77 G. Bosoni, *Italian Design. MoMA Design Series* (New York: The Museum of Modern Art, 2008), p. 34.
78 'Benefit Seen to Trade in Italian Loan', *Christian Science Monitor* (13 December 1947), p. 19.
79 'Italy Again Shows Handicrafts Here', *New York Times* (8 November 1949), p. 28.
80 FR, ACLR, CADMA. Fasc. 2, Commissione di presidenza 1945–1948. CADMA commissione di presidenza, circolare interna #2, 31 October 1947. Document 38/40 1898.
81 'Make It From A Pattern'. *Harper's Bazaar* June 1947, p. 97.
82 'Paraventi di Fornasetti'. *Domus* February 1949, p. 36.
83 HIH itself and its interiors were used as setting for fashion shoots in a few more instances by the *New York Times* (in 1949 and 1952) and *Vogue*: 'Vogue Designs for Dressmaking: Necktie Materials For All Day … Late Day'. *Vogue* 1 April 1949, pp. 168–69; 'Summer Cloths … More and Prettier'. *Vogue* 1 May 1949, pp. 125–29.
84 Mannes, 'Italy Looks Ahead', p. 141.
85 M. Soldi, *Rosa Genoni. Moda e politica: una prospettiva femminista tra '800 e '900* (Venice: Marsilio, 2019).
86 D.M. Lasansky, *The Renaissance Perfected. Architecture, Spectacle & Tourism in Fascist Italy* (University Park: The Pennsylvania State University Press, 2004).
87 'Italian Address Book'. *Vogue* 15 February 1949, p. 5.
88 Emphasis originally in the text.
89 B. Duffy, *Advertising Media and Markets* (Hoboken: Prentice-Hall, 1951), p. 288.
90 'Italian Address Book', p. 8.
91 'The Italian School', *Vogue* 15 November 1946, p. 97.

92 'Urges Moves to Boost Imports From Italy', *Women's Wear Daily* (23 May 1947), p. 10; J. Teague, 'Italian Election Results Held Spur to Handicrafts, Exports', *Women's Wear Daily* (21 April 1948), pp. 1, 44, 46; 'Survey Finds Good General Acceptance of Italian Goods', *Women's Wear Daily* (18 January 1949), p. 57.

93 'Handicraft Lines Recover in Italy', *New York Times* (1 October 1948), p. 37.

94 C. Rossi, *Crafting Design in Italy: From Post-War to Postmodernism* (Manchester: Manchester University Press, 2015), p. 13.

95 Its president was Ivan Matteo Lombardo, Italian Minister of Foreign Commerce. Ramy Alexander was the vice-president.

96 Original in Italian: 'Per il futuro più lontano, posso vedere HDI-CADMA prolungata fino al 1948, ma non ho la più pallida idea per il '49, anzi, per dir la mia, vorrei che nel '49 non ci sia più nulla o quasi di HDI o CADMA. Un piano, dunque, possibilmente biennale, ma non più in là.' FR, ACLR, Carteggio generale. Ascoli, Max (DOC 83) 1945–1980. Max Ascoli to Carlo Ludovico Ragghianti, 13 December 1946. Document 3 1955.

97 According to *Women's Wear Daily*, HIH closed the retail division Piazza on 19 June 1953, but kept its wholesale operations until at least 1956.

98 V. Steele, 'Italian Fashion and America'. In *The Italian Metamorphosis, 1943–1968*, edited by Germano Celant (New York: Guggenheim Museum Publications, 1994), p. 496.

3

Florence: old culture and new commerce

The 1951 First Italian High Fashion Show organized by Giovanni Battista Giorgini was the ending point of a long process that saw the re-establishment of Florence's cultural relevance after its Liberation in 1944. From that year on, several exhibitions and culturally relevant events hosted in the city expressed the whirl of international interest in the moral rehabilitation of Italy. This chapter focuses on the role of intermediary businesses based in Florence in the promotion of Italian fashion exports to the United States. It first discusses the role of CADMA and its staff in providing a close relationship between Italian handicraft makers and American retailers and considers the political affinity that Max Ascoli found with the city of Florence and Ragghianti, which preceded the establishment of CADMA and became one of the reasons why Ascoli chose Florence as the Italian operational base of HDI. In fact CADMA's two Florence offices at Palazzo Strozzi and Istituto d'Arte di Porta Romana were not its only Italian branches.[1] Nevertheless, the central organization of CADMA did revolve around its Florence headquarters.[2]

For this reason, contextualization of the presence of CADMA in Florence is crucial to the historical analysis undertaken in this book and to understanding the fertile cultural and commercial ground that prepared for Giorgini's successes in the 1950s. The chapter proceeds then to examine a case study of CADMA's concrete efforts, the return of Salvatore Ferragamo shoes to the American market. It finally interlaces Giovanni Battista Giorgini's biography with CADMA's initiatives and the cultural scenario of the time, discussing Giorgini's core business activities before the 1951 First Italian High Fashion Show and their overlapping with Italian and American promotions for the travelling exhibition *Italy at Work: Her Renaissance in Design Today*.

By the time he founded HDI in 1945, Max Ascoli had established friendships with several of Florence's anti-fascist intellectuals, particularly with Carlo and Nello Rosselli, Piero Calamandrei, and Gaetano Salvemini. His association with Carlo Ludovico Ragghianti, though, as Alessandra Taiuti has demonstrated, was likely initiated during Ascoli's Italian trip in the summer of 1945, during which CADMA was founded.[3] Ragghianti, born in 1910, was a young art critic and historian who graduated from the University of Pisa in 1932 and moved to Florence in the late 1920s. Ragghianti's anti-fascism was as strong if not stronger than Ascoli's, so much so that he quickly became one of the most important members of the Resistance and, in 1944, the president of the Comitato Toscano di Liberazione Nazionale (CTLN). The German troops had declared Florence an open city in July 1944, with Allied Forces entering the city at the beginning of August. Florentine members of the CTLN, led by Ragghianti, actively fought to obtain command of the city and negotiate terms with the Allies. They eventually managed to organize an exceptional form of self-government in Florence, reportedly the first in liberated Italy, which was acknowledged and accepted by the Allies.[4] From the Liberation of Florence in 1944 on, Ragghianti was involved in many cultural initiatives such as exhibitions, publications, and the establishment of councils such as La Strozzina, an association of local institutions whose primary aim was the organization of decorative arts exhibitions in Florence.[5] The 1948 exhibition *La casa italiana nei secoli*, organized per Ragghianti's initiative and with the curatorial direction of Licia Collobi Ragghianti, constituted a sort of parallel event in Italy to the exhibitions with which CADMA equipped the House of Italian Handicrafts, such as *Handicraft as a Fine Art in Italy* (1947) and *Vita all'Aperto* (1948). The intention was to put on display the same domestic dimension of decorative arts that would be later highlighted with *Italy at Work*, legitimizing the creativity of artisans, past and present, and the quality of their work.[6] CADMA, therefore, must be inscribed and discussed within the multitudes of cultural initiatives that aimed at placing Florence once again higher up in the rank of Italy's cultural capitals.

The cultural perspective of Ragghianti needed to be complemented by the experience of a business professional, possibly well-versed in the art trade market, in cultural policies relating to tourism and its fluxes, and in the transatlantic relationships that Italy had maintained in the prewar period. For these reasons, Ragghianti wanted the technical committee of CADMA in Florence to be headed by Mario Vannini Parenti. A former diplomat to South America, Vannini Parenti spent years in Peru, where he contributed to the opening of the Italian Art Museum of Lima (1922), and in Argentina until 1924, when he returned to Italy. He became involved with the Florentine public administration in roles related to tourism and handicrafts until 1941, and obtained a managerial role within the Cosulich steamship line. After a hiatus, in 1944 Vannini Parenti was appointed general commissioner of all Florentine tourist boards.[7] He would soon become an influential member of the executive committee of the local tourism board, Azienda Autonoma del Turismo, and later of the Ente Provinciale per il Turismo di Firenze. Before becoming a resident buyer figure of sorts acting as an intermediary between manufacturers and his HDI colleagues, Vannini Parenti had established strong connections with the Italian-American community in New York. An archival photograph from the 1930s (Figure 3.1) shows him presenting a ceremonial sash embellished with the symbol of Florence to New York mayor Fiorello La Guardia in his role as *consultore municipale* or consultant for the city of Florence.[8]

To promote only the best products possible from each production district of Italy, HDI wanted Vannini Parenti to create sub-commissions within CADMA that could deal with different categories of products: faience, glass, alabaster, textiles, leather, and so forth. Each sub-commission, it was suggested by the New York staff of HDI, could benefit from a series of interviews between CADMA and the Italian producers, something very common in the United States. This request came from the fact that Ascoli and Bruno Foà, executive director of HDI, were afraid that Vannini Parenti was centralizing the power of CADMA in his own hands. There were two motives for not wanting it to happen: the taste displayed by Vannini Parenti was not aligned with the artistic direction coming from Diamond first and Dinsmore later, and, more importantly, his reputation and business associations were not considered crystal clear. These issues slowly

3.1 Mario Vannini Parenti (left) with New York Mayor Fiorello La Guardia and Italian Consul-General Gaetano Vecchiotti, ca. 1937. Archivio fotografico del Museo di Palazzo Davanzati

exonerated Vannini Parenti and Ragghianti from the constitution of Compagnia Nazionale Artigiana (CNA), the semi-public organization that took over the work done by CADMA and HDI and, eventually, the planning of the exhibition *Italy at Work*. Born in 1887 and thus considerably older than Ragghianti (born in 1910) and Ascoli (1898), Vannini Parenti's taste and sensibility for modern styles differed significantly from his colleagues and created a few problems with HDI, whose staff in New York was often not happy with his selections: this issue is considered within a specific reference later in the chapter.

The second issue was a bit more problematic to solve, because Vannini Parenti showed a preference for establishing partnerships with the same businessmen over time, yet his network proved to be beneficial to the image of HDI and the roster of manufacturing firms associated with it. When Ragghianti headed the formation of the government of the city of Florence, the first local government set up by the CTLN, he vouched for Vannini Parenti to be a part of it. Notwithstanding, the correspondence between Ragghianti and Ascoli implies that Vannini Parenti's political background was challenging for the reputation of CADMA: it is arguable that his past administrative roles during the Fascist government had been discussed, although they did not represent the main issue at stake.[9] In fact, Ascoli was nonetheless optimistic when it came to Vannini Parenti's reputation, although cautious: 'rest assured', he confided to Ragghianti, 'that I did hear disparaging rumours about him, and hints to his speculative motives in every possible way. I asked everyone to provide evidence, but I would be very surprised if they could bring actual proofs'.[10] In particular, Ascoli commented on his reluctancy to link his name and that of his newly formed non-profit organization to certain Florentine businessmen such as Salvatore Ferragamo, who had been introduced to Ascoli in Rome during his 1945 trip as an acquaintance of Vannini Parenti. Their correspondence demonstrates that both Ascoli and Ragghianti feared that the affiliations of Vannini Parenti could haunt the good impact that Ascoli wanted HDI and CADMA to obtain over people's perception of Italian crafts in the United States. It is worth remembering here that the statutes of CADMA and HDI clearly specified their non-commercial scope. This element was emphatically emphasized over time and would become a key argument in the controversies experienced later with the already existing commission-aire businesses operating in the United States, discussed in the next section. Surviving private documents demonstrate that Ascoli was not worried by the possibility that Vannini Parenti could be attempting to profit directly from the organization. Rather, he was more concerned with keeping the business of CADMA and HDI as free as possible from monopolistic commitments to specific firms. This is because, he feared,

> now that we have samples, and that trade with Italy is possible again, Vannini tends to bond with similar commercial interests … in any ways I am following

a line of reasoning that resembles the decisions taken [during his 1945 visit to Rome]. That is, agreements with all possible commercial interests, but no strict bonds with anyone, and above all no monopoly to anyone.[11]

The 'line of reasoning' expressed by Ascoli found its application in the day-to-day business through the manufacturers aided by CADMA and promoted by HDI. In particular, an analysis of surviving archival documents and press of the time demonstrate that the firm Salvatore Ferragamo functioned as a driving force behind the fashion merchandise exported through HDI and HIH, but, at the same time, that the agencies supported other manufacturers as well.

In the postwar period, Ferragamo was among the very few Italian firms with a long-established reputation in the United States, as amply demonstrated by both the scholarship led by the Fondazione Ferragamo and the Museo Ferragamo's director, Stefania Ricci, and the many scholars that have investigated the shoemaker's business culture and his legacy in fashion museology.[12] Nonetheless, while several texts have reconstructed the rise to fame of this internationally famous fashion brand, little is known about its activities once the war ended. Present in the American market since the 1920s, the firm's luxury designs embodied ever since an astute compromise between the exoticism of European export products and a keen adaptability to the US market's needs. In addition to this and Ferragamo's own understanding as an entrepreneur of the taste of his overseas customers, the dissemination of Ferragamo footwear in the United States in the postwar years was supported by the expert intermediation of at least two specialized organizations: its commercial partner for distribution, the Gimbels company, and CADMA.[13] The autobiography of Salvatore Ferragamo provides only a few cues to how the firm managed to reappear on the US market after the Second World War: it barely mentions that a former Florentine supplier was generous enough to offer him the possibility to buy a batch of natural leather. Despite the quality was reportedly much lower than the raw materials that he used to work with, Ferragamo accepted it. The only other important consignment that aided Ferragamo's recovery in the earliest postwar years, according to the memoir, was a large batch of raffia from Madagascar.[14] While the memoir does not elaborate on the circumstances, business records pertaining to CADMA document how the organization acted as an intermediary with the Italian Government and thus might be associated with the transaction highlighted in the memoir. Leather was considerably difficult to retrieve during and immediately after the war, but the brokerage of Vannini Parenti, a personal acquaintance of Salvatore Ferragamo, obtained two import licenses from the Ministry of Foreign Commerce, requesting to import leather from the United States for Ferragamo. They served the scope of producing a batch of 10,000 shoes, destined for an unspecified market, and a batch of novel shoe samples to be sold to the Fifth Avenue department store Saks in New York. In addition to these, the documents record how Vannini Parenti requested another license to import leather for other Florentine artisanal workshops, among which was one of the suppliers to Guccio Gucci. Sensing the timely needs of the manufacturers, eager to return to production, Vannini Parenti added in its communication to HDI that it was crucial for the leather to reach Florence from New York via Leghorn 'as soon as possible'.[15]

It is reasonable to presume, then, that some of the Ferragamo and Gucci merchandise photographed by Clifford Coffin for the British and American editions of *Vogue* in the summer of 1946 were samples manufactured thanks to the intermediary aid of Vannini Parenti for CADMA, providing a glimpse into the new production of Florentine leather artisans. Marya Mannes added further information on the items photographed in the quintessential editorial 'Italian fashion' of January 1947, a slightly different version of her earlier British *Vogue* article 'The Fine Italian Hand'.[16] Gucci was represented in the photographed selection by a 'sturdy' bucket bag (Figure 3.2), made of leather tinted in a dark natural hue, closed at the top with a latch threaded into the bag's top half. It was reported that the design had already been 'copied everywhere' and represented one of the most important 'accessory news' from Florence.[17]

At the same time, though, Ferragamo chose to present shoe designs already known to his international customers through advertisements and coverage in the American press. Half of the page (Figure 3.3) was taken by a large, horizontal photograph of a 'Turkish-toed mule', a model from 1938 called 'Moorish'; a version of it, made for the UK luxury department store Fortnum and Mason, is still preserved in the archive at Fondazione Ferragamo. This mule, with its wedge heel, the quirky pointed toe, and the padded tubular decoration circling the upper, sported a reminiscence of the commodification of generic 'oriental' features, meaning really a North African and Middle Eastern 'fabrication of the West'.[18] Popular in 1910s fashion, such features can be observed in other Ferragamo models from the same period.[19] The materials used were cork, suede, and kid leather.[20] With a more contemporary take and perhaps referencing the recent Occupation of Italy, the calfskin boot in the lower-left corner of the page was said to be a model adapted from the idea of an officer's boot, 'very handsome in a conservative way' and deemed 'sensational' by Mannes. The article concluded by saying that Ferragamo had been 'able to return to the manufacture of fine shoes only eight months [prior to January 1947], after the usual vicissitudes of war and occupation': this final note confirms the support received from Vannini Parenti, CADMA, and HDI in the spring of 1946.

When, in 1947, *Vogue* published an imposing, full-page photograph of two slender legs wearing two different models of black shoes, the image celebrated the return of Ferragamo shoes in the United States,

Leather pouch, leather thong

the **I**talian school

This is what Italy makes, and what it has made for centuries: shoes, bags, perfections in leather. Interrupted by war, Italian leather-masters have returned to their craft—and from the celebrated school of shoemaking that gave us the wedge sole, the thong-sandal, come these handmade leather accessories. The scene: Florence, the banks of the Arno, the Ponte Vecchio, where Italian women (whose beautiful legs and feet are possibly the best in Europe) wear shoes like the ones shown here. *Above:* Gucci's pouch: dark, natural leather threaded through with a leather thong. *Opposite:* Shoes by Ferragamo. A Turkish mule. An adaptation of an officer's boot. An Oxford of pink fishskin, surprising source, surprisingly hardy.

3.2 Gucci bag. *Vogue*, November 1946. © Condé Nast

'*from* Ferragamo *to* America … the first to be exported since 1940'.[21] They maintained the same handmade quality expected from 'Italy's celebrated leather master', it was said, plus the new models now featured a lighter structure that would perfectly complement the recent trend of longer skirts launched by Christian Dior with his line 'Corolle'. The collection was exclusively available at Sacks Fifth Avenue, as it had been anticipated by Vannini Parenti in his business correspondence to HDI in New York, and to further spread the news the department store published several full-page advertisements in different US fashion magazines and newspapers, announcing the world-famous shoemaker returning to the store with 'an entire gamut of his beautiful, hand-sewn shoes' (Figure 3.4). Those included an 'interlaced suede ankle strap' pump, probably the model 'Ninfea'; the model 'Cortina' featured in the *Vogue* photo cited above; and the 'Invisible' model.[22]

167

Turkish-toed mule

Calfskin boot

Fishskin Oxford

3.3 Three Ferragamo shoes. *Vogue*, November 1946. © Condé Nast

The penetration of the advertising campaign and the diffusion of the new Ferragamo designs through the most exclusive department store chains in the United States received further media resonance when, in the same year, the Salvatore Ferragamo firm and its founder were awarded the Neiman Marcus Award for Distinguished Service in the Field of Fashion. Marking the fortieth anniversary of the Neiman Marcus store in Dallas, Texas the 1947 celebrations were the first to host international professionals from the world's fashion industries and thus honoured the talents of Irene (Lentz) of Hollywood, Norman Hartnell of London, Christian Dior of Paris, and Salvatore Ferragamo of Florence. The official press release particularly

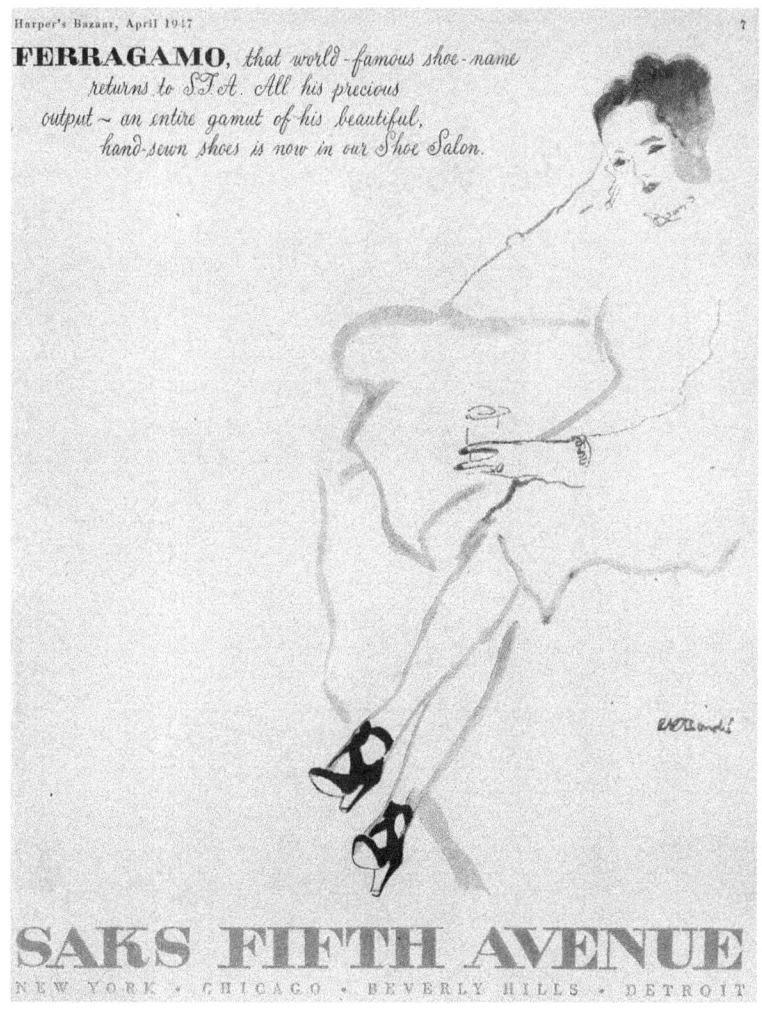

3.4 Ferragamo advertisement by Saks Fifth Avenue. *Harper's Bazaar*, April 1947. Courtesy of *Harper's Bazaar*, Hearst Magazine Media, Inc. Image published with permission of ProQuest LLC. Further reproduction is prohibited without permission

emphasized the practical aspects of Ferragamo's construction theory, derived from his anatomy studies, somehow also grounding his exoticism and artisanal skills in the high culture of medicine studies. The beauty and ingenuity of the shoes derived from an 'orthopedic understanding' that mirrored the study of the human body's proportions typical of classic art studies.[23] In his combining 'Italian classicism and age-old hand-craftmanship with prophetic inventiveness so modern as to be almost fourth dimensional in concept', Ferragamo and, by extension, Italian fashion were included in a poker of fashion capitals in which Paris was flanked by three emergent

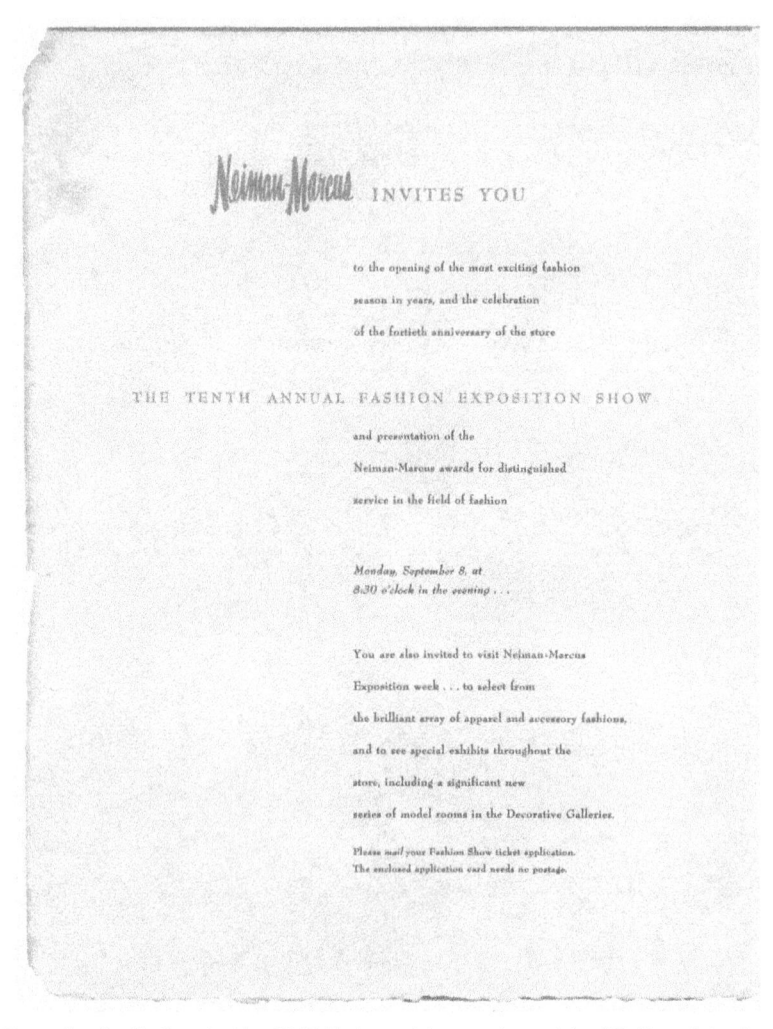

3.5 From the invitation to the 1947 Neiman Marcus Award for Distinguished Service in the Field of Fashion: description of the event. DeGolyer Library, Southern Methodist University

competitors, now worthy of recognition (Figures 3.5 and 3.6).[24] News of this validation was promptly received at the HDI headquarters and, right after his participation in the celebrations in Texas and on his way back to Italy, Ferragamo stopped in New York where a cocktail party was held at HIH in his honour.[25] The ceremony of the 1947 Neiman Marcus Award connected two aspects discussed in this book so far. It consolidated Stanley Marcus' vision for an internationally competitive fashion market, outlined in his 1946 lecture to the Fashion Group of New York previously discussed in Chapter 1. It additionally celebrated the fruitful mobilization

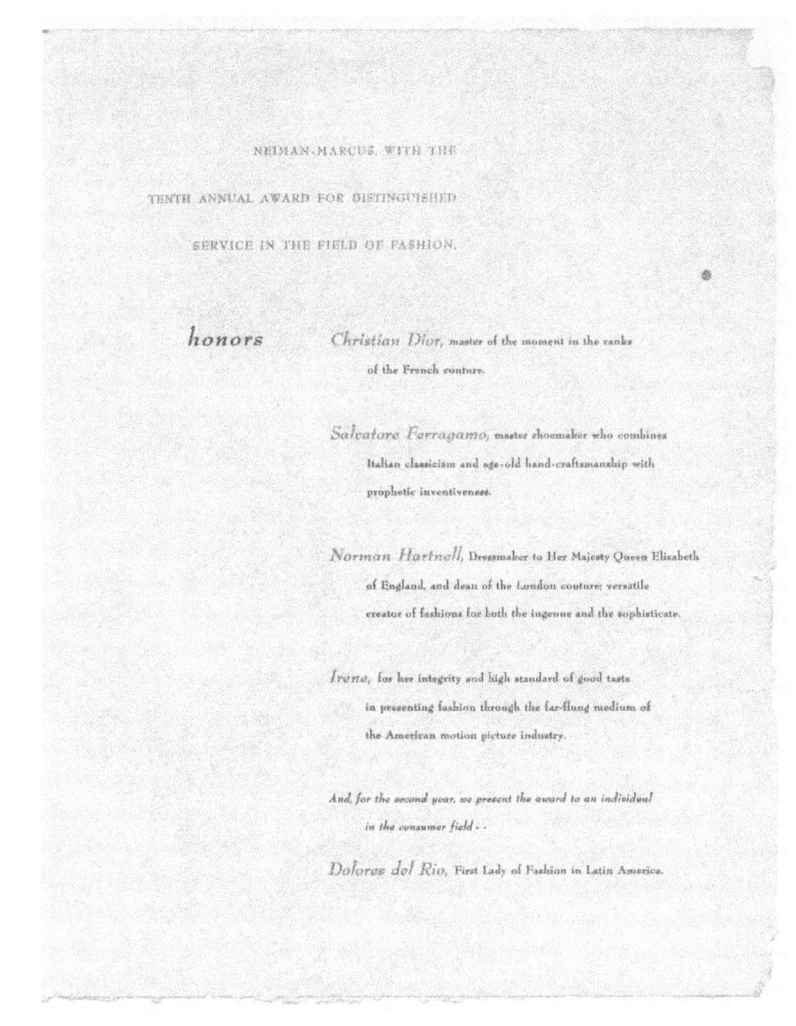

NEIMAN-MARCUS, WITH THE

TENTH ANNUAL AWARD FOR DISTINGUISHED

SERVICE IN THE FIELD OF FASHION,

honors   *Christian Dior*, master of the moment in the ranks
of the French couture.

Salvatore Ferragamo, master shoemaker who combines
Italian classicism and age-old hand-craftsmanship with
prophetic inventiveness.

Norman Hartnell, Dressmaker to Her Majesty Queen Elizabeth
of England, and dean of the London couture; versatile
creator of fashions for both the ingenue and the sophisticate.

Irene, for her integrity and high standard of good taste
in presenting fashion through the far-flung medium of
the American motion picture industry.

*And, for the second year, we present the award to an individual
in the consumer field - -*

Dolores del Rio, First Lady of Fashion in Latin America.

3.6 From the invitation to the 1947 Neiman Marcus Award for Distinguished Service in the Field of Fashion: list of honorees. DeGolyer Library, Southern Methodist University

of the intermediary work of CADMA, who made it possible to concretely produce the prized shoes, and Gimbels, who distributed Ferragamo to Neiman Marcus in Dallas and other stores in the United States.

Ironically, though, even if the award celebrated the spirit of rebirth epitomizing the 'new' Italy through the inventiveness of its most prominent fashion artisan, the original invitation for the award show featured the Fascist emblem to symbolize Italy (Figure 3.7), involuntarily confirming the continuity of those few professionals able to export Made in Italy merchandise in the United States in both inter- and postwar times.[26]

3.7 From the invitation to the 1947 Neiman Marcus Award for Distinguished Service in the Field of Fashion: cover reproducing the symbols of the honorees' home countries. DeGolyer Library, Southern Methodist University

From CADMA to Compagnia Nazionale Artigiana

The case study of Ferragamo offers a perspective on the temporary coexistence of commissionaires and buying offices with the non-commercial scopes of HDI and its associated agencies. In reality, the contrasts experienced by these professionals in opposition to HDI, HIH, and CADMA are central to a more general discussion on the importance of intermediary professionals to the close network of Florentine artisanal workshops. Florence was traditionally home to a thick network of buying offices, thanks to its convenient location in Central Italy, which made it easy to reach production centres in other regions and the many artisanal workshops in the neighbouring areas (e.g. Doccia, Signa, Impruneta, Arezzo, Santa Croce, etc.). The network of commissionaires and intermediaries was competitive and included both independent agencies and local branches of foreign distributors and retailers: among the American ones, Gimbels and AMC (American Merchandising Corporation) opened their offices between 1928 and 1933 and remained active even after the effects of the economic crisis of 1929 shut down many of the Italian independent offices.[27] Within this complex scenario, the archival sources confirm that neither HDI nor CADMA ever intended to be perceived as commercial buyers or intermediaries: their revenue was only meant to pay operational expenses such as rent, shipping costs, insurance coverage, and salaries to clerks and assistants, as members of both committees reportedly worked pro bono. Furthermore, the presence of HDI and CADMA in the market was never conceived to be in competition with commercial buying offices. Many of these offices had ceased their activities during the Second World War, interrupting commerce between Italy and the United States. In Ascoli's own words, professional buying agents and commissionaires could not return to their businesses unless unpaid brokers went before them and paved their way.[28] The intentions of HDI's staff for the years 1946–47 pointed out that the agency's official position as a business facilitator might have looked flawless on paper, yet it still needed to demonstrate its scope for commercial buying offices

> and eliminate any source of misunderstanding. For instance, we could call a meeting with a group of commissionaires, resident buyers, and some export firms, not only to clarify the controversial points in their minds about our business, but also to obtain their support for the New York exhibition [read: the opening of HIH]. We need to erase any suspicion that we buy samples to compete against them. We could ask them to present some of their goods in the exhibition [at HIH], while we advertise their distribution system.[29]

The suspicion mentioned above most likely arose at the press event that introduced HDI to the general public in the summer of 1945. An article in *Women's Wear Daily* mentioned potential plans for purchasing and distribution, and the possibility of using the local division of a buying office.[30] This possibility was never mentioned again and, instead, it became quite clear that CADMA would be the intermediary between Italian artisans and US buyers. Still, the word 'intermediary' was actively avoided as it suggested that HDI was trying to set up an alternative service between producers and retailers.[31] An informational pamphlet printed by CADMA for artisans interested in approaching its services specified clearly that neither CADMA nor HDI were commercial enterprises or intermediaries and that they did not intervene as intermediaries, agents or commissionaire agents between producers and buyers.[32] It is clear that if using the language and the definitions of their professional categories, HDI and CADMA could have given the impression to the already existing buying offices, resident buyers, and commissionaires that their agencies were trying to replace their position in the market. It was paramount to keep relations cordial and collaborative: while there are no records of meetings held with representatives from buying offices, in 1947 HIH organized at least two exhibitions of fashion merchandise and giftware for the specific purpose of extending an offer of diplomatic collaboration. These were the fashion exhibitions of autumn 1947, discussed in Chapter 2, and a *Christmas Gift Exhibition*, put together with the contribution of twenty-six exporters and without the technical advice of CADMA.[33]

The analysis of the business records and the correspondence between HDI and CADMA reveals that numerous disagreements occurred between executives. Their cultural and personal differences eventually led to the dissolution of the original arrangement between Ascoli, Ragghianti, and Vannini Parenti. The quality and taste of the objects selected by CADMA for the American market and to be put on display at the HIH represented the most pressing issue. As previously discussed, Ascoli's biggest concern towards Italian handicrafts was that the majority of those imported into the United States were deemed to be of poor quality, a statement echoed in many letters to the Italian staff since the beginning of HDI's operations. At the time, US department stores were inclined to mistrust Italian merchandise, reported Ascoli, and expressed his preoccupation several times during his visit to Italy in 1945. He was particularly worried about one fact: 'American taste has improved infinitely in recent years. Today, competition for quality goods comes from all over the world. If Italian production remains at the level of shoddy goods, it is screwed forever. The general idea here is that *it is* at the level of shoddy goods.'[34]

The only way to change this negative perception, he recommended, was the continuous production of samples that US customers would perceive as genuinely Italian. By keeping the desires expressed by the US market in mind, yet still retaining a certain Italian quality, recognizable as exotic and European, HDI would contribute to correcting the perception of Italian goods for American consumers. This required that CADMA's technical committee in Florence demonstrated an adequate sensibility to recognize modern designs that could be approved and considered useful by American consumers. Aligned with the three goals established by HDI's Bruno Foà in 1946 and outlined in Chapter 2, CADMA's chief responsibilities until 1947 included selecting handcrafted artistic objects to be exported to the United States and providing assistance to American buyers travelling to Italy. While relationships between CADMA and HDI got tenser over time, the opening of HIH increased what Ragghianti and Vannini Parenti perceived as an interference of HDI over the selection of merchandise, which could now be proposed directly by Italian manufacturers to HDI without the intermediate approval of CADMA.[35]

The acme of the tension between the two agencies was the appointment of an American-based expert, enforced by Ascoli and Foà, who
would take control over the decisions formally attributed to the technical committee of CADMA and, in practical matters, formerly executed
by Vannini Parenti alone. Despite the good intentions and the exceptional energy that he put into his role, Foà and Ascoli did not think that
Vannini Parenti was capable of modern sensibility when it came to taste
in arts and crafts, nor that he could move beyond the mainstream dimension of Italian handicraft as an accessory to tourism. When he asked to
be formally made solely responsible for the selection of merchandise,
Foà baulked at the idea of Vannini Parenti shipping 'another museum
of horrors' to the HDI offices: 'he lacks modern taste', confided Foà to
Ragghianti, 'demonstrating in this regard preferences that I would say
are almost *umbertine*', a reference to Vannini Parenti's old age and the
cultural milieu of his formative years.[36] The whole CADMA lacked vitality
and a peculiar style, an urgent matter that needed quick solutions, as Foà
informed Ragghianti:

> Taking a kind of mental assessment of CADMA's activities in its first year of
> existence, I note that while much has been done to kick-start the different
> phases of its work there is still something missing – I would be going to say
> the bite or if you prefer its 'style' ... Max has some ideas in this regard, includ-
> ing the possibility, which I am telling you in strict confidentiality, of looking
> for someone who could serve as the permanent technical director for that
> position.[37]

A new person was needed, someone who could supervise the technical and
artistic qualities of the handicrafts selected by mediating and interpret-
ing Italian and American tastes. It is not surprising, then, that his arrival
upset the staff in Florence, as the description above mirrored the functions formerly intended for CADMA and, by and large, for Vannini Parenti.
The 'permanent intermediary working in collaboration between HDI and
CADMA' was Ramy Alexander, who arrived in Italy in January 1947 and
was introduced by Ascoli to the CADMA staff with the hope of 'getting
along and loving one another'.[38] A former 'consultant for UNESCO on the
reconstruction of museums and art damaged during the war', Alexander
was born Avraam Goldstein in Odessa; he emigrated to Italy in the late
1930s and then moved to the United States, where he became an American
citizen in 1943.[39] A thorough analysis of the Florentine CADMA records
demonstrates that Alexander never appeared to get along with his Italian
colleagues. Ragghianti complained about his lack of experience, his tendency to refuse the samples selected by CADMA, and his possessiveness
over the authority that Ascoli granted him as a resident HDI officer in
Florence. Reportedly, Alexander began to take over the decision-making
processes, increasing his power and neglecting to include his Italian colleagues. Because of this, Ragghianti and Vannini Parenti slowly began to
take a back seat, later relinquishing their positions at CADMA and taking

no part in its successor CNA, of which Alexander would become vice-president. By assuming a role of direct intermediation within the industry of Made in Italy exports, Alexander would position himself in a competing role with Florence's most industrious commissionaires, among which the business biography of Giovanni Battista Giorgini (1898–1971) will be examined in the next section.

The G.B. Giorgini buying office

The Giorgini archive richly documents how the profession of a commissionaire was organized in postwar years, offering a considerable number of documents that tell stories of downfalls and successes alike. Commissionaires existed in the field of *haute couture* trade and had been regularly employed by Parisian houses since before the First World War.[40] Their role was to be intermediaries between the couture houses and the foreign buyers, assisting in the selection of designs, management of transactions and arrangements of shipping and customs fees. With structured expertise in the brokerage of Italian handicraft exports to the United States, the G.B. Giorgini office of Piazza S. Trinita in Florence was among those commercial buying offices with which HDI and CADMA felt the need to establish a collaboration.

Before his rise to fame in 1951 with the Italian High Fashion Show series, Giovanni Battista Giorgini was first and foremost a prominent commissionaire, an intermediary between store buyers and manufacturers.[41] Not particularly active within the Italian fashion industry, Giorgini never worked with couture before the end of the Second World War but acted as a commissionaire for his clients in the United States selling artistic handicrafts, furniture, antiques, ceramics, home décor and textiles. The G.B. Giorgini buying office was established in 1922 when 24-year-old Giovanni Battista split ways with the marble quarry business owned by his family near Forte dei Marmi, Lucca, and moved to Florence. A member of the Waldensian community from his mother's side, Giorgini grew up in a multilingual network of relatives and acquaintances, counting on a network of fellow Protestants, and sharing the belief that moral values can be translated into one's own business activities, contributing to the advancement of society.[42] His multicultural upbringing and acquaintances in the religious community in Europe and the United States greatly helped him to set up a network of business contacts that sustained his buying office in Florence.[43]

Since the 1930s Giorgini showed a preference for a specific business model in which he could combine retail and wholesale, inspired by his direct experience with American department stores and his acquaintance with the promotional policies adopted by Ente Nazionale per l'Artigianato e le Piccole Industrie (National Agency for Handicrafts and Small Industries, ENAPI). ENAPI, a governmental agency established in 1925 to advance the production and promotion of handicrafts Made in Italy, exerted some forms of control over the artistic quality of handicrafts to facilitate and intensify their circulation within domestic and international markets, thus displaying an early example of intermediation function in the field.[44] As pointed out by Claudio Alhaique and Manuela Soldi, ENAPI established a display practice for Italian handicrafts through its permanent showroom in Florence first and in other Italian cities later,[45] an *esposizione campionaria permanente*, in which samples from different Italian artisans rotated regularly and informed buyers and manufacturers on the latest developments of the field.[46] The establishment of such a 'flagship' showroom of sorts went beyond ENAPI's participation in collective exhibitions, such as the Biennale in Monza and the Triennale in Milan, and rather aligned with the later, modern experience of HIH in New York in its aiming for an official role as intermediary of the Italian handicraft segment.

Giorgini's take over ENAPI's showroom became his early 1930s project for a series of specialty shops, displaying luxury handicrafts Made in Italy, and modelled against his own shop in Florence's Lungarno Guicciardini, called Le Tre Stanze (the three rooms), which specialized in the 'practical objects that are requested for the necessities of a home, or the kind custom of the "gift"'.[47] The project was drafted in 1931 in preparation for a national conference of buying offices, held in Rome on 15 December 1931 and organized by Confederazione del Commercio (National Confederation of Commerce).[48] The shops were envisioned by Giorgini as located in the biggest Italian cities, functioning as retail and wholesale spaces at the same time and thus attempting to accommodate the needs of commercial buyers and to absorb part of the 'invisible exports' brought in by tourism.[49] In private, Giorgini expressed bitter remarks against ENAPI and its ineffectiveness in helping artisans in a practical way.[50] To counteract his resentment, Giorgini presented the specialty shop project to ENAPI stressing both his loyalty to Fascism and to the advancement of Italian *artigianato* and his experience with US buyers. In particular, locating the specialty shops in different Italian cities meant changing the display according to the taste and sensibility of each city, something Giorgini probably grasped in his experience of how American store chains carried different selections in different locations.[51] The project failed to materialize and in 1935 even Le Tre Stanze closed after a bankruptcy declaration.[52] As Giorgini blamed the 'massive crisis in America', it can be argued that Le Tre Stanze and the 'Italianness' of its products had failed to attract American customers and that the cultural capital of Made in Italy had not been fully expressed by the artisanal production of Italian handcraft workers, also considering the impact of the quality issues in the perception of American buyers mentioned by Ascoli and previously discussed.

Giorgini would develop ideas for showrooms inspired by his own reinterpretation of American department stores at different times in his career. In 1932 he opened a showroom in Paris in collaboration with the French commissionaire firm Adolphe Schloss Fils & Cie.[53] Its director

Lucien Schloss (1881–1962), son of the founder, worked as resident advisor in Paris for the Textile Color Card Association,[54] and had originally contacted Giorgini in 1927 with the possibility of opening a Schloss branch in Florence.[55] *Women's Wear Daily* reported that the aim of Giorgini's showroom in Paris was to serve the purposes of American buyers who did not have the time nor the intention to go to Italy and to present merchandise in accordance with the taste of US retailers and wholesalers.[56] This same issue would later be tackled by HDI, as discussed in Chapter 2, especially as after the Second World War it became 'virtually impossible for the individual American buyer to go over and do a thorough job of rounding up handicraft among the widely-scattered Italian craft centers'.[57] The selection of fashion merchandise presented appeared to be specially curated and comprised:

> [s]hoe, bag and belt sets [that] are among the items of interest to WOMEN'S WEAR DAILY readers ... White metal jewelry looking like old silver hand-wrought pieces ... Real silver jewelry set with pearls, is shown in similarly artistic rather than ultra fashionable designs ... a large collection of staple kid gloves ... reported as wanted by the American market.[58]

Schloss provided Giorgini with legitimization by being a steady fixture in the couture business and an enterprise well-known to American buyers in Paris.[59] The location of the showroom assured the buyers that the Italian fashion merchandise on display was approved by Schloss and thus a viable complement to the usual Parisian shopping spree.

As previously noted in the case study of Le Tre Stanze, in the interwar period the G.B. Giorgini firm and its wholesale import–export trade suffered from the 1929 economic crisis. Giorgini was aware of the main issues that characterized the exports of the Italian handicraft industry: in particular, he had direct experience of artisans not being quick enough to produce what was required from them, resulting in shipment delays and disappointed customers. This was a frequent cause of dissatisfaction among his US clients and, eventually, it led to the withdrawal of many of them. As a result, Giorgini invested in diverse business ventures to be able to sustain his family and their living standards, including owning stocks in an ice cream parlour in downtown Florence, named VeroGlacia.[60] Similarly, the Giorgini residence would often times accommodate foreign students from the United States or Switzerland as paying guests, something that Giorgini reportedly did to keep the family afloat as, still in 1935, 'the export trade [was] almost totally halted, due to the political climate'.[61] Giorgini's middle son, the late architect Vittorio Giorgini, would later recall how the family economy was greatly helped by a steady flow of female students from wealthy American families coming to Florence to attend the study abroad programme at Smith College: their rent allowed Giorgini to employ a cook and a maid to help his wife Nella run the house.[62]

The archival sources demonstrate clearly that Giorgini never ceased to be interested in trading with the US market, as his letters from the interwar period are constantly referring to '[keeping] the contacts with my American clients and do by myself that little amount of export trade that I have always kept with the United States'. Even though the frustration of not being able to conduct business with his preferred international partners hassled him greatly, his hopes to see the export business take off with great stability never wavered, and many of the relationships developed during the early years endured.[63] The experience accumulated over almost twenty years was briefly stored away only during the Second World War when Giorgini was enrolled in the Italian Army for about two years. In the fast-paced and high-risk environment of the commissionaire business, Giorgini consistently sought out the best deals and opportunities; specifically, his aesthetic sensibility and social upbringing led him to focus on the trade of high-level handicrafts, antiques, and homeware. His familiarity with the United States and a penchant for the business approach of his US clients became a trademark of his own work, especially when he attempted to replicate promotional strategies seen in department stores abroad. The experiences of Le Tre Stanze and the Parisian showroom help contextualize Giorgini's subsequent business venture with the management of Florence's Allied Gift Shop from 1944 to 1946. Here Giorgini reprised his occupation in trade and tested once again the specialty shop format that he had envisioned in the 1930s.

'A miniature Macy's' in Florence

The presence of US military forces on the Florence territory between 1944 and 1946 can be usefully examined to contextualize both the atmosphere in the city of Florence and the developments of Giorgini's business ventures in the immediate postwar years. In occupied Europe, there existed a general strategy adopted by the US military to keep morale high among the troops deployed overseas. In 1944 the Allied troops' morale in Florence was hitting rock bottom and the harshness of winter was taking a toll on already battered divisions. *Life* magazine reported how 'most of the troops in Italy have convinced themselves that theirs is the "forgotten front" and that all the glory of the European war will go to the troops that are now fighting on the Western Front'.[64] Entertainment was thus provided to the troops in the different divisions of the military in theatres of war. For instance, the habit of holding football games between divisions of the Army in occupied territories was quite diffused.[65] The organization of specialty shops represented another strategy in the bigger scheme of keeping the troops entertained and required the set-up of appropriate facilities. Shopping for fashionable merchandise seemed to be a common diversion for GIs stationed in Europe, as acknowledged by sources of the time. In Paris, American officers queued outside famous perfumer shops such as Chanel in Rue Cambon and Guerlain in Champs Elysees, purchasing gifts for their loved ones in time for Christmas.[66] In her autobiography

Shocking Life Elsa Schiaparelli described how the end of the Occupation brought several US officials to her fashion house 'queuing up to buy presents to take home'.[67] In Florence, military medic Minoru Masuda, passing through Florence in 1944 with the 442nd Regimental Combat Team of the United States Army, recorded in his diaries how Florence appeared to him as 'teeming with people ... It is a clean, neat town as Italian cities go and the people are in marked contrast to the southern Italians, being of a higher class and dress'. He bought a 'mystical ring' to hold his neckerchief, as the city seemed to be a good place to shop, so much so that Masuda could not manage to see much artwork either in museums or churches 'because of all the time we spent in [sic] shopping. I don't think that my time was lost, though'.[68] As the GIs developed a habit of sending home gifts and trinkets from Europe, local shops provided the exotic giftware that, once again, contributed to the 'invisible exports' of Italy.

The Allied Gift Shop of Florence, open between 1944 and 1946, responded to this unusual need caused by the war. Florence had been officially liberated by the Allies in August 1944, and by October Giorgini, on behalf of the Headquarters Florence Command of the Allied Military Government, opened the shop in a building confiscated by the Allied troops in Via dei Calzaiuoli 56/r.[69] Located in downtown Florence, halfway between the Duomo and Ponte Vecchio, the building had housed the oldest and most prestigious department store in Florence, the Bazar Bonajuti, and later the general store Grande Emporio Duilio al 48. Elsie McNeil, manager of the Fortuny boutique in New York and a long-time client of Giorgini, described the Allied Gift Shop as 'a miniature Macy [sic], run for the benefit of [Anglo-American] soldiers on leave in the convenient premises of a former general store'.[70] The shop sold Made in Italy merchandise to Allied military personnel stationed in Florence, including a large selection of fashionable accessories such as stockings, sunglasses, costume jewellery, silk lingerie, embroideries, and various items of clothing.[71] When military officials questioned why the prices were considerably higher than in other shops in Florence, Giorgini would detail the superior quality of the merchandise sold, including pure silk fully fashioned stockings, sold at 576 lire, and watch straps in real leather.[72] Nevertheless, since the building had been confiscated by the Army and Giorgini had no rent expenses, the Welfare Office asked him to lower the markup on the Gift Shop's prices from 50 to 35 per cent and no utility bills were to be paid.[73]

Two peculiarities distinguished this venture. First, only Anglo-American military personnel were permitted to shop in the store; no civilians were allowed, besides sales-clerks and Giorgini himself.[74] Second, the Headquarters Florence Command of the Army Welfare Services, a British contingent within the Allied Military Forces, officially owned the shop and appointed Giorgini as its general manager, an occupation that he held from 4 October 1944 to 15 March 1946.[75] Surviving documents are unclear and make it difficult to determine how the Gift Shop came into being. Giorgini's daughter Matilde recollected that, after being interrogated by a purge commission set up by the Allies, Giorgini was asked to put together the Gift Shop.[76] Apparently, Giorgini at the time did not have the money to buy merchandise to set up the Gift Shop.[77] He resorted to recruiting local artisans and manufacturers who had managed to salvage their production and asking them to sell directly in the Gift Shop, earning a 50 per cent commission on each sale.[78] The configuration of the shop suited the project: it consisted of 'a long balcony and, all around it, a great many small rooms shaped like horseshoes. In every room was a craftsman'.[79] Thanks to the Gift Shop downtown and its subsequent branches in Barberino del Mugello (Florence), Montecatini, Monza, and Milan, Giorgini was able to earn considerable sums of money, which he strenuously defended from allegations brought in by military staff that he 'did nothing but coordinat[e] the stalls'.[80] Frequent deposits into his wife's bank account, averaging 800,000 lire each, and expensive shopping sprees, such as two tailored ladies' coats worth 9,000 lire each, suggest that the Giorginis were faring far better than the average Florentine family during the AMGOT occupation.[81] Employees of the Gift Shop enjoyed respectable salaries, with cashiers earning 1,558 lire a month and English-speaking sales assistants earning 1,290 lire. According to the Army Welfare Services, between 5 October and 31 December 1944 alone Giorgini grossed a net profit of $16,477 and 53 cents.[82]

While the shop should only have remained open for three months, Giorgini managed to keep it open for almost a year and a half. His request to open a second Allied Gift Shop at Le Cascine, the city park within the immediate outskirts of Florence, was halted in 1945, but Giorgini managed to run other Allied Forces Gift Shops, including one in Trieste, recruiting collaborators within his circle of family members and old acquaintances. At the beginning of March 1946, the Welfare Office ordered the closure of the shop in Via de' Calzaiuoli, and Giorgini was ready to reprise his old profession, enriched with both a new experience and, apparently, a considerable economic profit. The Command congratulated him by writing that '[d]uring the period you have worked for the "Army Welfare Services" our Gift Shop has had the name of "the best in Italy". Everyone from the Supreme Commander C.M.F. [Central Mediterranean Forces] downwards was loud in their praise of the efficiency and display as shown in our establishment'.[83] The efforts of Giorgini in the organization of this venture mirrored the plans outlined with Le Tre Stanze, his project for ENAPI, and the Parisian showroom at Schloss. Despite the temporary interruption of his export business during the war, Giorgini managed to maintain his relationships with local workshops and manufacturers through the Gift Shop. He also demonstrated shrewd financial planning by saving some funds for future business ideas. Additionally, he made a significant strategic shift by aligning his conduct with the winning coalition of the Allies, even though he previously subscribed to the cultural and commercial politics of Fascism.[84] Within Giorgini's biography, the Allied Forces Gift Shop represents a peculiar case study in the overall discourse on the many ways in which postwar Italy started to become a reputable source of fashion merchandise. Its history also supports the case for a discussion on the inclusion of fashion-related merchandise within the broad notion of 'entertainment' to the troops. Previous research has not acknowledged any instances of similar official businesses, making Giorgini's management of the Gift Shop a rare instance of Allied-sponsored business activity in Europe during wartime. The shopping experiences of deployed militaries complement the stories of fashion houses that remained open during the Occupation, contributing to a better understanding of how wartime in Europe could still encompass glimpses of everyday life.

'Excellent connections, fine reputation'

The excitement brought by the reopening of transatlantic travel routes at the end of the Second World War inspired many Italian merchants to venture again to the United States: 1946 was a particularly important year for the reopening of the transatlantic fashion trade between Europe and the United States. The excitement was well evident to those in the business: commissionaire firm Roditi & Sons, well-established and renowned in Florence long before the war, had already arranged a shipment of assorted novelty items, selected from a few hundred samples of 'artistic Italian merchandise' to arrive in New York in the spring of 1946.[85] Max Ascoli and the HDI headquarters had been aware of this reprise of commerce and monitored its developments with the help of CADMA's Mario Vannini Parenti. Vannini Parenti reminded his colleagues overseas that the goal for CADMA was not to compete with commissionaire firms, but rather to watch over their activities with benevolence, and be happy that their non-profit agencies inspired and excited the people currently interested in trading Italian handicrafts.[86] Later that same year, Vannini Parenti travelled to New York 'on a trade mission, to rekindle commercial relationships between Italy and America, especially in the handicraft sector, after the long interruption brought by the war'.[87] Giorgini, too, detected the trend that had brought Roditi and Vannini Parenti back to the United States before him. A few months after closing the Allied Forces Gift Shops, he published a classified in *Women's Wear Daily*, proposing his expertise to American firms looking for commissionaires: promising his 'excellent connections, fine reputation, financial rating, office and showroom in Florence', Giorgini offered his service in the fields of 'ready to wear, accessories, cosmetics, home decorators' lines'.[88] During the summer, he prepared for his first important trip after the end of the war, visiting his Italian suppliers in Bassano, Nove, and Milan.

The trip served to connect Giorgini with old and new clients alike. The first stop was in New York, where he visited the luxury department store B.

Altman, a recently acquired client.[89] Further stops included Washington, Dallas, Kansas City, St Louis, Chicago, and Cleveland, where he met with store representatives and small retailers alike. When he returned at the end of January 1947, Giorgini was 'very satisfied with [his] trip'. His intention to rekindle the links between Italian manufacturers and American sellers as quickly as possible proved effective and the years to come would see a significant improvement in the volume of his transactions. Already in 1948, the surviving correspondence shows how Giorgini had increased his activities and enlarged his staff. Besides his daughters Matilde and Graziella, Graziella's husband Giovanni Maria Fadigati, and the assistant Franca, Giorgini was aided in Milan by Domenico Orsi, his nephew. When Orsi left Milan in 1950 and became the New York agent of Terragni (Figure 3.8), the textile manufacturer of Como, the decision was approved and directed by Giorgini, who came to consider Orsi's new job as a way for his firm to have an 'office in New York'.[90]

The number of American clients represented by Giorgini significantly increased after the 1946 trip, with a particular rise in the number of department stores recognized for their fashion departments. In October 1948 Giorgini travelled again to New York and stayed for a few months, spending most of his time working at B. Altman, where the management set up for him an office within the import division to hold meetings with the store buyers.[91] His primary contact at Altman was James A. Keillor, vice-president, of whom Giorgini spoke with great respect and gratitude in his letters and who kept reminding him that in 1948 he would send him 'even more buyers than [the previous] year'.[92] It was Keillor who introduced him to Alex Pollack, director and general manager of Henry Morgan's, the Canadian department store, of which Giorgini became the resident buyer in Italy with a monthly salary of $250.[93] Via Henry W. Morgan, Giorgini was put in contact with Halle Brothers Co., a department store in Cleveland, who at the time was represented by another commissionaire firm in Italy, but was not happy with their service. Giorgini thrived with the idea of having so much work that he needed to reorganize the office and hire more buyers.[94]

As Giorgini's interests increasingly moved towards fashion, his clients in Italy included more and more manufacturers within this area, with an initial focus on textiles. In a series of letters from early 1946, Giorgini's brother Carlo, a commercial agent at AGIP (the General Italian Oil Company), pushed him to acquire DuPont as a client, helping Giorgini to gain a technical insight into the state of the textile industry in Italy.[95] Giorgini's connections in the textile industry strengthened through the following years and provided him with important US clients. In the spring of 1949, he personally accompanied Wesley Simpson and his wife, fashion designer Adele Simpson, to Como and Milan, as they were looking for textile suppliers:

3.8 Advertisement for Terragni of Como textile manufacturer and its New York agent Domenico Orsi. *Bellezza*, March 1951. By permission of the Ministry of Culture – Pinacoteca di Brera – Biblioteca Braidense, Milan

> At 9 I met with Mr. Simpson with whom I [visited suppliers in] Milan in the morning ... This morning I woke up at 7 to be at [Hotel] Principe at 8 and meet the Simpsons for the last details; they left for [Nice] ... After breakfast [we went to] a silk factory for a complicated discussion on behalf of Mrs. Adele Simpson who is the famous American designer. Mr. Simpson cabled to New York and opened a letter of credit for 15 thousand doll [sic] ... Simpson seems to be a very good client, in any way he is an important client, big and very well-known.[96]

The prestige of Italian silk had not been lost on Adele Simpson, who was among those American fashion manufacturers visiting Italian textile suppliers for their postwar collections. Although the fashion history canon would later affirm that, before the Second World War, '[t]here was no such thing as Italian fashion', it is more accurate to say that 'there was no overall strategy'[97] to establish a synergy between the unrecognized Italian fashion designers and the more established textile manufacturers, now on a 'path of growth and recognition almost uninterrupted since the 1930s'.[98] The first-hand experience gained through the partnership with Terragni of Como, documented in his archive and strengthened by the family link provided by Domenico Orsi, opened possibilities to Giorgini that other Italian agencies and councils were pursuing at the same time, though all of them lacked financial support and *ad hoc* policies by the Italian Government. The improvement brought by Giorgini was the idea of one big event to attract the interest of foreign markets with specific promotions, an idea that he developed based on the continuous travelling he had done for years across the Italian peninsula in search of suppliers for his clients. The many years of experience in the US market and the wholesale of Italian handicrafts, plus the connections in Italy and abroad, were instrumental in creating a new project that this time would involve fashion merchandise and couture. Nevertheless, it resonated clearly with the themes that he had brought up in the past to promote different activities, such as the will to 'give a new impulse to a field of work of prime relevance to the Nation', by directing the endeavours of artisans and manufacturers so to 'mould ourselves towards fashion which is constantly evolving'.[99] The final impulse will be clearly seen when examining the connections between Giorgini and the touring exhibition *Italy at Work* in the next chapter.

Notes

1 L. Mingardi and D. Turrini, 'Il Made in Italy come atto politico. HDI e CADMA, Max Ascoli e Carlo Ludovico Ragghianti 1945–1948'. *LUK* 27, 2021, pp. 85–95, 89.

2 P. Cordera, 'L'incantesimo Della Casa. L'arte e l'industria in Vetrina'. In *Storytelling. Esperienze e Comunicazione Del Cultural Heritage*, edited by Sandra Costa, Paola Cordera, and Dominique Poulot (Bologna: Bologna University Press, 2022), pp. 221–34, 225.

3 A. Taiuti ed., 'La "Rimessa a Foco" Dell'Italia. Il Carteggio Tra Max Ascoli e Carlo Ludovico Ragghianti (1945–1957)'. *Nuova Antologia* 141(2237), 2006, pp. 5–45, 8.

4 F. Cavarocchi and V. Galimi, eds. *Firenze in Guerra, 1940–1944: Catalogo Della Mostra Storico-Documentaria* (Florence: Firenze University Press, 2014), pp. 119–28.

5 The impact of La Strozzina as Ragghianti's organizational apparatus is particularly relevant to the postwar discourse of Florence regaining its cultural capital with the Frank Lloyd Wright exhibition, accurately detailed by Lisa Carotti. See L. Carotti, *Del disegno e dell'architettura: il pensiero di Carlo Ludovico Ragghianti. Analisi critica delle mostre di Wright, Le Corbusier e Aalto a Palazzo Strozzi* (Lucca: Edizioni Fondazione Ragghianti Studi sull'arte, 2020).

6 C. Baskins and S. Bottinelli, '"La Casa va Con La Città": Lorenzo the Magnificent and the Arts, 1949'. *California Italian Studies* 7(1), 2017, pp. 1–30.

7 I am indebted to Emanuele Greco who generously let me read his detailed bio-graphical work on Mario Vannini Parenti: E. Greco, 'L'Attività Culturale di Mario Vannini Parenti (1887–1983)' (Research paper, Università di Firenze, 2010–11).

8 'Ordini dei SS. Maurizio e Lazzaro e della Corona d'Italia', *Gazzetta Ufficiale* (22 July 1936), p. 2380.

9 Confirmed also in Greco, 'L'Attività Culturale di Mario Vannini Parenti (1887–1983)', 69–70.

10 Fondazione Ragghianti, Archivio Carlo Ludovico Ragghianti, Lucca (hereafter FR, ACLR), Carteggio generale. Ascoli, Max (DOC 83) 1945–1980. Max Ascoli to Carlo Ludovico Ragghianti, 18 July 1946. Document 5 2036b.

11 FR, ACLR, Carteggio generale. Ascoli, Max (DOC 83) 1945–1980. Max Ascoli to Carlo Ludovico Ragghianti, 31 May 1946. Document 2015a.

12 C.M. Belfanti and E. Merlo, 'Patenting Fashion: Salvatore Ferragamo Between Craftmanship and Industry', *Investigaciones de Historia Económica – Economic History Research*, 12(2), 2016, pp. 109–19; M. Dahlen, 'Ferragamo Wedge'. In *A History of Intellectual Property in 50 Objects*, edited by Claudy Op den Kamp and Dan Hunter (Cambridge: Cambridge University Press, 2019), pp. 200–07; E. Palomino, 'Indigenous Arctic Fish Skin Heritage: Sustainability, Craft and Material Innovation' (PhD Dissertation, London College of Fashion, University of the Arts London, 2022); M. Martin, 'Fashion in the Art Museum: A Case Study of Salvatore Ferragamo Shoes'. In *L'Italia al Lavoro. Un Lifestyle da Esportazione*, edited by Paola Cordera and Chiara Faggella (Bologna: Bologna University Press, 2023), pp. 187–94.

13 C. Faggella, 'Il nuovo Rinascimento della moda italiana: Ferragamo e il dopoguerra'. In *Salvatore Ferragamo 1898–1960*, edited by Stefania Ricci (Milan: Skira, 2023), pp. 482–89.

14 S. Ferragamo, *Shoemaker of Dreams. The autobiography of Salvatore Ferragamo* (London: George G. Harrap & Co., 1957), p. 195.

15 FR, ACLR, CADMA. Fasc. 3, Mario Vannini Parenti to Max Ascoli, 23 February 1946. Document 1923b.

16 M. Mannes, 'Italian fashion'. *Vogue* 1 January 1947, pp. 118–21, 155–56; M. Mannes, 'The Fine Italian Hand'. *Vogue UK* September 1946, pp. 44–9.

17 Mannes, 'Italian fashion', 155.

18 R. Martin and H. Koda, *Orientalism. Visions of the East in Western Dress* (New York: The Metropolitan Museum of Art, 1994), p. 9.

19 A. Geczy, *Fashion and Orientalism. Dress, Textiles and Culture from the 17th to the 21st Century* (London: Bloomsbury, 2013), pp. 136–41.

20 K. Aschengreen Piacenti, S. Ricci, and G. Vergani eds., *I Protagonisti Della Moda. Salvatore Ferragamo (1898–1960)* (Florence: Centro Di., 1985), p. 108.

21 'Ferragamo Shoe Return'. *Vogue* 15 March 1947, p. 192.

22 Advertisement. *New York Times* (27 April 1947), p. 53.

23 DeGolyer Library, Southern Methodist University, Stanley Marcus Papers. Box 64, Folder 27, Neiman Marcus Award Press Release, 1947.

24 DeGolyer Library, Southern Methodist University, Stanley Marcus Papers. Box 64, Folder 27, Neiman Marcus Award Press Release, 1947.

25 'Italian Handcrafts Honor Ferragamo', *Women's Wear Daily* (23 September 1947), p. 3.

26 DeGolyer Library, Southern Methodist University, Stanley Marcus Papers. Box 64, Folder 27, 'Tenth Annual Fashion Exposition Show Invitation', 1947.

27 R. Marcucci, *ANIBO e Made in Italy. Storia dei Buying Offices in Italia* (Florence: Vallecchi, 2004), p. 13.

28 BMA, PUB, Press Releases, 1947–1952. 'Statements by Dr. Max Ascoli at the Opening of the Exhibition, "Italy at Work" at the Brooklyn Museum, Wednesday evening, November 29th, 1950', Document 07–09/1950, p. 109.

29 FR, ACLR, CADMA. Fasc. 3, Bruno Foà to Carlo Ludovico Ragghianti and Mario Vannini Parenti, 14 September 1946. Document 38/21 1861b.

30 'To Return with Facts on Italian Handicrafts', *Women's Wear Daily* (3 August 1945), p. 16.

31 FR, ACLR, CADMA. Fasc. 1, Memo, undated [1946–1947]. Document 39/35 1942a.

32 FR, ACLR, CADMA. Fasc. 1, 'Per gli artigiani esportatori' pamphlet, undated [1946], p. 14.

33 FR, ACLR, CADMA. Fasc. 2, Commissione di presidenza 1945–1948. CADMA commissione di presidenza, circolare interna #2, 31 October 1947. Document 38/40 1896.

34 Original in Italian: 'L'ho detto molte volte quando sono stato in Italia. Il gusto americano si è infinitamente scaltrito durante questi ultimi anni. La concorrenza di roba di qualità viene oggi da tutti i paesi del mondo. Se la produzione italiana rimane al livello paccottiglia, è fregata per sempre. L'idea generale qui è che sia al livello paccottiglia.' FR, ACLR, CADMA. Fasc. 3, Max Ascoli to Mario Vannini Parenti, 18 February 1946.

35 FR, ACLR, CADMA. Fasc. 2, Commissione di presidenza 1945–1948. CADMA commissione di presidenza, circolare interna #2, 31 October 1947. Document 38/40 1898.

36 FR, ACLR, CADMA. Fasc. 3, Bruno Foà to Carlo Ludovico Ragghianti, 4 December 1946. Document 19 2258b.

37 FR, ACLR, CADMA. Fasc. 3, Bruno Foà to Carlo Ludovico Ragghianti, 4 December 1946. Document 19 2258b.

38 FR, ACLR, CADMA. Fasc. 2, Commissione tecnica 1946–1947, relazione della commissione tecnica, 31 January 1947. Document 38/30 1879; FR, ACLR, Carteggio generale. Ascoli, Max (DOC 83) 1945–1980, Max Ascoli to Carlo Ludovico Ragghianti, 13 December 1946. Document 3 1955.

39 R.M. Cook, *Alfred Kazin: A Biography* (New Haven: Yale University Press, 2007), p. 119.

40 N. Troy, *Couture Culture: A Study in Modern Art and Fashion* (Cambridge: MIT Press, 2003), p. 240. See also Edith L. Rosenbaum, 'American Offices in Paris', *Women's Wear Daily* (3 January 1912), pp. 1, 12.

41 The word *commissionaire* is a loan from French and indicates someone that is entrusted with a duty.

42 L. Pagliai, 'Giovan Battista Giorgini: Alle Origini Del "Made in Italy". Economia e Modernizzazione Tra Fascismo e Repubblica' (PhD Dissertation, Università degli Studi di Pisa, 2007), p. 3.

43 C. Faggella, 'Before 1951: setting up the network of G.B. Giorgini and the launch of Made in Italy'. *Italian American Review*, 14(1), 2024, pp. 95–109.

44 Pagliai, 'Giovan Battista Giorgini', 140.

45 C. Alhaique, *Le esportazioni dei prodotti artigiani e la Compagnia Nazionale Artigiana nel suo primo anno di attività* (Rome: Scuola Tipografica 'Don Luigi Guanella', 1950), p. 49.

46 M. Soldi, 'Mostrare l'artigianato. L'attività espositiva dell'ENAPI'. In *Design Esposto. Mostrare La Storia / La Storia Delle Mostre*. Atti Del Convegno AIS/Design 2021, edited by Fiorella Bulegato and Maddalena Dalla Mura (Venice: Università IUAV di Venezia, 2021), pp. 64–83, 70.

47 Archivio di Stato di Firenze, Archivio della Moda Italiana di Giovanni Battista Giorgini (hereafter ASF-AMIGBG), Carteggio. Draft of an Invitation for the Inauguration of Le Tre Stanze, undated.

48 'Il Convegno delle Case Import-Export'. *Commercio: rivista mensile della Confederazione Nazionale Fascista del Commercio* December 1931, p. 801.

49 A. Pellegrino, *La Città Più Artigiana d'Italia. Firenze 1861–1929*. Studi e Ricerche Storiche (Milan: FrancoAngeli, 2012), pp. 84.

50 ASF-AMIGBG, Carteggio. G.B. Giorgini to his brother Mario, 26 July 1934.

51 Faggella, 'Before 1951', 101–02.

52 ASF-AMIGBG, Carteggio. G.B. Giorgini to Arthur Taylor (secretary-general of YMCA in Italy from 1922 to 1937), 28 February 1935.
53 B.J. Perkins, 'Glimpses of Paris: Plan Italian Showing in Paris for U.S. Buyers', *Women's Wear Daily* (22 March 1932), p. 6.
54 R.L. Blaszczyk, *The Color Revolution* (Cambridge: MIT Press, 2012), p. 180.
55 'Lucien Schloss', *Women's Wear Daily* (14 August 1962), p. 31; Pagliai, 'Giovan Battista Giorgini', 135.
56 'Italian Accessories Grouped in Paris Salon for Benefit of American Buyers', *Women's Wear Daily* (3 June 1932), section II, p. 8.
57 J. Teague, 'Italian Handcraft House Now Stocks and Sells Direct', *Women's Wear Daily* (26 August 1949), p. 7.
58 'Italian Accessories Grouped in Paris Salon for Benefit of American Buyers'.
59 V. Pouillard, *Paris to New York. The Transatlantic Fashion Industry in the Twentieth Century* (Cambridge: Harvard University Press, 2021), p. 110.
60 ASF-AMIGBG, Carteggio. G.B. Giorgini to Alberto Passigli, 6 October 1939.
61 ASF-AMIGBG, Carteggio. G.B. Giorgini to his brother Carlo, 17 January 1935.
62 B. Tognetti, 'Vittorio Giorgini Architetto (1926–2010). Un Viaggio Con La Natura: Dalla Costruzione Della Casa Esagono al Mondo Della Spaziologia' (MA Dissertation, Università degli Studi di Pisa, 2016), p. 12.
63 Faggella, 'Before 1951', 99–101.
64 'The Spaghetti Bowl'. *Life* 29 January 1945, p. 75.
65 One such event took place in Florence on New Year's Day 1945, when the Fifth Army faced the Twelfth Air Force in what was called the 'Spaghetti Bowl'.
66 B.J. Perkins, 'Propose French-U.S. Parleys To Improve Buying of Models', *Women's Wear Daily* (20 November 1944), pp. 1, 6.
67 E. Schiaparelli, *Shocking Life* (London: J.M. Dent & Sons, 1954), p. 171.
68 M. Masuda, *Letters from the 442nd: The World War II Correspondence of a Japanese American Medic*, edited by Hana Masuda and Dianne Bridgman (Seattle: University of Washington Press, 2008), p. 83.
69 ASF-AMIGBG, Altre Attività. Unknown Welfare Officer to G.B. Giorgini, 4 October 1944.
70 ASF-AMIGBG, Altre Attività. Elsie McNeil to G.B. Giorgini, November 1945.
71 ASF-AMIGBG, Altre Attività. 'List of Artisans that Operate under the Allied Forces Gift Shop', undated.
72 ASF-AMIGBG, Altre Attività. G.B. Giorgini to Captain K.L.E. Budden, 23 July 1945.
73 The shop occupied the premises of former general store Grande Emporio Duilio al 48, established in 1902 by Joseph Siebzehner. Siebzehner was deported to Auschwitz in January 1944 and died on the way there.
74 ASF-AMIGBG, Altre Attività. Major M.G. Beckett to G.B. Giorgini, 17 March 1945.
75 ASF-AMIGBG, Altre Attività. G. Kay Lt. RAC, Gift Shop Guestbook, undated.
76 G. Vergani, 'The Sala Bianca: The Birth of Italian Fashion'. In *The Sala Bianca: The Birth of Italian Fashion*, edited by Giannino Malossi (Milan: Electa, 1992), p. 30.
77 ASF-AMIGBG, Altre Attività. G.B. Giorgini to Captain Herbert S. Lauterstein, undated [probably April 1945].
78 ASF-AMIGBG, Altre Attività. Capt. Herbert S. Lauterstein, QMC, to G.B. Giorgini, 4 April 1945.
79 Vergani, 'The Sala Bianca', 30.
80 ASF-AMIGBG, Altre Attività. Capt. Herbert S. Lauterstein, QMC, to G.B. Giorgini, 4 April 1945.
81 ASF-AMIGBG, Altre Attività: Bank deposit Receipt, G.B. Giorgini to Zaira Augusta (Nella) Nanni Giorgini, 10 December 1945; ASF-AMIGBG, Altre Attività. Receipts from dressmaking shop Sartoria Carlo Cattaneo to G.B. Giorgini, 24 December 1945.
82 ASF-AMIGBG, Altre Attività. Herbert S. Lauterstein, Captain, QMC, to G.B. Giorgini, 4 April 1945.
83 ASF-AMIGBG, Altre Attività. S. Lieut. G. Kay, Welfare, to G.B. Giorgini, undated.

84 Pagliai, 'Giovan Battista Giorgini'; Faggella, 'Before 1951', 98–99.
85 'Italian Merchandise for Roditi's Arrives', *Women's Wear Daily* (12 April 1946), p. 41.
86 FR, ACLR, CADMA. Fasc. 3, Mario Vannini Parenti to Bruno Foà, 22 February 1946.
87 M. Olschki, *Oh, America!* (Palermo: Sellerio, 1996), pp. 40–41.
88 'Business Opportunities', *Women's Wear Daily* (8 May 1946), p. 54.
89 C. Faggella, 'Dietro Le Quinte Alla G.B. Giorgini. Le Assistant Buyers e l'esportazione Di Moda Italiana Negli Stati Uniti, 1946–1956'. In *Un Oceano Di Stile. Produzione e Consumo Di Made in Italy Negli Stati Uniti Del Dopoguerra*, edited by Simone Cinotto and Giulia Crisanti (Milan: Mimesis edizioni, 2023), pp. 163–80.
90 ASF-AMIGBG, Carteggio. G.B. Giorgini to Nella Giorgini, 1 November 1949; 'Terragni of Como to Open Permanent Sales Office here', *Women's Wear Daily* (25 May 1950), p. 39.
91 ASF-AMIGBG, Carteggio. G.B. Giorgini to Nella Giorgini, 17 October 1948.
92 ASF-AMIGBG, Carteggio. G.B. Giorgini to Nella Giorgini, 24 October 1948.
93 L.F. Sharman, 'Fashion and Refuge: The Jean Harris Salon, Montreal, 1941–1961'. In *Fashion: A Canadian Perspective*, edited by Alexandra Palmer (Toronto: University of Toronto Press, 2004), pp. 270–90, 274.
94 ASF-AMIGBG, Carteggio. G.B. Giorgini to Nella Giorgini, 24 October 1948.
95 ASF-AMIGBG, Carteggio. Carlo Giorgini to G.B. Giorgini, 23 March 1946.
96 ASF-AMIGBG, Carteggio. G.B. Giorgini to Nella Giorgini, 19 March 1949.
97 Vergani, 'The Sala Bianca', 38.
98 L. Savi, *A New History of 'Made in Italy'. Fashion and Textiles in Post-War Italy* (London: Bloomsbury Publishing, 2023), p. 38.
99 ASF-AMIGBG, Altre Attività. G.B. Giorgini, Untitled Draft for Unnamed Project (16 November 1934).

4

Across the United States: *Italy at Work*

In the spring of 1950, fashion photographer Karen Radkai visited Rome on account of *Harper's Bazaar* to photograph 'people and things considered important in America', as reported by Irene Brin in *Bellezza*. Brin, a prolific writer, a gallerist, and a fashion journalist, would become Rome editor of *Harper's Bazaar* in 1952 thanks to the support she provided to Radkai in the making of this same photoshoot.[1] The *Bellezza* article exemplifies Brin's unconventional style, through which she captured current news on contemporary fashion and rendered them through a 'biographical representation of the character, being it authentic or fictional', who narrated the story.[2] What we also find in the article is perhaps one of the earliest anticipations of what the organizers of the travelling exhibition *Italy at Work: Her Renaissance in Design Today* would choose to pick from shops and boutiques to represent the contemporary Italian fashion scene. The core of the article sees Brin empathizing with Radkai's longing for a preconstructed, US-based image of Italy in her visit to Rome, which she managed to find in many aristocratic 'women, with face and body features perfectly Italian, dressing the Italian way, [such as] princess Borghese by Fernanda Gattinoni, princess Boncompagni by Gabriellasport, baroness Uberta d'Avanzo by Fontana, donna Esmeralda Ruspoli by Fabiani'.[3] By preferring these 'sophisticated' Italian ladies, whose promotional role was previously identified in Chapter 1 and here acknowledged by Radkai, the photographer chose to avoid those Roman women who inadequately persevered in wearing French fashion and those dressmaking shops' owners who were either in Paris buying toiles or busy in Rome over-decorating evening dresses that no one, except someone in a 'minor republic of South America' would buy, commented Brin with a 'critical provocation tinged with a vein of irony'.[4]

Brin then proceeded to list the items that Radkai thought looked 'Italian enough' and bought for herself, which represented and summarized what all American women looked for when in Italy: big, supple leather bags and comfortable, fun, cheap shoes in Rome and Florence; 'dozens of scarves and shawls by Tessitrice dell'Isola' from Capri; necklaces by Luciana; umbrellas by Gucci; Gegia Bronzini's artisanal textiles; Giuliana Camerino's bucket bags; artistic ceramics made at the outskirts of Rome at the Valle dell'Inferno workshop;[5] and textiles by Tessitura di Rovezzano of Florence,[6] managed by Marinetta di Frassineto. Whether Radkai's shopping spree was fictionalized or not, these same items would later constitute the core fashion merchandise on display during *Italy at Work*. They included items of *moda boutique*, the practical ready-made garments suitable for leisure and sports sold in the 'boutique' shops that introduced clients to the dressmaking atelier: Brin defined those batch collections as 'swift, ready-made, rational sets'.[7]

This all corresponded, noted Brin, to an image of Italy that already existed in the mind of Radkai, a further development of the 'Italian Look' described by the US press by the end of the German Occupation of Italy, as outlined earlier in this book. It also comprised a certain Italian style in dressmaking, blossoming as the local *sartorie* gained ground in those daring American stores willing to try a new European import, as it will be explored in the next chapter. Although high-end clothing did not officially appear among the categories identified by the organizers of *Italy at Work*, the promotion of Italian fashion merchandise was nevertheless included in the exhibition given the attention and efforts that both HDI and HIH had spent to increase the visibility of this merchandise category in the US market.

The reconstruction of the events that enabled the organization of the travelling exhibition *Italy at Work* is extremely complex, given the number of professionals involved in its set-up, of artisans, architects, and designers whose works were featured, and the cultural and political ramifications that the exhibition originated both in Italy and the United States as a forerunner in the promotion of Made in Italy abroad.[8] On the one hand, several studies acknowledge the key role of *Italy at Work* in revitalizing the modernity of Made in Italy exports abroad, led by Penny Sparke's pioneering 'The Straw Donkey' article of 1998 and chiefly focusing on the perspective of decorative arts and history of design.[9] On the other hand, the interdisciplinary approach currently advocated for by many fields of studies in the humanities and the discovery of a complex network of Italian archives, so far overlooked in favour of the American ones, are at the forefront in the development of more recent studies that analyze the exhibition from different points of view, including its role in the development of an independent Italian fashion scene.[10] Much is still in need of being discussed, nevertheless: this chapter thus summarizes the aspects, so far mapped out in the book, key to the formation of an identity of Italian fashion and connects them to the exhibition, considered an establishing event for the recognition of Italian originality in fashion and a threshold in preparation for the international acceptance of Italian couture. The chapter analyzes the fashion merchandise displayed in *Italy at Work* and how it changed as the exhibition moved from city to city in the United States; the power relationships between organizers, intermediaries, and the fashion market of the United States; and the exhibition's impact on both the career and the legacy of fashion intermediary Giovanni Battista Giorgini.

The selection procedure

In 1948 Max Ascoli was no longer in charge of the operations connected with HDI and had officially resigned to resume his academic and journalistic careers. In his inaugural talk held for the opening of *Italy at Work* at the Brooklyn Museum on 29 November 1950, Ascoli stressed that

> C.N.A. absorbed all the functions of H.D.I., which, in the accomplishment of its task, had spent approximately $370,000. At that stage, I considered that my job had been done. It was no longer a matter of philanthropy. It was business. That had been the aim of H.D.I. all along: To do its work as an unpaid broker, set up its pilot projects, spread carefully its seed money, and then give to business the role that belongs to business.[11]

By that time HDI had merged with CADMA in a new Italian-American conglomerate, the Compagnia Nazionale Artigiana (CNA), whose president and vice-president were, respectively, right-wing socialist Ivan Matteo Lombardo, Italian Minister of Foreign Commerce and former trade agent for textile manufacturer De Angeli Frua, and Ramy Alexander, as explained in Chapter 3. Former HDI consultant Gertrude Dinsmore was appointed general manager of HIH, while financial consultant David Freudenthal became its president in March 1950.[12] Freudenthal, who previously worked at Bloomingdale's department store in a management position, was the special assistant to the chief of the Economic Cooperation Administration mission in Rome, with duties as 'adviser on capital investments and on industrial and agricultural developments'.[13] Links with the Allied administration and the fashion industry were thus unequivocally secured once again. The network of professionals that Ascoli built around the venture appeared solid and well-geared into the most relevant business channels in Italy and the United States. For these reasons, before closing permanently, HIH became a key retail point in New York, and the publicity that it received in the printed press contributed to a widespread acquaintance with Italian design among American consumers.

The results obtained by HDI had opened an interesting venue for those Italian businesses that sensed the opportunity for establishing or reacquainting a commercial relationship with the United States. In particular, the Italian department store La Rinascente attempted a similar venture with its private label APEM (Artigianato Produzione ed Esportazione Milano): its American agent was Ann Roberts, who left HDI in 1947 and started freelancing as a trade consultant for the export of Italian handicrafts.[14] Established under the artistic direction of architect and designer

Gio Ponti and supported by the financial structure of a large commercial enterprise as La Rinascente,[15] APEM was originally in HDI's bad graces at the outset of CADMA's operations, as it represented to Ascoli 'the clutches of the harpies ... [grappling the Italian artisans] from the inside like the Borlettis of Milan'.[16] Ragghianti was of the same opinion, and believed that the non-profit nature of HDI and CADMA often crumbled in comparison to the commercial possibilities of the monopolistic tendencies displayed by personalities such as industrialist Borletti and architect Gio Ponti: 'They can do what we cannot: that is, they can secure exclusives on the best and most affordable products.'[17] Yet, collaborations with APEM did in fact ensue shortly after this correspondence, as well as the involvement of HIH with Gio Ponti and many of his associates in the preparation of HIH's exhibitions.[18]

The partnership with HIH was thus ready to evolve with a more comprehensive and pervasive strategy of promoted visibility for Made in Italy handcrafted goods and artistic wares, which nevertheless required additional funds and a new operational structure with stronger financial assets. The *New York Times* reported in December 1947 that Ascoli had obtained from the Export-Import Bank 'credit in favor of Istituto Mobiliare Italiano, an Italian public credit institution engaged in public financing, for the account of an Italian handicraft industries corporation in the process of establishment which will include representatives of both private and public interests'.[19] The corporation mentioned in the article was Compagnia Nazionale Artigiana, or CNA, the conglomerate originated by the merge of HDI and CADMA briefly introduced in the previous chapter. The credit amounted to a $4,625,000 loan to be distributed to those artisanal businesses that intended to purchase either raw materials or technical equipment in the United States exclusively. The loan, recalling the distribution strategies of raw material originally envisioned by HDI through the support of CADMA, was meant to help only those workshops that already had a consolidated presence in the United States or, alternatively, manufacturers willing to become exporters, but lacking the internal competences allowing them to do so.[20] Additionally, the press reported news of this loan stressing how this financial support would have helped develop and diversify

> those lines of goods which have always been imported by the United States and which have been eagerly sought by consumers and trade circles. The new organization will help in the production of articles for the American market. It will assist in styling and designing and in the development of new lines of merchandise. The organization will work in close cooperation with importers and all selling outlets ... the situation is further brightened by the reductions in United States tariffs, which are expected to become effective on Jan. 1.[21]

To streamline the process of instructing manufacturers in Italy and to administer the loan as efficiently as possible, HIH sent a questionnaire to 4,000 retail stores, department stores, specialty shops, and gift shops across the United States asking to determine the type of merchandise most appreciated by American retailers.[22] When it came to fashion merchandise, the results highlighted a preference for traditional designs, bright colours, and styles suitable for 'casual or country living'.[23] On the contrary, reported flaws were the fact that lingerie, fabrics, and straw items were perceived as somewhat overpriced and of lower importance in comparison to pottery, alabaster and leather.

The idea of setting up a travelling exhibition to showcase the newly developed merchandise came from Meyric R. Rogers, curator of decorative and industrial arts at the Art Institute of Chicago, who reportedly matured it after visiting HIH in New York in 1949.[24] The key role of Rogers is confirmed by a report that he wrote and submitted to Charles Nagel, director of the Brooklyn Museum, in which he chronicled how he spoke to the Director of the Art Institute of Chicago Daniel C. Rich and to officials of the Museum of Modern Art in New York before contacting Ramy Alexander, vice-president of CNA, to inquire about the 'possibilities of obtaining material for an exhibition illustrating the present achievement of Italian designers and craftsmen in the various fields of the decorative industrial arts'.[25] Rogers initially acknowledged the involvement of the Museum of Modern Art in New York, whose director René d'Harnoncourt had been a board member of HDI, but the partnership did not occur and, instead, the Brooklyn Museum agreed to host the inaugural leg of the exhibition.[26] In 1949 the Art Institute of Chicago 'authorized a field survey of Italian crafts and industrial arts to see whether conditions were favourable for an exhibition of [Italy's] postwar production to be held in the United States', so during that summer Rogers joined Alexander in Italy for a tour of various workshops and artisan schools.[27] Ivan Matteo Lombardo, Italian minister for Industry and Commerce, provided substantial support to the project by promising to deliver the chosen items free of charge to the American exhibitors and to help with shipping and insurance.[28] Lombardo's involvement in the different planning stages of *Italy at Work* was coherent with his presidency of both CNA and the Triennale, the international art and design exhibition held in Milan since 1933,[29] and with what he deemed a sentimental connection that he had with the export of handicrafts, one of his earliest professional occupations.[30] Moreover, it demonstrated a certain cohesiveness in the promotional plans envisioned by the management of the HIH and CNA, who tended to surround themselves with professionals equally competent in the Italian and American sides of the operations. A second trip followed in the spring–summer of 1950, during which Rogers and Alexander were joined by the rest of the newly formed committee of American experts in charge of selecting the objects to be displayed: it included Charles Nagel, director of the Brooklyn Museum, industrial designer Walter Dorwin Teague, and their respective wives. The purpose of this trip was to finalize the selection of artefacts for the exhibition and so the committee, 'working with the facilities of CNA, met in Italy from April fourth to June fourth 1950, making its selection in a tour of over three thousand miles'.[31]

An ever-changing selection

While *Italy at Work* did not comprise a dedicated fashion section, visitors could spot plenty of fashionable ideas in the vast selection of dress textiles and fashion merchandise, incorporated in two of the twelve categories identified by the organizers. Dressmakers were, however, missing, since the bulk of objects to be shown in *Italy at Work* were selected in the summer of 1950, a time in which Italian couture was still not considered suitable for exporting. The international fashion system was still based on Parisian *haute couture*, which dictated its trends all over the world and whose designs were employed by Italian dressmakers too.[32] Italian dressmakers who tried to break free from this production paradigm by creating original garments were proportionately still few and had not yet received recognition of originality from international buyers. For this reason, American trade buyers did not attribute creative self-sufficiency to Italian dressmakers, whose success with American clients heavily relied on purchases from individual clients travelling to Italy. As a result, the fashion merchandise chosen by the selection committee of *Italy at Work* was also oriented toward these types of objects, tracing the trends highlighted by the American press that had interested American buyers since 1944.

The exhibition catalogue confirmed the emergence of a preferred style in Made in Italy fashion merchandise, already circulating in American glossy magazines and fashion columns in local newspapers. Fashion in *Italy at Work* comprised a selection of pioneering items distinguished by the Italian practical and creative traits that American clients recognized. The exhibition chiefly showcased a broad range of accessories, particularly costume jewellery and leather goods, as well as various clothing fabrics. However, there were limited examples of readily available garments, and the photographic section of the catalogue only featured one item. As such, it fails to provide a comprehensive reflection regarding the encompassing fashion choices exhibited during the three-year nationwide tour. The catalogue dedicates five pages to fashion accessories and textiles, beginning with photographs of four costume jewellery sets designed by Luciana Aloisi, Emma Ivancich, Carlo Barbasetti di Prun, and Eva Carocci Vedres, respectively. It follows with samples of satin and silk fabrics provided by the Roman boutique Myricae, and one full-page photograph of a handmade skirt made in black cotton and hand-printed in green and gold, executed by artist Irene Kowaliska (Figure 4.1).

Irene Kowaliska, a Polish artist, immigrated to Italy in 1931 and joined the influential German community that defined the ceramics industry in Vietri.[33] After relocating to Positano in 1942, she started experimenting with hand-printing techniques on cloth and collaborating with Teresa Massetti's Roman boutique Myricae. Massetti relied heavily on the creations of independent artists, usually painters hired out to manufacturers in the fields of decorative arts, fashion accessories, and illustration for the manufacture of

4.1 Skirt by Irene Kowaliska, from the exhibition catalogue of *Italy at Work: Her Renaissance in Design Today*, 1950.

distinctive ready-made items of *moda boutique* quality. Kowaliska's artistic style, described by Lisa Ponti in *Domus* as a 'pleasant and genuine Salerno dialect infused with Nordic influences', reflected her distinctive viewpoint as an immigrant and thus her individual gaze towards crafts and fashion.[34] In her comprehensive study of Naples and Campania in the establishment of a Made in Italy style stemming from the South, Ornella Cirillo argues that one of the main contributions of Kowaliska to the image of Italy's postwar fashion scene was contributing to 'spread the name of Positano in decorative art exhibitions all over the world' at a time in which the work 'of local creatives [was] still silent and anonymous, while the singular landscape [was] the value of strong communicative impact attracting a vital circulation of visitors'.[35] In 1950, the designer created a skirt for Ingrid Bergman which featured on the cover of the French publication *Cinémonde*, boosting the appeal of Italian style after the war (Figure 4.2).

Tessitrice dell'Isola enjoyed the same fame in the American press and embodied the same taste for the almost primitive design well represented by the selection carried by the Roman boutique Myricae, but while Massetti relied mostly on painted and hand-printed fabrics, Maria Chiara Gallotti of Tessitrice achieved striking effects of decoration through weaving. The aristocratic upbringing of Gallotti and her financial misfortunes after the war enticed US journalists further, while the beginning of her entrepreneurship bore the remnants of Italy's colonial past, as noted by *Harper's Bazaar*: '[i]n 1945 Baronessa Clarette Galotti ... was evacuated from Africa with other Italian colonists. She returned to her native land widowed and penniless, with only one asset – a knowledge of weaving acquired in African villages'.[36] In the photographs that accompany the short piece, originally shot in 1949 by Karl Bissinger for a *Flair* assignment, Gallotti and American-Italian socialite Consuelo Crespi pose gracefully modelling the finished woven skirts; yet the female workers employed by Gallotti photographed while operating the looms (Figure 4.3), indicated as 'native girls', were the ones concretely producing the garments. This combination of aristocratic female entrepreneurship and 'philanthropic' involvement with the local community, nevertheless, helped Italian fashion gain considerable traction in the press, since it corresponded to that 'aristocratic-nostalgic' stereotypical representation of Italy that Americans were looking for during the postwar years.[37]

Other ready-made garments had been selected and exhibited during *Italy at Work*, as it can be inferred from archival sources pertaining to the exhibition's publicists and from museums' collections. The exhibition included a hand-painted skirt by Florentine artist Dianora Marandino and a blue and red cape jacket decorated with white fringes in wool and synthetic fibres by Tessitrice dell'Isola, both made with textiles from the Bevilacqua manufacture of Venice and currently in the collection of the Costume Institute at the Metropolitan Museum of Art in New York. Furthermore, sample Angora wool garments arrived in December after the installation was completed and were thus not included. When they were sent to Chicago for the second leg, they were excluded from the display selection altogether for unspecified reasons, probably related to the fact that the exhibition comprised originally of more than 2,500 pieces and thus it could have been complicated to insert new ones and replace others.[38]

An additional large hand-woven shawl decorated by a large band in lurex and fringes in the same material was photographed and included in the printed materials for the opening of the exhibition at the Brooklyn Museum. Two photos recently found in the press kit of the Brooklyn Museum's press officers, Richard Pleasant and Isadora Bennett, display

4.2 Ingrid Bergman wearing a Kowaliska skirt. *Cinemonde*, 30 January 1950.

two stylings of the garments, emphasizing its ingenuity and transformability, presented as unique when compared to typical mass-manufactured goods made in the United States, yet still functional for the wearer because of its versatility. In one photograph the model faces away from the camera to reveal the shawl's width and the decorative details

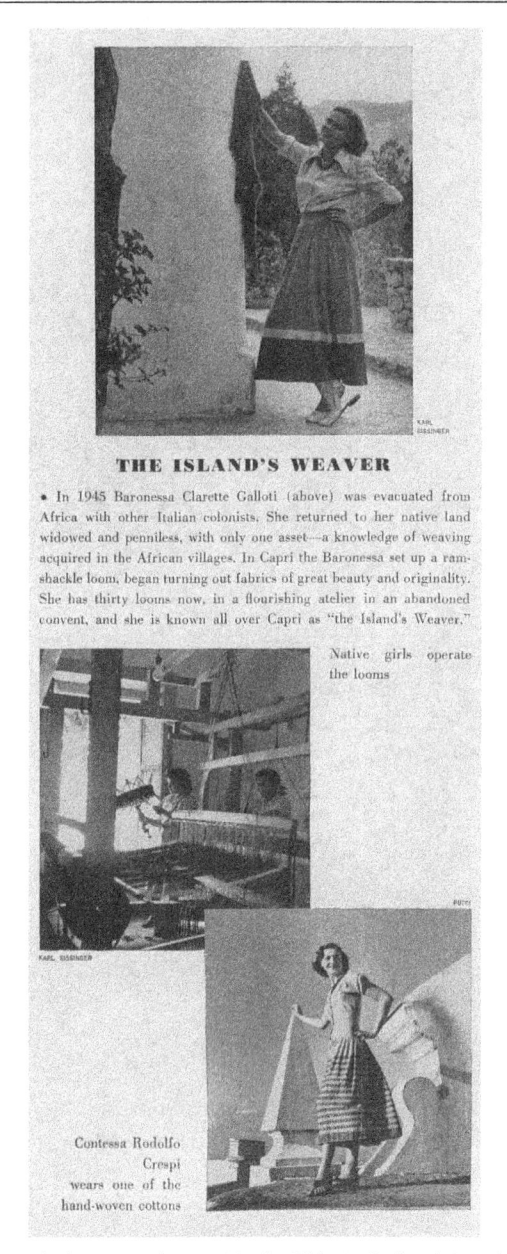

THE ISLAND'S WEAVER

• In 1945 Baronessa Clarette Galloti (above) was evacuated from Africa with other Italian colonists. She returned to her native land widowed and penniless, with only one asset—a knowledge of weaving acquired in the African villages. In Capri the Baronessa set up a ramshackle loom, began turning out fabrics of great beauty and originality. She has thirty looms now, in a flourishing atelier in an abandoned convent, and she is known all over Capri as "the Island's Weaver."

Native girls operate the looms

Contessa Rodolfo Crespi wears one of the hand-woven cottons

4.3 Short article and photographs on Maria Chiara Gallotti, Tessitrice dell'Isola. *Harper's Bazaar*, March 1949. Courtesy of *Harper's Bazaar*, Hearst Magazine Media, Inc. Image published with permission of ProQuest LLC. Further reproduction is prohibited without permission

within it (Figure 4.4), while in the other she stands with her left side facing towards the camera, wearing the stole more closely to her body, to resemble a full-length dress (Figure 4.5). In a recent work, Alessandra Vaccari retraces the persistence of garments specifically designed to

4.4 Full shot of a woman modelling a Tessitrice dell'Isola shawl. From the press pack of *Italy at Work: Her Renaissance in Design Today*, 1950. Courtesy of Princeton University Library

transform their appearance in the history of Italian fashion and its stylistic independence, outlining their being intrinsically related to a modernist conceptualization of fashion that somehow surpasses chronologies and the temporality of fashion itself.[39] Within this frame of reference, the appearance of transformable garments in the fashion merchandise selection of *Italy at Work* speaks of the continuum that existed, from a historiographical perspective, between Fascist fashion and the postwar Made in Italy produced in a liberated, democratic country. This invisible thread

4.5 Alternate styling of a Tessitrice dell'Isola shawl. From the press pack of *Italy at Work: Her Renaissance in Design Today*, 1950. Courtesy of Princeton University Library

that connected 'Fascist fashion' and the products of Italy's 'Renaissance in design' (from the full title of the *Italy at Work* exhibition) was not detected by the American press, which was greatly interested in these unusual garments. The *New York Times* praised a special transformable and 'unfinished woven dress' also made by Tessitrice dell'Isola that perfectly met the definitions of an ingenious and practical new Italian Look. The dress consisted of a large portion of 'handsome rough hand-woven silk', on top of which the buyer would have to cut an opening for the neck, sew the sides under the sleeve openings, and possibly complete it with a belt: it was, according to the reporter, 'one of the most interesting objects in the fashion section'.[40]

The functional elegance of this creation echoed the widespread narrative circulating among American journalists since the late 1940s, which had been adapted in the press releases chiefly produced by Pleasant and Bennett about the new creativity of Italy showcased by *Italy at Work*. Richard Pleasant explained it clearly, when he could not obtain good quality photographs suitable for the press from Meyric R. Rogers, that the largest amount of publicity for the exhibition had to be produced in connection with the opening, so it would have been possible to capitalize on it in connection with the following stops, Chicago being second in line: 'If magazine publicity isn't generated on the basis of the Bklyn [sic] show he'll have a hard time reviving the patient afterwards. If he doesn't know it, 95% of the national editors are provincial New Yorkers and edit accordingly.'[41] The narrative employed focused quite significantly on the materials used and the unusualness of some of them: in this sense, the models included from Florentine firms Salvatore Ferragamo and Edoardo Frattegiani were exemplary, as both shoemakers specialized in novelty designs combined with uncommon materials.

The innovation found in their footwear samples was mostly employed in displays that enhanced their materials, especially raffia, straw, and nylon, in the case of Ferragamo's 'Invisible' model.[42] The same principle of selection evidently applied to Gucci, represented solely by a selection of cloth and straw walking umbrellas, rather than leather footwear and luggage. They were not included in the catalogue, but a recently uncovered photo of the exhibition's setting at the M.H. de Young Memorial Museum in San Francisco shows them displayed in an octagonal construction together with other Mediterranean-inspired fashion accessories in straw and raffia, such as a bag and a hat by Florentine straw artisan Emilio Paoli, and six pairs of Ferragamo shoes (Figure 4.6). The exhibition catalogue offers no information about the Ferragamo shoes on display either, possibly due to a specific choice by curator Meyric R. Rogers, according to whom an exhaustive catalogue would have been unfeasible given the 2,500 objects on display.[43] At the end of the exhibition in 1953 some of the objects remained in the United States and, among them, were nine pairs of Ferragamo shoes, now in the collection of the Costume Institute of the Metropolitan Museum of Art.[44] While some of these can be recognized in Figure 4.6, including the 'Mercury' sandal and the 'Valle' espadrille, others are not part of the group that did remain in the United States. Among the six pairs of Ferragamo shoes placed at the base of the octagonal structure displayed in San Francisco one can also recognize a pair of sandals with an 'F' shaped wedge and Tavarnelle needle lace uppers, sandals with raffia heels and ankle laces, and a pair of lace-up shoes with raffia uppers.[45]

4.6 'Mediterranean fashion accessories' at the M.H. De Young Memorial Museum of San Francisco display of the *Italy at Work: Her Renaissance in Design Today* exhibition, 18 June–31 July 1951. Archives of American Art, Smithsonian Institution

It is quite possible that the objects displayed changed as the exhibition progressed in its path through the years, presumably based on the availability of local department stores that organized commercial 'Italian festivals' in parallel to *Italy at Work*.[46] This was true for Ferragamo, whose exhibited items required updating after each seasonal release and could therefore be eligible for seasonal sales such as with the clearance summer sale (Figure 4.7) at The White House department store in San Francisco that coincided with the conclusion of *Italy at Work* at the De Young Museum.

The partial rotation of the fashion merchandise was an additional confirmation of the attractive nature of those designs and their being in

4.7 Ferragamo advertisement for The White House department store. *San Francisco Examiner*, 30 August 1951

tune with the contemporary trends of the American market. One of the display cases at the Brooklyn Museum, for example, contained two additional pairs of Ferragamo shoes that are not among those that remained in the United States after the exhibition closed, and which ended up in the collection of the Brooklyn Museum first and later at the Costume Institute (Figure 4.8). Even more interestingly, the vitrine included also a Giuliana Camerino red calfskin bucket bag, unusually topped with a fabric cap that could be knotted like a handkerchief to create a handle. Yet, neither the names of the firm nor of its owner, Giuliana Coen, appear in the catalogue of the exhibition. The same bag, called 'Apache', had appeared in *Bellezza* a few months earlier (Figure 4.9), and it was part of a far-West inspired collection that included other transformable bucket bags, in leather and textiles, called 'Muciacitos'.[47] A possible explanation for this inclusion in Brooklyn is that personal relationships did play a relevant part in business transactions of the time, as demonstrated by the history of *Italy at Work*.[48] The staff at Fondazione Ferragamo confirm that Giuliana Coen's bags were frequently featured in the Ferragamo shops at the time, a relationship supported also by the study of Irina Inguanotto on Elda Cecchele, a specialist embroiderer based in Veneto whose work was commissioned by both Coen and Ferragamo in the 1950s.[49] It seems plausible, therefore, that both the proximity of Ferragamo and Coen as acquaintances and the sale of Coen's fashion merchandise in Ferragamo's stores ultimately led to the inclusion of the Giuliana Camerino 'Apache' bag in the Brooklyn display, as a demonstration of its fashion currency.

Curator Meyric R. Rogers justified the choice of favouring practicality and innovation over the stereotypical motifs with a purely folkloric flavour. Of the latter kind, he singled out traditional Florentine leatherwork, now a 'stereotype vulgarized by its very success as an article of commerce' because of the incessant demands of foreign buyers, who were pushing on this type of product so unnecessarily decorated.[50] While, in his opinion, this type of production was part of the large category of souvenirs, Rogers and the rest of the selection committee had sought to

4.8 Installation view of *Italy at Work: Her Renaissance in Design Today* at the Brooklyn Museum with Giuliana Camerino bucket bag 'Apache', 1950. Brooklyn Museum Libraries and Archives

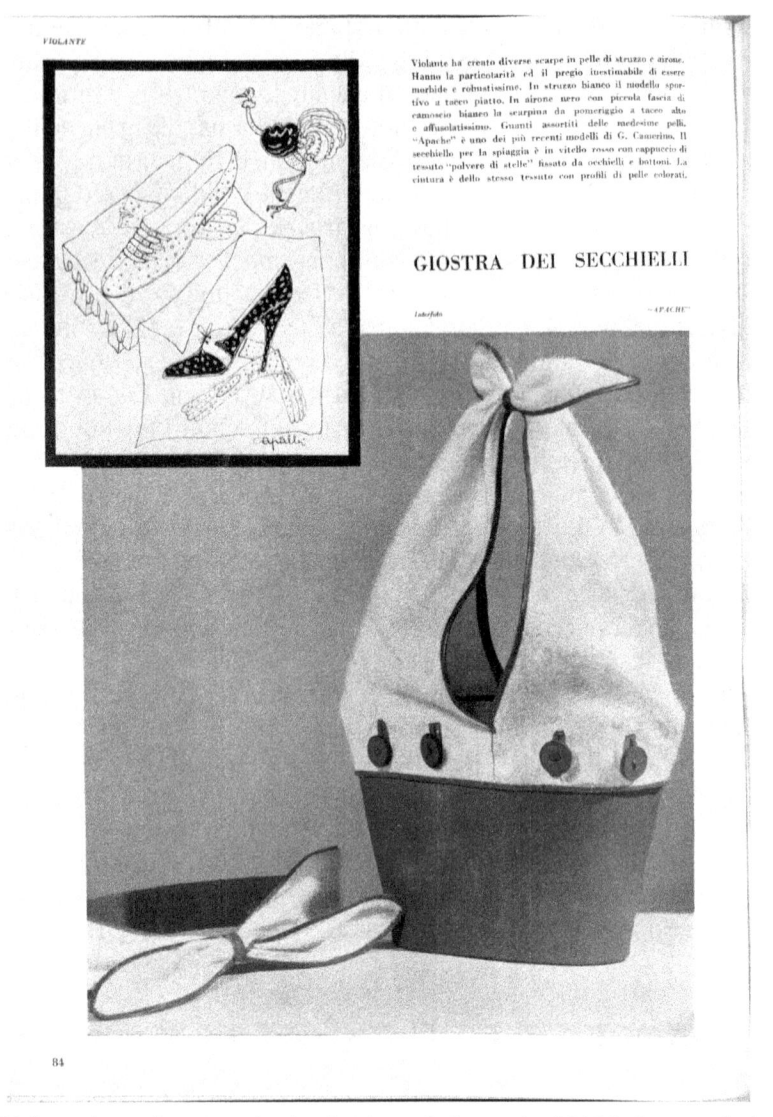

4.9 Giuliana Camerino, 'Apache' bucket bag. *Bellezza*, April 1950. Cameraphoto Epoche/©Vittorio Pavan. By permission of the Ministry of Culture – Pinacoteca di Brera – Biblioteca Braidense, Milan

compose a picture, albeit a heterogeneous one, in which American consumers recognized a certain Italianness in fashion craftsmanship. The events that led him to pre-approve the project of an Italian couture fashion show at the Brooklyn Museum demonstrate Rogers' conviction that the exhibition could exert the authority necessary to legitimize the creativity of Italian fashion exports.

The fashion show that never was

In the summer of 1950, after completing the second field survey and selecting the objects to be displayed in *Italy at Work*, Meyric R. Rogers and his wife Helen met Giovanni Battista Giorgini, who immediately pitched to Rogers the idea of presenting a selection of the current best Italian dress-makers to the public of *Italy at Work* in New York. In this ideal setting, in which state-of-the-art Italian industrial design and craftsmanship merged, they would have been able to introduce the promising creativity of Italian fashion, an emerging sector of Made in Italy, to an audience of interested connoisseurs.[51] The show, according to Giorgini, would combine ancient and modern clothes in a seamless integration of the celebrated past of Italian costume traditions and the new emerging style, simple yet creative and striking. Giorgini's vision, heavily influenced by the traditional histori-cal re-enactment popular in Florence and in Tuscany, combined different eras to emphasize Italy's glorious past and its ability to influence interna-tional fashions,[52] as contemporary garments would have been paired with authentic period costumes dating back to the fourteenth, fifteenth, and sixteenth centuries, along with two servant uniforms dating back to the seventeenth century to be worn by real exhibitions staffers.[53]

Rogers and Charles Nagel, the director of the Brooklyn Museum, responded enthusiastically to Giorgini's flamboyant proposal and agreed that the fashion show should be held at the Brooklyn Museum to highlight its direct connection with *Italy at Work*.[54] At the same time, however, they stressed the pressing need to find a sponsor willing to finance the event, ideally an upscale department store in the New York area. The set-up and preparation costs for the Brooklyn Museum were proving to be quite sub-stantial, and it was deemed necessary to solicit additional contributions in the form of sponsorship.[55] The exhibition publicist Richard Pleasant was already well aware of the issue in June 1950 as he corresponded with the Assistant Secretary of State for Public Affairs Edward W. Barret, trying to have a free boost of publicity by requesting that Ambassador Dunn mention *Italy at Work* to the press on his arrival in New York on the first Italian com-mercial flight since the war. He added that '[e]xpenditure of ECA funds, as you know, stops at the water's edge, and therefore, money must be raised locally for the presentation of the exhibition in America'.[56] *Women's Wear Daily* estimated that the expenses incurred in preparing the exhibition amounted to some $370,000, underscoring an operation that, although it was considered successful within days of its opening, had turned out to be decidedly expensive.[57] A special committee created for the opening was trying to raise funds for the exhibition and make access free for as many visitors as possible.[58] It was certainly not possible to recover financial sup-port for such an expensive ancillary event that was not in the original plan-ning, mostly concerning the promotion of a still emerging merchandise sector in the eyes of American buyers.

In addition to incurring costs that the organizers could not afford, the support of a department store would also have facilitated the logistics of the show, especially regarding transportation and storage of costumes and couture garments in the United States. Being the experienced commissionaire that he was, Giorgini promptly requested information from Rogers regarding duties and import conditions already at the outset of their written interaction, asking whether he contemplated the goods entering the United States free of duty or as a temporary importation.[59] Nagel and Rogers asked Giorgini to investigate among his retail acquaintances in each of the eleven other cities that would have hosted the exhibition and ask the sponsors to contact them directly to discuss the organization. Confident of his business partnership with department store B. Altman on Fifth Avenue, less than two months before the opening of the exhibition Giorgini confirmed to Nagel that he had forwarded the proposal to the vice-president of B. Altman, James A. Keillor and that some leading Italian couturiers responded enthusiastically to participate in the show at the Brooklyn Museum.[60] The show would be structured along the lines of the seasonal presentations held in American department stores, presenting multiple brands together grouped according to different categories of garments: outerwear, daywear, sportswear and leisurewear, and eveningwear, complemented by a plush selection of accessories such as hats, hairstyle accessories, gloves, bags and footwear. In preparation for the Show, in 1950 Giorgini attended the fashion shows held during the Venice Film Festival and the Roman couture openings of Visconti, Fontana, Carosa, and Schuberth; he also reportedly obtained financial support from some unspecified influential Turinese professionals who were willing to sponsor the New York fashion show.[61]

Despite this, B. Altman's response was negative. Keillor estimated that the event would cost between $25,000 and $35,000, 'far beyond anything we would be willing to undertake at this time'.[62] Furthermore, since the store was unable to see the garments beforehand via its ready-to-wear merchandising buyer, Violet Meison, it could not take on the responsibility of backing a couture runway show with models that could potentially be unfit for the American market, or worse yet, a blatant imitation of Parisian designs.[63] While the postwar reconfigurations of power were about to end the undiscussed monopoly of French couture in the transatlantic fashion trade, at the time Paris was still the only reputable source for designs. As observed by fashion historian Véronique Pouillard, the American ready-to-wear industry and the European businesses of couture copying could not afford to disseminate styles and designs that did not correspond to the trends approved in Parisian *maisons de haute couture*.[64] Keillor's response to Giorgini's proposal reflected the current market situation. Although the store was keen on the idea of an opening towards Italian couture, the public act of sponsoring a fashion show without first allowing buyers to preview the garments would have been counterproductive to B. Altman. Giorgini would later explain that a misunderstanding probably occurred and that he did not mean that B. Altman should buy the garments outright, as they would usually do for their seasonal fashion festivals; Giorgini would obtain the garments through a consignment agreement with the couture and fashion firms, and at the same time he would be able to finance the set-up of the show thanks to his sponsors in Turin.[65]

Research consultant and curator Michelle Murphy discussed the situation at length with Keillor before the store's decision.[66] Murphy, the research consultant of the Edward C. Blum Industrial Design Laboratory at the Brooklyn Museum, was an influential fashion expert of her time: a member of the Fashion Group, she was responsible for one of the largest costume collections in a museum at the time, contributing significantly to its growth. In 1951 she was awarded the Neiman Marcus Award during their fourteenth annual Fashion Exposition, with the motivation that she had 'assembled the most complete collection of fashion and design source material in America, making the museum an actual working laboratory for United States designers'.[67] Investigating the archival sources held at the Brooklyn Museum, Lucia Savi provides a complementary explanation to Keillor's refute by pointing out that Murphy had already investigated the feasibility of such a show with her contact at *Women's Wear Daily*, journalist Alice B. Perkins, and received her unfavourable opinion.[68] In March 1950, *Women's Wear Daily* European correspondent Perkins had authored five articles on Italian dressmakers illustrating their spring collections, 'in view of American trade interest in the Italian fashion market'.[69] In the articles, published between 21 to 31 March 1950 after the spring showing season of Italian dressmakers, Perkins profiled nineteen fashion houses in three Italian cities, highlighting what she considered the best features of each and the reasons why they could represent interesting fashion ideas for the US market. The articles mentioned several dressmaking houses that carried a selection of identical reproductions and adaptations of Parisian models: in Milan, they were Biki, Rina Modelli, Vanna and Villa; in Florence, Marianna sold exclusively Parisian models, while Adele Aiazzi Fantechi would do 'half and half', as it was the case for Galitzine and Gattinoni in Rome. Two major Milan-based 'model houses' featured were Rina Modelli and Villa: their business consisted mainly of identical reproductions of Parisian models, although they also carried adaptations and a few original creations.[70] Carla Guido of fashion house Villa was quoted as saying that

> American buying is too small and scattered as yet to make it profitable to create original models for them. The time element is another factor, she comments. To attract substantial American buying, Italian collections should be shown in July and January, she believes, but she doubts if Americans would be

willing to risk much money on models until they know the silhouettes on which Paris would set its approval for the season. She suggests that if Americans are really interested in the Italian market, and would organize a small group to visit Milan at the same time, it might be profitable both for them and the Italian houses to show special interseason collections with distinctive Italian flavour, such as outdoor clothes for summer resorts.[71]

American buyers, thus, could not make much use of Italian collections because the spring lines were usually shown in mid-March (in Milan) or much later (in Rome), with just a few exceptions from more export-savvy houses, like Simonetta Visconti.[72] If the Italian Shows kept being organized after the French ones, accusations of derivativeness could not be effectively stopped. This observation resonated with the decision that Giorgini made to proceed with the Italian fashion show project anyway. Once he lost the opportunity to take part in a US-based sponsored event, he strategically planned his fashion presentation to open before the Parisian shows, preventing possible accusations of plagiarism, cutting down expenses by asking the participating Italian couturiers to contribute with 25,000 lire each, and eliminating customs, insurance, and shipping issues by organizing the event in Florence.[73] By condensing the positive results obtained by other promotions, among which the recent *Italy at Work* was key, and somehow imposing an acceleration to the acceptance of Italian couture designs, Giorgini's venture would eventually become such an integral part of the Italian fashion industry that it would lead to the establishment of the Centro di Firenze per la Moda Italiana first and later of the Pitti Immagini conglomerate.[74]

Despite the result of their interaction, the archival sources and the press indicate that Giorgini found a champion of the Italian fashion cause in Meyric R. Rogers: in his private conversations with Giorgini and in his public speeches and appearances alike, he clearly showed an interest in the subject of Italian fashion novelties. When *Italy at Work* opened at the Art Institute of Chicago in March 1951, Rogers wore an elegant white jacket made entirely of straw (Figure 4.10), with which he was photographed for the *Chicago Daily Tribune*.[75] As the garment was so unique, it was presumedly passed on to Rogers by Giorgini, who donned it himself a few months later during the celebrations of the Second Italian High Fashion Show of Florence in July 1951.[76] While in Italy during the previous year, Rogers reportedly found a new interest in Italian custom-made clothing, praising its quality of materials, style, and moderate prices, an irresistible combination that led him to purchase four bespoke suits. Forecasting a parallel with the growing recognition of Italian high fashion tailoring, Rogers said that anyone curious about the making of the new suits from Italy should keep being interested to find out: 'you'll have to watch me'.[77]

4.10 Meyric R. Rogers wearing a straw jacket. *Chicago Daily Tribune*, 8 April 1951

Whose idea?

One of the most compelling narratives that still circulates about Giorgini and his pre-1951 achievements is that he was responsible for either organizing or developing the original idea for the exhibition *Italy at Work*. Several works in the fields of design history, contemporary art history, and museology have amply demonstrated the chief involvement of CNA and Chicago-based curator Meyric R. Rogers. Even the role of Gio Ponti, for long indicated as one of the key inspirers and a behind-the-scenes organizer of the exhibition, has been recently reconsidered and inscribed in a more complex scenario of influences and transatlantic collaborations.[78] Within this set of ascertained participants, the exact dynamic of interactions that prompted the organization of *Italy at Work* remains unclear today, but it is possible to contribute to its understanding by summing up the numerous attributions of responsibility claimed so far. The result of these reflections aims to make clear to the reader that the interest towards Italian handicrafts and 'ready-for-export' objects in the late 1940s to the early 1950s was a shared trait among private businesses, cultural institutions and governmental agencies.

Early announcements of the exhibition had appeared already in 1949 and early 1950. In August 1949, *Women's Wear Daily* announced that HIH was arranging 'exhibitions of Italian goods in many sections of the country by late 1950 as a means of giving further impetus to distribution here which is concentrated largely on the Eastern seaboard at present. It will be a consumer promotion'.[79] In March 1950 the *Christian Science Monitor* reported that HIH was planning displays of 'leading lines of Italian handicraft goods … in Chicago and other leading cities in the United States'.[80] HIH had thus publicly acknowledged its desire to further develop its promotional strategies for the Italian handicraft industry with a series of exhibitions. Its involvement in *Italy at Work* was further reinforced by the opening words of the exhibition catalogue, where Meyric R. Rogers introduced the readers to the pivotal role of HDI in America, CADMA in Italy, and the initiatives propelled by Ascoli in general.[81]

The role of *Italy at Work* in the development of promotional discourses for Italian fashion has also a historiographical value. While the roles of CNA, HIH, the Art Institute of Chicago, and Meyric Rogers in setting up the exhibition are confirmed by primary sources pertaining to diverse archives and international scholarships, the fact that Giorgini claimed to have had the original idea for *Italy at Work* certainly discloses interesting information about the postwar market for Italian goods in the United States, its publicity, and its key players. A promotional booklet printed for the Second Italian High Fashion Show, held between 19 and 21 July 1951, explained that Giorgini organized two exhibitions of Italian modern arts and crafts in Chicago after the end of the Second World War. It is reasonable to think that they were the sort of display that Giorgini was most familiar with, intended for commercial sale and reflecting the experience developed with both Le Tre Stanze and the Allied Gift Shop in Florence. Taking place in the showroom of Chicagoan home decorators Watson & Boaler, with whom Giorgini collaborated since 1925,[82] these exhibitions supposedly spurred so much interest towards Italian products that, in the words of Giorgini and his publicists, they gave 'rise to the initiative of Mr. Rogers of the Museum of Modern Art in Chicago, for the exhibition "Italy at work"'.[83] Founded in 1916 and based in Chicago, Watson & Boaler was a consulting firm, providing personalized advice on furniture, remodelling, and home décor, but also represented by a large store in the Historic Michigan Boulevard District of downtown Chicago since 1933. Two of the four floors of the building occupied a permanent exposition space dedicated to silver, china, glass, and 'better accessories' for the home, featuring unique merchandise that matched the mid-luxury style usually sold by Giorgini.[84] In the autumn of 1948, Giorgini was invited by Watson & Boaler to take part in some promotional activities by head decorator Albert C. Hagmayer, an event to which the firm was reportedly planning to invite the Italian Consul-General.[85] An advertisement for Watson & Boaler in the *Chicago Daily Tribune* from the same period shows that the shop was having a promotion on modern fabrics, supposedly upholstery textiles, 'just received from Italy', but there are no further details on special exhibits held there.[86]

The following January the exhibition *Italian Artisans Exposition* (Figure 4.11) opened in the modern furniture department of the Watson & Boaler establishment.[87] It was presented by the press as 'the first show of its kind to be held here since the war', and displayed furniture, pottery, artistic crafts, and leather objects in both modern and traditional styles, with a preference for decorations done in 'a new vein'.[88] The design and architecture magazine *Interiors* dedicated a short editorial to the exhibition, as highlighted by Maria Cristina Tonelli,[89] yet the brokerage of Giorgini was not acknowledged by the publication, as it was usually the case with buying offices and commissionaires.[90] Meyric Rogers, a relevant presence in the cultural scene of Chicago due to his job at the Art Institute, was also familiar with Watson & Boaler, as he reportedly held at least one lecture on their premises.[91] In September 1950, while enquiring about the possibility of setting up an Italian fashion show at the Brooklyn Museum, Giorgini passed onto Rogers a message from Hagmayer who wanted to know 'what the committee [of *Italy at Work*] wanted Watson and Boaler to display of Fornasetti's', the all-around craftsman and artist based in Milan introduced in Chapter 2 and promoted by HIH and CNA, also present in *Italy at Work*.[92] Thus, there undoubtedly had been contacts between Giorgini and Chicagoan arts and crafts dealers of Italian exports, in parallel to the organization of *Italy at Work*.

Nonetheless, with reference to Giorgini's later claim to have inspired or even initiated *Italy at Work*, the 'authenticity' of the claim is not the type of contribution that this chapter wishes to make. Inaccuracies have arisen whenever previous research has claimed that Giorgini *did* organize *Italy at Work*, ignoring the popularity of the topic in the several previous scholarships that have discussed at length the exhibition. Rather, this chapter demonstrates that the documentation preserved in the Giorgini archive needs to be historically·contextualized within its time and with complementary primary sources from external collections. In this sense, Giorgini's provoking words demand a reflection on his constant drive for self-promotion: by affirming to have inspired *Italy at Work* Giorgini demonstrated to have a well-informed business vision. His claim filled the purpose of setting the

4.11 Advertisement for the *Italian Artisans Exposition* at Watson & Boaler. *Chicago Daily Tribune*, 2 November 1949

Italian High Fashion Shows within a frame of references that allowed its American audience to appreciate Italian fashion designs as something in vogue at the time. In particular, the overlap with *Italy at Work* put the Italian High Fashion Shows in close connection with a successful touring exhibition, itself the culmination of a long process of publicity for the Italian handicraft industry, comprising many categories of fashion merchandise. Knowing the American market as he did and having the possibility of being in contact with other intermediaries, such as competing buying offices and non-profit agencies like CNA, Giorgini benefited from the privilege of being able to dialogue with both demand and supply, fine-tuning his initiatives in a way that would satisfy either side of the Atlantic.

The road to couture

The *Italy at Work* exhibitions were the culmination of the last phase of a five-year-long series of promotional enterprises for the Italian handicraft industry, the initial scope of HDI. By providing the 'first comprehensive view of a new cultural renaissance burgeoning in an old civilization', Rogers and his collaborators publicly displayed the exhibition's political potential. The average citizen of the United States who did not have the possibility to travel, they argued, could nonetheless benefit from the exhibition as it represented 'a receipt for his kindnesses – and his tax money spent abroad'.[93] The exhibition was a step forward in the battle against Communism, Nagel affirmed in a press release, as it made it possible for Italian workers to desire 'Democracy, American style'.[94]

The handicraft industry of Italy, within which fashion and apparel in general constituted a relevant portion, demonstrated a great capacity for adaptability to the needs of the average American. Artisans could be willingly directed according to the current taste of US consumers, it was often reported. Furthermore, the selection of the 2,500 goods displayed in the exhibition, and eventually in stores, was entirely put in the hands of an all-American committee.[95] As to reinforce the commercial purpose of the whole operation, it was announced that each object would be accompanied by an approximate retail price established by HIH, and, by the time *Italy at Work* opened in Brooklyn, most of them were already on display in the main department stores of the cities whose museums would host *Italy at Work* in the following months.[96]

The tension between modernity and tradition, at the core of fashion as a modern phenomenon, was one of the elements that characterized exports of Italian handicrafts in the United States, and this would later be addressed in the characterization of Italian fashion wrought by Giorgini himself and the US press. By bridging artisanal tradition and modern novelty, *Italy at Work* embodied the vastly homogenous and fragmented nature of Made in Italy in the postwar period. In writing one of the earliest academic accounts on the exhibition, design historian Penny Sparke reflects on the reasons why *Italy at Work* included a seemingly kitsch object – to contemporary taste, that is – like a straw donkey.[97] With *Italy at Work* being partially a trade show, Sparke argues that the donkey's presence could be imputed to several reasons, among those the fact that it gave access through consumption to 'a country and a culture which was still seen to be in touch with its rural and artisanal traditions'. This same characterization was deliberately sought by the organizers, as Rogers stated that

> [t]hrough the ages the Italian has kept an intimacy with the earth and its products that is almost animistic in its quality … There is an unselfconscious personification of his material which leads him to work with it, at times even talk to it as with another individual not unlike himself.[98]

In this sense, the use of natural materials in the artisans' work was considered a given. 'With this', argues Sparke, 'went the retention of handmaking, the use of natural, indigenous materials'.[99]

According to fashion scholar Valerie Steele, among the reasons why Italian fashion did not appear in the transatlantic market until the 1950s was because Italy 'has a long tradition of elegant craftsmanship, but craft per se is not equivalent to art, not even the art of fashion'.[100] Conversely, this chapter demonstrated that the promotion of Made in Italy fashion merchandise in the immediate postwar years was deeply connected to the handicraft industry, which benefited from a promotion circuit ingrained in the ERP efforts and in a large transatlantic project of visibility in the United States. Within the sounding board of *Italy at Work*, its coverage in different types of magazines and local newspapers, the relationships that it established for manufacturers and buyers, and the recognition that it provided to fashion as a collective creative industry, the fashion merchandise manufacturers were catering to the needs of the United States to refuel of original ideas that would nonetheless fit in the mass production system of capitalism,[101] since, as stated by Rogers,

> [t]he mass of our material needs can be supplied by mechanized industry. Beyond this there remains and will continue to remain for the indefinite future a portion of our needs, material as well spiritual, which can be supplied only by the enjoyment and practice of individual skills. Here Italy has a tremendous constructive potential.[102]

Notes

1 V.C. Caratozzolo, '1952–1968: *L'Italia esplode*. Considerazioni sull'inedito di Irene Brin'. In *L'Italia esplode. Diario dell'anno 1952*, edited by Claudia Palma (Rome: Viella, 2014), pp. 191–208, 199.
2 Caratozzolo, '1952–1968: *L'Italia esplode*', 193.
3 I. Brin, 'Obiettivi puntati sull'Italia'. *Bellezza* May 1950, pp. 73–8.
4 V.C. Caratozzolo, *Irene Brin: Italian Style in Fashion* (Venice: Marsilio, 2006), p. 59.
5 M. Barrese, 'Il dialogo Roma-Stati Uniti per la promozione dell'artigianato artistico italiano'. In *L'Italia al Lavoro. Un Lifestyle da Esportazione*, edited by Paola Cordera and Chiara Faggella (Bologna: Bologna University Press, 2023), pp. 193–202.
6 Barrese, 'Il dialogo Roma-Stati Uniti', 195.
7 Barrese, 'Il dialogo Roma-Stati Uniti', 195.

8 P. Cordera and C. Faggella eds., *L'Italia al Lavoro. Un Lifestyle da Esportazione* (Bologna: Bologna University Press, 2023).

9 M. Casciato, 'Between Craftmanship and Design: Italy at Work'. In *La Arquitectura Norteamericana, Motor y Espejo de La Arquitectura Espanola En El Arranque de La Modernidad (1940–1965)* (Pamplona: T6 Ediciones, 2006), pp. 9–18; C. Rossi, *Crafting Design in Italy: From Post-War to Postmodernism* (Manchester: Manchester University Press, 2015); C. Marfella, 'Tra Arte e Arte Applicata. Gli Artisti Alla Mostra "Italy at Work: Her Renaissance in Design Today", New York 1950'. *Annali Delle Arti e Degli Archivi* 1, 2015, pp. 41–48; E. Dellapiana, 'Italy Creates. Gio Ponti, America and the Shaping of the Italian Design Image'. *Res Mobilis* 7(8), 2018, pp. 20–48; A. Gamble, *Cold War American Exhibitions of Italian Art and Design: 'Italy at Work: Her Renaissance in Design Today'* (New York: Routledge, 2023).

10 C. Faggella, '"Not So Simple": Reassessing 1951, G.B. Giorgini and the Launch of Italian Fashion' (PhD Dissertation, Stockholm University, 2019); C. Faggella, 'Il nuovo Rinascimento della moda italiana: Ferragamo e il dopoguerra'. In *Salvatore Ferragamo 1898–1960*, edited by Stefania Ricci (Milan: Skira, 2023), pp. 482–89; C. Faggella, 'Dietro Le Quinte Alla G.B. Giorgini. Le Assistant Buyers e l'esportazione Di Moda Italiana Negli Stati Uniti, 1946–1956'. In *Un Oceano Di Stile. Produzione e Consumo Di Made in Italy Negli Stati Uniti Del Dopoguerra*, edited by Simone Cinotto and Giulia Crisanti (Milan: Mimesis edizioni, 2023), pp. 163–80; C. Faggella, 'Prima della couture: la promozione della moda italiana in *Italy at Work*'. In *L'Italia al Lavoro. Un Lifestyle da Esportazione*, edited by Paola Cordera and Chiara Faggella (Bologna: Bologna University Press, 2023), pp. 87–96; L. Savi, *A New History of 'Made in Italy'. Fashion and Textiles in Post-War Italy* (London: Bloomsbury Publishing, 2023), ; M. Martin, 'Fashion in the Art Museum: A Case Study of Salvatore Ferragamo Shoes'. In *L'Italia al Lavoro. Un Lifestyle da Esportazione*, edited by Paola Cordera and Chiara Faggella (Bologna: Bologna University Press, 2023), pp. 187–94.

11 Princeton University Library, Special Collections, Richard Pleasant Papers (hereafter PUL, RPP). Box 1, Folder 2, 'Outline of Talk by Dr. Max Ascoli at The Brooklyn Museum November 29, 1950'.

12 'Handicraft Lines Recover in Italy', *New York Times* (1 October 1948), p. 37.

13 'Freudenthal in ECA Post', *New York Times* (19 October 1948), p. 14; 'Elected to Presidency Of Italian Handicrafts', *New York Times* (8 March 1950), p. 8.

14 'Italy's Bid for Export is the Work of her Skilled Craftsmen'. *Harper's Bazaar* March 1948, pp. 296–97.

15 E. Dellapiana, *Il design e l'invenzione del Made in Italy* (Turin: Einaudi, 2022), p. 111.

16 Original in Italian: 'bisogna anche aiutarli a sfuggire alle grinfie delle arpie di dentro e di fuori – di dentro come i Borletti di Milano': FR, ACLR, Carteggio generale. Ascoli, Max (DOC 83) 1945–1980. Max Ascoli to Carlo Ludovico Ragghianti, 6 November 1946. Document 47 2229a.

17 Original in Italian: 'possono fare ciò che noi non possiamo fare: e cioè assicurarsi delle esclusive sui prodotti migliori e più convenienti'. FR, ACLR, Carteggio generale. Ascoli, Max (DOC 83) 1945–1980. Carlo Ludovico Ragghianti to Max Ascoli, 8 December 1946. Document 22 2261c.

18 A. Filippini, 'Paolo De Poli e l'America: 1947–1967. Gli Smalti Verso Il "Nuovo Mondo"'. In *L'Italia al Lavoro. Un Lifestyle da Esportazione*, edited by Paola Cordera and Chiara Faggella (Bologna: Bologna University Press, 2023), p. 134.

19 'Italian Trade Aid Seen in Bank Loan', *New York Times* (8 December 1947), p. 42.

20 Claudio Alhaique, 'Problemi attuali del credito all'artigianato'. *Moneta e Credito*, 1(3), 1948, pp. 327–33. Compagnia Nazionale Artigiana provided additional fiscal and trade advisory to those firms who wished to enter the export market.

21 'Italian Trade Aid Seen in Bank Loan'.
22 'Survey Conducted for Italian Goods', *New York Times* (29 March 1948), p. 31.
23 'Survey Finds Good General Acceptance of Italian Goods', *Women's Wear Daily* (18 January 1949), p. 57.
24 Rossi, *Crafting Design in Italy*, 16.
25 Brooklyn Museum Archives, Office of the Director records, Charles Nagel records, 1946–1955 (hereafter BMA, DIR-CN). Exhibition: Italy at Work (1), Meyric R. Rogers, 'Italian Contemporary Industrial Arts'. Reports on a survey made in Italy, 2 June–5 July 1949, Document 1949–02/1951.
26 Rogers, 'Italian Contemporary Industrial Arts'.
27 Rogers, 'Italian Contemporary Industrial Arts'; Meyric R. Rogers, *Italy at Work. Her Renaissance in Design Today* (Rome: Compagnia Nazionale Artigiana, 1950), p. 16.
28 Rogers, *Italy at Work*, 16.
29 R. Pepall, '"Il buon design è un buon affare." La promozione del design italiano del dopoguerra in America'. In *Il Modo Italiano: Italian Design and Avant-garde in the 20th Century*, edited by Giampiero Bosoni (Milan: Skira, 2006), pp. 78–89, 85.
30 I.M. Lombardo, 'Prefazione'. In *Le esportazioni dei prodotti artigiani e la Compagnia Nazionale Artigiana nel suo primo anno di attività*, edited by Claudio Alhaique (Rome: Scuola Tipografica 'Don Luigi Guanella', 1950), pp. 7–8, 7.
31 Rogers, *Italy at Work*, 17.
32 V. De Buzzaccarini, *La Sartigianeria. L'Artigianato Dell'abbigliamento Nel Tempo* (Monza: Modart, 1985), p. 83; E. Tosi Brandi, *Artisti Del Quotidiano: Sarti e Sartorie Storiche in Emilia-Romagna* (Bologna: CLUEB, 2009), p. 88; C. Faggella, 'Itinerari di moda fiorentina fra il dopoguerra e la fine degli anni sessanta: dal guardaroba alla memoria storica'. In *Moda, città e immaginari*, edited by Alessandra Vaccari (Milan: Mimesis edizioni, 2016), pp. 148–59, 154.
33 V. Pinto and G. Grattacaso, *Irene Kowaliska – 1939* (Cava de' Tirreni: Areablu Edizioni, 2018), pp. 11–16.
34 L. Ponti, 'La Kowaliska', *Domus* April 1950, p. 58.
35 O. Cirillo, 'Fashion and Tourism in Campania in the Middle of the Twentieth Century: a Story with Many Protagonists'. *Almatourism. Journal of Tourism, Culture and Territorial Development* 9(9), 2018, p. 33.
36 'The Island's Weaver', *Harper's Bazaar* March 1949, p. 238.
37 R. Bedarida, 'Ceramiche per ricostruire l'Italia: Lucio Fontana nelle mostre americane del dopoguerra'. In *L'Italia al Lavoro. Un Lifestyle da Esportazione*, edited by Paola Cordera and Chiara Faggella (Bologna: Bologna University Press, 2023), pp. 107–15, 114.
38 BMA, DIR-CN. Exhibition: Italy at Work (2) (CN 50–51), Charles Nagel to CNA's Claudio Alhaique, 6 August 1951. I am extremely grateful to Lucia Savi for providing me with this reference.
39 A. Vaccari, *Indossare la trasformazione. Moda e modernismo in Italia* (Venice: Marsilio, 2022).
40 B. Pepis, 'For the Home: Italian Crafts in Museum Exhibit', *New York Times* (29 November 1950), p. 52.
41 PUL, RPP. Box 1, Folder 2, Richard Pleasant to Ben Hall, 1 September 1950.
42 In the collection of the Costume Institute at The Metropolitan Museum of Art, New York. S. Ferragamo, 'Liuto', 1947–50. Acc. N. 2009.300.1244a, b.
43 Rogers, *Italy at Work*, 12.
44 Martin, 'Fashion in the Art Museum'.
45 The designs of the wedges and the sandals, respectively, correspond to the Ferragamo design patents 28482 (20 May 1948) and 35850 (20 November 1950).

46 C. Rossi, 'Made in Italy and Made for America: Craft in Italy at Work.' In *L'Italia al Lavoro. Un Lifestyle da Esportazione*, edited by Paola Cordera and Chiara Faggella (Bologna: Bologna University Press, 2023), pp. 59–66.

47 The 'Muciacitos' are oddly forecasting the earliest 'O bag' models first launched in 2012 by Paduan entrepreneur Michele Zanella.

48 P. Cordera and C. Faggella, 'Italy at Work, un laboratorio per la modernità'. In *L'Italia al Lavoro. Un Lifestyle da Esportazione*, edited by Paola Cordera and Chiara Faggella (Bologna: Bologna University Press, 2023), pp. xvii–xxiv, xix–xx.

49 One of the most comprehensive works on the relationships between Ferragamo, Coen, and Cecchele can be found in I. Inguanotto and G. Tattara, 'Innovazione, reti di comunicazione e di competenze. Elda Cecchele, Roberta di Camerino e gli artigiani della campagna veneta'. *Rivista di storia economica* 1, 2010, pp. 93–120.

50 Rogers, *Italy at Work*, 43.

51 Archivio di Stato di Firenze, Archivio della Moda Italiana di Giovanni Battista Giorgini (hereafter ASF-AMIGBG), Album 2. Meyric R. Rogers to G.B. Giorgini, 24 August 1950.

52 D.M. Lasansky, *The Renaissance Perfected. Architecture, Spectacle & Tourism in Fascist Italy* (University Park: The Pennsylvania State University Press, 2004).

53 ASF-AMIGBG, Album 2. G.B. Giorgini to Meyric R. Rogers, 15 September 1950.

54 ASF-AMIGBG, Album 2. Charles Nagel to G.B. Giorgini, 24 August 1950.

55 BMA, PUB, Press Releases, 1947–1952. 'Statements by Dr. Max Ascoli at the Opening of the Exhibition, "Italy at Work" at the Brooklyn Museum, Wednesday evening, November 29th, 1950,' Document 07–09/1950, p. 121.

56 PUL, RPP. Box 1, Folder 2, Richard Pleasant to Edward W. Barrett, 25 June 1950.

57 J. Teague, 'High Cost of Promotion Here Hard to Surmount'. *Women's Wear Daily* (1 December 1950), p. 41.

58 PUL, RPP. Box 1, Folder 6, Brochure with information on a fundraiser, undated [November 1950] .

59 ASF-AMIGBG, Album 2. G.B. Giorgini to Meyric R. Rogers, 29 August 1950.

60 ASF-AMIGBG, Album 2. G.B. Giorgini to Charles Nagel, 5 October 1950.

61 ASF-AMIGBG, Album 2. G.B. Giorgini to Nella Giorgini, undated [19 October 1950].

62 ASF-AMIGBG, Album 2. B. Altman to G.B. Giorgini, 11 October 1950.

63 ASF-AMIGBG, Album 2. James A. Keillor to G.B. Giorgini, 11 October 1950.

64 V. Pouillard, 'Keeping Designs and Brands Authentic: The Resurgence of the Post-War French Fashion Business under the Challenge of US Mass Production'. In *Made in Europe: The Production of Popular Culture in the Twentieth Century*, edited by Klaus Nathaus (London: Routledge, 2015), pp. 815–35.

65 BMA, DIR-CN. Exhibition: Italy at Work (1). G.B. Giorgini to B. Altman, 19 October 1950, Document 1949–02/1951. My gratitude to Marcella Martin who kindly provided me with this reference.

66 ASF-AMIGBG, Album 2. Charles Nagel to G.B. Giorgini, 20 October 1950.

67 'Winners of Fashion Awards Are Named by Neiman-Marcus', *Women's Wear Daily* (13 August 1951), p. 4.

68 Savi, *A New History of 'Made in Italy'*, 43.

69 A.K. Perkins, 'Report From Italy on Dressmaker Showings', *Women's Wear Daily* (21 March 1950), p. 3.

70 Perkins, 'Report from Italy'.

71 A.K. Perkins, 'Report from Italy on Dressmaker Showings', *Women's Wear Daily* (22 March 1950), p. 3.

72 A.K. Perkins, 'Report from Italy on Dressmaker Showings', *Women's Wear Daily* (30 March 1950), p. 3.

73 ASF-AMIGBG, Album 2. G.B. Giorgini to Carosa, 28 December 1950.

74 K. Fallan and G. Lees-Maffei, 'Introduction: The History of Italian Design'. In *Made in Italy: Rethinking a Century of Italian Design*, edited by Grace Lees-Maffei and Kjetil Fallan (London: Bloomsbury Academic, 2013), pp. 1–34, 22.

75 A. Lynch, 'Curator Tours Italy Seeking Revitalized Art', *Chicago Sunday Tribune* (8 April 1951), part III, p. 3.

76 G. Braggiotti Etting, 'Florence in Fashion'. *Town & Country* September 1951, p. 177.

77 J. Cass, 'Art Institute Beneficiary of Their Travels', *Chicago Daily Tribune* (17 September 1950), part VII, p. 6.

78 M.C. Tonelli, 'Italia e Stati Uniti, 1948–1954: un percorso di opportunità'. In *L'Italia al Lavoro. Un Lifestyle da Esportazione*, edited by Paola Cordera and Chiara Faggella (Bologna: Bologna University Press, 2023), pp. 21–8; E. Dellapiana, 'Una "sala da pranzo che è più da guardare che da usare"'. In *L'Italia al Lavoro. Un Lifestyle da Esportazione*, edited by Paola Cordera and Chiara Faggella (Bologna: Bologna University Press, 2023), pp. 77–84.

79 James Teague, 'Italian Handcraft House Now Stocks and Sells Direct', *Women's Wear Daily* (26 August 1949), p. 7. The will to expand distribution in other Northern American states is consistent with the observations made by Pagliai, according to which the majority of Italian buying offices and trade agents concentrated their business activities within the New York area.

80 Edmund Stevens, 'Italy to Push Handicraft Sale In Effort to Capture Dollars'. *Christian Science Monitor*, (9 March 1950), p. 6. The article reports of a press conference in which Ivan Matteo Lombardo (1902–1980) participated as Minister of Foreign Trade.

81 Rogers, *Italy at Work*, 15–16.

82 L. Pagliai, 'Giovan Battista Giorgini: Alle Origini Del "Made in Italy". Economia e Modernizzazione Tra Fascismo e Repubblica' (PhD Dissertation, Università degli Studi di Pisa, 2007), p. 133.

83 ASF-AMIGBG, Album 4. Booklet for the Second Italian High Fashion Show, 19–21 July 1951.

84 'Watson and Boaler Will Modernize Boul Mich Store', *Chicago Daily Tribune* (22 January 1933), part III, p. 8.

85 ASF-AMIGBG, Carteggio. G.B. Giorgini to Nella Giorgini, 30 October 1948.

86 Advertisement', *Chicago Daily Tribune* (18 December 1948).

87 The name of this small commercial exhibition has been erroneously referenced as 'Italy at Work' in a recent edited volume: D. Calanca, 'Italy at Work, From Craftmanship to Fashion, 1923–1950/Italy at Work, dall'artigianato alla moda, 1923–1950'. In *G.B. Giorgini and the Origins of Made in Italy*, curated by Neri Fadigati (Florence: Gruppo Editoriale, 2023), pp. 40–54, 52.

88 E. Weigle, 'Italian Craftsmen's Work Is on Display Here', *Chicago Daily Tribune* (19 January 1949), part II, p. 1.

89 Tonelli, 'Italia e Stati Uniti, 1948–1954', 23.

90 'Retail Story. Italian Modern in Chicago'. *Interiors* April 1949, pp. 122–25.

91 'Here and There', *Chicago Daily Tribune* (17 October 1949).

92 ASF-AMIGBG, Album 2. G.B. Giorgini to Meyric R. Rogers, 15 September 1950.

93 Giorgini to Rogers, 15 September 1950.

94 Giorgini to Rogers, 15 September 1950.

95 Rogers, 'Italian Contemporary Industrial Arts'.

96 BMA, PUB, Press releases, 1947–1952. Document 10–12/1950, p. 97.

97 P. Sparke, 'The Straw Donkey: Tourist Kitsch or Proto-Design? Craft and Design in Italy, 1945–1960'. *Design History Society* 11(1), 1998, pp. 59–69.

98 Rogers, *Italy at Work*, 22.

99 Sparke, 'The Straw Donkey', 60.

100 V. Steele, 'Italian Fashion and America'. In *The Italian Metamorphosis, 1943–1968*, edited by Germano Celant (New York: Guggenheim Museum Publications, 1994), p. 496.
101 S. Gundle, *Glamour: A History* (Oxford: Oxford University Press, 2008), p. 232.
102 Rogers, *Italy at Work*, 14.

5

Fashion councils of Turin, Milan, and Rome

> In the midst of many negativities, of many disbeliefs and slanders, of many silly things that people think and say about us Italians, we have an unshakable faith in the new *Risorgimento* of Italy, which we feel is already underway, while other countries are only starting to glimpse it and they are amazed by it and sometimes they also fear it.[1]

The postwar scenario of fashion promotion in Italy was tumultuously characterized by several disconnected initiatives, supported by the interests of different professionals and parts of the industry within the country. Namely, Turin, Milan, and Rome appeared to be the cities holding the greatest stakes. Despite the will to further their own interest groups and agendas, the three cities hosted self-appointed fashion councils that were particularly concerned over the development of foreign trade and, especially, the establishment of steady agreements with the US fashion market.[2] Retrieving their historical vicissitudes challenges the notion that, before Giorgini, Italian fashion did not exist and that the Fashion Shows in Florence were the first instances of promotion of Italian fashion directed to international audiences.[3] In connection with the 'preoccupation with origins' inspired by Bloch and outlined in the Introduction, the following pages challenge the conventional historiography of fashion and enrich its structure with overlapping networks of intermediaries and professionals competing for the same goal: making Italian fashion profitable as an export and establish its endurance in the international market. In the following pages, the book outlines and discusses the different initiatives that started taking place in Italy as soon as the Second World War drew to an end. The ways in which the different fashion professionals of Turin, Milan, and Rome operated to gain the attention of United States buyers are highlighted in relation to the role that Giorgini would establish for Florence and his own business.

Councils in the three cities are thus presented as predecessors and competitors of Giorgini's private organization, each one of them characterized by a specific configuration of interests: the 'American colony' in Rome, the industrial scene of Milan, and the reconstitution of the remnants of a Fascist fashion council in Turin, a city that was once the only legitimized fashion capital of Italy. In this regard, my additional aim is to highlight the postwar historical trajectory of Ente Nazionale della Moda (ENM), the official Italian fashion council established during Fascism, and demonstrate the ways its staff strived to remain a relevant reference in the postwar reconfiguration of the Italian fashion system. The chapter also serves as a presentation for the dressmakers and fashion firms that caught the attention of the American press before 1951, and who in turn would take part in the early establishments of Giorgini's Italian High Fashion Shows.

The magazine *Bellezza* and the impact of the war

In 1944 Italy was enduring German Occupation, later followed by a temporary military government led by the Allied Forces. Yet, despite the brutal images that the Occupation conjures up in our mindset of posterity, historical research suggests that the business of fashion in certain parts of Italy continued during wartime and that a study of this activity details the impact of the war over the industry's stages of development. Between the declaration of an armistice, proclaimed by Italy on 8 September 1943, and the end of April 1945, the Anglo-American Allied Forces progressed from the shores of Campania to the mountains of Valle d'Aosta, in the pursuit of liberating the peninsula from German troops. As the Allies pushed their enemies towards the north, the Liberation of Italy happened gradually and over a wide span of months. Naples was liberated in October 1943, while Rome followed in June 1944 and Florence in August of the same year. By the end of April 1945, the SS surrendered the last territories of Northern Italy, including Milan, Bologna, and Turin. Those months of Occupation would encompass long-lasting difficulties for the population, particularly in sourcing fuel, food, and water for many months to come. In this context, the traditional historiography has focused on the narratives of those Italian fashion creators whose businesses flourished after the end of the Second World War. For instance, Simonetta Colonna di Cesarò, owner of fashion houses Simonetta Visconti (Rome) and later Simonetta et Fabiani (Paris), reported in her autobiography that she managed to put together her first collection in 1946, two years after the Liberation of Rome, even if '[i]n 1946 Italy lacked bare necessities, let alone fabrics and equipment to create a high fashion collection'.[4] Similarly, designer Roberto Capucci, who made his debut in the early 1950s, has frequently emphasized how the postwar years allowed his fashion house to flourish thanks to abundant workmanship and, particularly, Italian women's renewed will to 'get dressed again'.[5]

By emphasizing the efforts and success of the 'new' postwar Italian fashion, the memoirs of those designers contributed to creating a historiographical divide between inter- and postwar Italian fashion. The resulting impression is that the 'new' Italy required new (and politically untainted) protagonists, even in the fashion business. Instead, the pages of *Bellezza*, the most prestigious Italian high fashion magazine of the 1940s, reveal how several reputable and long-standing Italian dressmaking firms managed to remain open during the war, making sure that Italian women would 'not, despite everything, become savages yet'.[6] Publishing of *Bellezza* fell under the duties of Ente Nazionale della Moda (ENM), the national fashion council, originally founded in 1935 to discipline the production, circulation, and promotion of Italian fashion, and formally dissolved in 1944.[7] With the establishment of ENM the Fascist regime had bestowed additional official authority upon Turin, a city whose cultural influence in fashion was mainly represented by a number of local court dressmakers revolving around the Royal House of Savoy. Though its functions could not be compared to those of the Chambre Syndicale de la Couture Parisienne, scholars agree on attributing to ENM a passive role of surveillance and reprimand, its official main activity being the supervision of the processes of both production and reproduction of models and accessories.[8] The influence exerted by ENM was additionally disseminated through the publication of the glossy magazine *Bellezza* through a controlled company called EMSA, Edizioni Moda Società Anonima (Anonymous Society of Fashion Publishers). The magazine's editorial concept had been originally conceived by architect and designer Gio Ponti, who envisioned it as the Italian alternative to the American magazines *Vogue* and *Harper's Bazaar* to finally promote an Italian taste pervading fashion, the arts, and culture, to make it visible for other countries to see and appreciate.[9] EMSA published the magazine since its inception in 1941, when *Bellezza* became the official magazine of ENM, until the early months of 1945. As pointed out by historian Silvia Vacirca, the various issues of *Bellezza* published between 1943 and 1945 transmit the sense of urgency that the editorial team – including Gio Ponti himself, Elsa Robiola, and illustrator Federico Pallavicini – felt while keeping the magazine in operation despite the conflict.[10]

The magazine continued reporting on the fashion showings and on the fashion houses that were actively working notwithstanding the war. The effects of the war in Rome, discussed in Chapter 1 from the point of view of the first American journalists visiting the city with the Allies, did not significantly impact the lives of the wealthy and the upper classes, allowing many dressmakers to keep their businesses active and undisturbed. In Milan, where the editorial office of *Bellezza* was located and the few correspondents left could still reach for fashion news, the war had hit way harder and for longer. Mrs Manette Valente of the dressmaking firm Vanna had to close her atelier, destroyed during bombing incursions, and instead use her private apartment to host co-workers and run a temporary dressmaking workshop.[11] By using this location to keep her business running she ensured that her new collections would appear in *Bellezza* even between 1943 and 1945, at the highest point of the conflict on Italian territories. Other Milanese dressmakers who could not relocate anywhere else in the city would move their dressmaking firms to the relatively more tranquil locations around Lake Como, while some ateliers were spared by the bombings and could remain open in their original locations. This was the case of Ferrario in via Montenapoleone who, in the autumn of 1943, managed to organize a small showing of its winter collection including furs and evening pieces.[12]

In the spring of 1945, EMSA ran out of funds so there was an attempt to sell *Bellezza* to an industrial 'concern', a third party that would have been able to 'guarantee the nobility of the magazine, as it had been in the past' and, most of all, to keep the headquarters of the magazine in Turin and reprise the collaboration with ENM, once the latter resumed its activities.[13] In fact, the now dissolved ENM had been put under controlled administration by the Italian Social Republic, the shadow government led by Mussolini in Salò near Lake Garda: its commissioner decided not to reintegrate the financial participation in EMSA, alleging a lack of funds, and additionally argued that EMSA did not have the power to dispose freely of the publication since *Bellezza* was first and foremost 'the official magazine of Ente Nazionale della Moda. Thus, considering the present situation [the controlled administration of ENM], we think that [*Bellezza*] should suspend its publication. To this end we request you to act accordingly'.[14]

Following the shutting down of EMSA, a new publishing company resumed the publication of *Bellezza* in November 1945: the hiatus had lasted less than a year and most of the editorial staff remained the same, now led by editor-in-chief Michelangelo Testa.[15] Towards the last pages of the magazine, a caption confirmed that publishing of the 'new' *Bellezza* was authorized by the Psychological Warfare Branch and thus by the Allies. The magazine took a different publishing turn and started implementing a more significant coverage of Rome-based dressmakers and increasing its coverage of Parisian fashion, often with photoshoots done by its own collaborators, such as Elsa Robiola. The new editorial guidelines contrasted with the direction previously imparted by Ponti, whose anti-fashion and anti-frivolities stance had been embedded since the establishment of *Bellezza* in 1941, when the focus was more consistently on the (often nameless) dressmakers of Milan and Turin in particular.[16] The demise of ENM, thus, shifted the focus of attention from Turin to whichever other city proposed itself with fashion exhibitions and promotional initiatives. *Bellezza* recognized this momentum and increased mentions of Rome-based dressmakers and articles penned by journalist and art gallerist Irene Brin. Brin, who owned the art gallery L'Obelisco with husband Gaspero del

Corso, became a crucial figure in the promotion of the Roman fashion scene, and her talent was eventually recognized by the US fashion press when she was hired to correspond from Rome for *Harper's Bazaar*.[17] Already in the first issue of the 'new' *Bellezza*, Brin wrote about the differences perceivable in the fashionable women of Turin, who were more inclined to follow the predicaments of a French magazine, and those of Rome, who were loyal to the American ones. Their dissimilarities, wrote Brin, reflected two almost separatist ways to interpret fashion that nevertheless found a common ground in their acknowledgement that Luciana's costume jewellery, made by Baroness Luciana Aloisi de Reutern and later sold in the United States thanks to the exhibition *Italy at Work*, represented the universal style of Italian fashion merchandise of the postwar period.[18] The inception of the new editorial team of *Bellezza* marks the beginning of a new series of articles, mostly by Brin but not exclusively, in which the readers become acquainted with Roman names that would become increasingly popular in Italy and particularly abroad.

Turin and Ente Italiano della Moda

ENM was one of the many public agencies created during Fascism, thanks to which the city of Turin had enjoyed a significant position in the Italian fashion system until the mid-1940s. The war and the Occupation had worsened both the state of the industry and the finances of ENM: the funding that it had received from the government, around 2 million lire, ceased in 1943.[19] Following the armistice of 1943, the Italian Social Republic formally dissolved ENM, as discussed earlier, and its bureaucratic remnants were put under controlled administration in May 1944.[20] It took a while for the Ministry of Industry and Commerce, headed by Ivan Matteo Lombardo of CNA, to become aware of the survival of ENM: it wasn't until 1945 that the government in Rome received information from Turin, still occupied by German troops, and agreed that, while ENM and its ties to the Fascist administration needed to be dissolved, Italy nevertheless required a national fashion council.[21] A national fashion council was needed for multiple reasons: to safeguard the creation of original models; to launch collaborations between different branches of the fashion industry, such as textile manufacture and dressmaking; and, most importantly, to promote exports abroad.[22] It was suggested to convert the once state-controlled fashion council into a simple association, recognized by but not part of the new Italian Government.[23] Even Turin's Palazzo della Moda, the distinctive 'fashion palace' of ENM inaugurated in 1938 to host fashion showings and exhibitions, had been severely damaged by the war bombings of 1943 and ENM was in a critical operational state because its existence was now seen as a shameful display of favouritism. Nonetheless, as soon as 1945 part of ENM's original staff and its former general manager Vladimiro Rossini promptly migrated into a new association, called Ente Italiano della Moda

(Italian fashion council, from now on EIM).[24] Despite not being a governmental agency, the creation of EIM was approved by the provisional Government of Italy, therefore partially reprising the appealing connotation of authority that Turin had enjoyed in the previous years. Its activities remained under cover for more than a year, so much so that, since its establishment had not been publicly announced, other associations and professionals attempted to replace the role of its predecessor ENM.

As previously discussed, at the outset of the Liberation many Italian professionals in the field of fashion acknowledged that the damages inflicted to the Parisian fashion industry by the German Occupation created the occasion for Italy to claim a spot in the export market. Industry and retail professionals alike agreed that a national council, modelled against the paramount example of the Chambre Syndicale de la Couture Parisienne, could greatly improve the modernization of the Italian apparel sector. For this reason, a few attempts were made to replace the now-defunct ENM and several letters were addressed to the Ministry of Industry and Commerce from associations willing to supersede the politically outmoded council of the recent Fascist past. Among those, the Associazione Nazionale Produzione Artistica Abbigliamento (National Association for the Artistic Production of Apparel) in Rome was promising integrity and a streamlined configuration if chosen to become the new national fashion council.[25] Its president Carlo De Gaspari, owner of fashion house De Gaspari Zezza, argued that it was time to 'take advantage of this moment in which, for different reasons, France … is in serious difficulties because of a lack of resources'.[26] In a letter, De Gaspari expressed his concerns towards the former staff of ENM and their reconstitution of the organization under a similar name, EIM, with the support of 'a local group of so-called carnettisti from Milan and Turin'.[27] Carnettisti, whose role in the transition that the Italian fashion industry underwent from dressmaking to luxury ready-to-wear is cleverly analyzed by Lucia Savi, were intermediaries who provided a service to fashion houses by selecting textiles from manufacturers to create sample books, hence the name derived from the French word *carnet*.[28] This letter confirms that De Gaspari, as many others by then, was aware of the fact that the 'new' EIM was restarting its operations and was aiming to restore Turin's old prestige as a fashion capital, together with the help of other intermediary professionals and possibly their economic support.

Mostra Nazionale Arte Moda in Turin, 1946

This muster of efforts between intermediaries produced the first exhibition of fashion and art organized by EIM, the *Mostra Nazionale Arte Moda*. This large exhibition took place in October 1946 in the salons of the former Royal Palace of Turin, now the headquarters of EIM, and reportedly gathered sixty-five Italian fashion houses and six French milliners.[29] The exhibition was promoted with a newsreel made by Italian newsreel production company INCOM: it showed several models parading in the palace, recently abandoned by the House of Savoy and transformed into a rich and lavish setting.[30] Commentator Guido Notari concluded the newsreel by noting how the autumn/winter collections of 1946–47 displayed a reminiscence of the styles that were popular at the end of the First World War, but with a major difference: 'Unlike in 1918 when fashion had to bear a [French] cachet, today it is Turin and Milan, Florence, Bologna and Rome that are inventing the silhouette, the shape of the woman that we will love next season.'[31] The newsreel enhanced the creativity of Italian couture houses and the fact that the war had brought them unprecedented freedom of expression, legitimizing the independence of their designs. The local press, emphasizing that the exhibition had indeed attracted interest from members of the national fashion scene, reported that news of it circulated in the press in Switzerland, France, Belgium, England, the United States and 'even Russia'.[32]

Bellezza celebrated the opening of the exhibition and its ingenious display (Figures 5.1 and 5.2), one that could effectively emphasize how Italian fashion could represent a national style embodying, 'rather than the expression of the taste of its time, the very expressive synthesis of an entire civilization'.[33] Such a standpoint was reminiscent of the editorial style so vehemently expressed by Ponti, according to which 'the goal of *Bellezza* was not so much to document the varying whims of fashion as to testify and help create an Italian style, understood as an expression – one which was universal – of the Italian civilisation'.[34] EIM had won a battle, affirmed *Bellezza*, demonstrating that fashion in Italy could benefit from exhibitions that favour an accurate preparation and selection of the objects displayed rather than exhibit frivolity, thus aptly framing the 'distinctive elements that make one people different from another, an era different from another, a civilization different, for better or worse, from another'.[35]

The main aim of the exhibition was thus the reinstatement of Turin as the original and sole fashion centre of Italy, especially according to Turinese newspaper *La Nuova Stampa*. Its journalists championed the supremacy of the original fashion capital, devoting a number of articles to the initiatives put in place by EIM. 'Will Turin regain her primacy in the field of fashion, for which it deserved in peacetime the name "little Paris"?', asked the newspaper rhetorically, shortly before the opening of *Mostra Nazionale Arte Moda*, in anticipation of which fashion creators and their workforces alike were filled with the excitement to reprise their trade.[36] Following the opening, *La Nuova Stampa* focused on the international hype created around the new Italian collections and pointed out how some Turinese fashion houses had been invited to send their latest creations to the United States.[37] Additionally, the Turin exhibition spurred the interest of Arthur Tarshis, director of the International Exposition of

5.1 Images from *Mostra Nazionale Arte Moda* in Turin. *Bellezza*, October 1946. By permission of the Ministry of Culture – Pinacoteca di Brera – Biblioteca Braidense, Milan

Textiles in New York.[38] *Women's Wear Daily* confirmed the participation of fifty-six Italian exhibitors in the 1947 edition of this trade fair, held in Lexington Avenue's exhibiting space of Grand Central Palace, where they appeared to constitute the largest foreign group represented.[39] Thanks especially to fashion journalist Anna Vanner, who would soon become one of the most prominent Italian fashion editors, *La Nuova Stampa* sympathetically covered the initiatives launched under the aegis of EIM. In

5.2 Images from *Mostra Nazionale Arte Moda* in Turin. *Bellezza*, October 1946. By permission of the Ministry of Culture – Pinacoteca di Brera – Biblioteca Braidense, Milan

early 1949, it was reported that the city of Turin was getting ready to host the *Esposizione Internazionale dell'Arte Tessile e dell'Abbigliamento* (International Exhibition of Textile Art and Apparel), whose organizational committee was headed by Filippo Alberto Giordano delle Lanze, president of EIM. Speaking about the recently restored potential of the Italian textile industry, Giordano delle Lanze declared that Italian textiles had acquired the skills needed to face competition from other foreign countries, particularly in the luxury segment where Italy 'had reached the forefront of world production'.[40] The exhibition was reportedly not a trade fair and therefore had only demonstrative purposes: it aimed to showcase what Italian mills and fashion designers could offer to international customers with a vast array of textiles, original couture models, and ready-to-wear, even if in this latter fashion area Giordano delle Lanze admitted: 'we still need to learn a lot, especially from America'.[41] In later years EIM continued to organize exhibitions and conferences, and in 1949 its *Esposizione Internazionale dell'Arte Tessile e dell'Abbigliamento* contributed to the exceptional ferment and visibility experienced by the Italian fashion industry in that year.[42]

Primo Congresso Nazionale della Moda in Rome, 1949

The reopening of international trade and travel in the immediate postwar years, as demonstrated so far, fostered a fruitful moment of expansion for private associations concerned with the promotion of Italian fashion. In an industry which will be characterized until the 1960s by scattered promotions, the need to update the structure of professional education, and the lack of continuity in the collaborations between designers and textile manufacturers,[43] the geographical disunity of initiatives remained a residual from the interwar times. Italian press reports of the time reflect this division as newspapers sided with different interests. Three years after the *Mostra Nazionale Arte Moda*, *La Nuova Stampa* of Turin reacted resentfully to the news that the Chamber of Commerce in Rome was organizing a suspicious conference on the status of Italian fashion.[44] This 'strange' conference was the May 1949 *Primo Congresso Nazionale della Moda*, which eventually endorsed the establishment of yet another fashion council, the short-lived Comitato della Moda. The anonymous article on *La Nuova Stampa* condemned the Roman initiative as a way to waste energy in a situation that should have required collective efforts to consolidate the role of Turin and EIM. The conference, instead, was meant to unite representatives from different areas of the fashion industry to discuss the most urgent problems they were facing. Keynote speakers included Carlo De Gaspari, of Associazione Nazionale Produzione Artistica Abbigliamento and fashion house De Gaspari Zezza, vice-president of the organizing committee; Carmine Cialfi, spokesperson for Confederazione Generale dell'Industria (General Confederation of Italian Industry); and EIM's vice-president Ernesto Mazzonis, owner of cotton manufacturing plant Mazzonis. The participants belonged to various categories, including industrialists, manufacturers, sketchers (*figurinisti*), journalists, artisans, and politicians. Registered attendees included the Italian division of German textile manufacturer Bemberg, from Milan; textile manufacturer Terragni of Como, an acquaintance of G.B. Giorgini previously introduced in Chapter 3; dressmakers Sorelle Fontana, Carosa, Montorsi, and Caraceni, from Rome; and dressmaker Sorelle Chiostri of Florence. A representative of the Ministry of Industry and Commerce introduced the conference on behalf of Minister Ivan Matteo Lombardo. Among the topics examined, a presentation by Giuseppe Ratti discussed how to successfully direct sales towards the United States, 'the only market not directly or indirectly under bureaucratic constrictions'.[45]

Ratti, a correspondent for Fairchild Publications and *Women's Wear Daily*, had been on the executive committee of the *Esposizione Internazionale dell'Arte Tessile e dell'Abbigliamento* hosted in Turin a month earlier by EIM.[46] During his talk 'Exporting Italian fashion in America', Ratti explained the potential offered by the North American market (mostly Canada and the United States) to Italian artisans and manufacturers. Citing from *Women's Wear Daily*, Ratti quoted New York-based designer Charles Armour who stated: 'You don't see one or two chic Italian women, you see so many that you can't possibly take them all in. They're not extreme or bizarre, but quietly elegant and lady-like.'[47] The quote rhetorically reinforced Ratti's statements on how 'Italian apparel has never been more appreciated, also because – this is the key aspect – American audiences find it often more suitable to their taste in comparison to French products'.[48] Key arguments in Ratti's talk were the simplicity and the restrained chic of Italian dressmaking as considered 'more wearable, more in tune with the lives Americans lead', as pointed out also by the *Women's Wear Daily*'s article he cited. The statements backed Ratti's recommendations to increase standardization of middle-range garments and accessories better suited to department stores. His talk aimed to encourage industrialists and designers to focus on ready-to-wear, since it represented a far better opportunity than attempting to challenge the unrivalled monopoly of traditional Parisian couture, and to consider the vantage point of the involvement of several Italian-American entrepreneurs in the US ready-to-wear industry. Regarding promotion, continued Ratti, there was no need to invest in publicity in Italy. The most efficient way to promote Italian products, he argued, was 'working on site [in the United States], using American methods'.[49] Ratti concluded his talk by recommending Italians to direct their efforts towards two main instruments: trade publications, indirectly referencing the one he represented, *Women's Wear Daily*; and fashion shows or fashion exhibitions to be held in the main US cities.

News of the conference was reported, probably by Ratti himself, in *Women's Wear Daily*, which highlighted the keynote speech given by Ratti and his advice to 'Italian fashion people not to compete directly with the French "*haute couture*", but dedicate themselves to medium-priced clothing production especially made for United States retailers'.[50] Both the conference proceedings and *Women's Wear Daily* reported that the result of the conference was the approval of 'a resolution calling for the constitution of a new organization of all branches of Italy's clothing and textile industries with the aim of coordinating, fostering, and protecting fashion production in Italy as well as of Italian garment exports'.[51] The Italian newspaper *Il Commercio d'Italia*, previously the official weekly periodical of Confederazione Nazionale Fascista dei Commercianti (National Fascist Association of Merchants) reported that the Chamber of Commerce of Rome was going to select the new organization's representatives among various professional categories, constituting the short-lived Rome-based Comitato della Moda in November 1949.[52] The decision to create a new council represented the productive outcome of a reportedly well-attended conference, with participants from all categories of business and regions of Italy that could have formed a fitted *super partes* council to direct the technical activities promoted by Turin's EIM, thus restoring the lost value of Turin as Italy's fashion capital.[53]

Milan and its Centro Italiano della Moda

Comitato della Moda never managed to become an authority within the industry but served the purpose of preparing for the later advent of Camera Nazionale della Moda, and only a few texts have since acknowledged its short-lived existence.[54] With the benefits of hindsight, it can be said that it could not do much to rival the political and industrial forces that came to support the two major fashion councils of the time, Turin's EIM and Centro Italiano della Moda di Milano (Milan's Italian Fashion Centre, from now on CIMM). The latter proved to be supported by a solid network of professionals and a series of efficient promotional activities. A direct emanation of the textile industry, CIMM was reportedly founded in 1948 by Franco Marinotti, head of fibre manufacturer SNIA Viscosa, and Aldo Fercioni, son of Milanese dressmaker Giovanni Fercioni.[55] CIMM had its headquarters in Piazza San Babila: its members, according to *Women's Wear Daily*, were thirty high-end manufacturers of dress and furs that included 'couturiers Ventura, Biki, Fercioni, Vanna, Veneziani, Noberasko and Tizzoni', while financial support came from textile manufacturers Marzotto, Rossi, Gavazzi, Tiziano, and Rosasco, among others.[56] The rivalry between CIMM and EIM, as well as between the two production centres that they represented, was well acknowledged by those in the business, and *Il Commercio d'Italia* reported in 1950 on how 'in the underground fight between Turin and Milan the problems of the fashion [industry] were running the risk of being forgotten by both contestants'.[57] 'The fight is on between the Centro Italian [sic] della Moda', reported *Women's Wear Daily* a few months earlier, 'whose members comprise about thirty Milan dress and fur garment creators, and the Ente Moda, the Turin association, which is understood to be financed in part by the big Fiat automobile concern'.[58]

Nevertheless, while EIM concentrated its promotional activities in Turin, CIMM was farsighted enough to enlarge its sphere of action and create an auxiliary centre in Venice, Centro Internazionale delle Arti e del Costume (International Center for Arts and Costume, from now on CIAC) where in 1951 renowned costume historians James Laver, Doris Langley Moore, and François Boucher coordinated the first international fashion conference held in Italy.[59] The two interconnected councils served CIMM's promotional purpose of appointing Venice as the perfect location to hold events with both cultural and commercial relevance, and in 1949 CIMM established an annual commercial fashion festival held in connection with the Venice International Film Festival. The efforts of local councils and the city administrative officers were highlighted by *Bellezza* with the first edition of 1949, commenting on how the structure of the fashion show imparted by CIMM's director Carmine Cialfi respected the individualism of each designer and, at the same time, conveyed the collective nature of the heterogeneous group of original models and adaptations.[60] The unique atmosphere provided by the city of Venice and the mixed environment of art (with the Biennale), cinema (with the Film Festival), and fashion provided an ideal promotional platform to include Italian couture creations in a wide scenario of national and international references.

The second edition of the Venice fashion festival, in 1950, was a four-day parade of Italian, French and British designers, hailed as an 'international festival of fall and winter Haute Couture' by *Women's Wear Daily*.[61] According to Giovanni Battista Giorgini, who attended the show in preparation for the one that he planned to organize in connection with *Italy at Work* in New York, 'the general opinion was that the Italian Show was the best'.[62] Irene Brin and Elsa Robiola, reporting for *Bellezza*, emphasized the link between art and the newly found sumptuousness of Italian dressmaking with a photoshoot held at the Venice Biennale. Here a cocktail dress by Roman dressmaking atelier Carosa (Figure 5.3) was photographed against a billboard sign claiming *il mondo cambia*, the world changes, somehow echoing the novel position of Italian couture on the transatlantic fashion stage. It was probably not a coincidence that the dress was made of rayon, the artificial fibre that constituted the core business of SNIA Viscosa, chief backer of CIMM and CIAC.[63] Two outfits that do not appear in this fashion spread were instead circulated to *Women's Wear Daily* by CIMM, linking them to the fact that they had been recently purchased by 'American movie stars'.[64] The designs and their descriptions emphasized characteristics immediately ascribable to a certain Italianness: rich embroideries (though machine-made), supple volumes reminiscing of Renaissance costumes, and the inspiration from art. The article particularly noted a dramatic cape, in the style of a Venetian Doge, by Adriana Cerri of Milan, and an Etruscan decorative pattern in sequins, on a Germana Marucelli evening dress, designed by Piero Zuffi.

5.3 Carosa cocktail dress shown during the Venice Film Festival. *Bellezza*, October 1950. Cameraphoto Epoche/©Vittorio Pavan. By permission of the Ministry of Culture – Pinacoteca di Brera – Biblioteca Braidense, Milan

In addition to its headquarters in Milan, CIMM set foot in Rome, too. Although financially backed by couturier Fercioni of Milan and industrialist Marinotti of SNIA, both based in Northern Italy, CIMM formally inaugurated its establishment by sponsoring a grand collective fashion show in Rome, only a few weeks before *Primo Congresso della Moda*. The fashion magazine *Bellezza* reported that CIMM aimed to be the propelling force of coordination and discipline of Italian fashion, organizing fashion showings that would represent 'the test stand of production and the demonstration of its agreement with the public's taste'.[65] The show was documented in a newsreel, which remarked on the newly gained independence of Italian designers from the constraints of Parisian fashion trends.[66] The newsreel also emphasized the American stamp of approval, showing actress Linda Christian, the new bride of Tyrone Power, in attendance; 'Hollywood on the Tiber' had just begun.

The impact of the Holy Year

While the organizers of *Italy at Work* favoured the handcrafted fashion merchandise and textiles that could better speak of the exoticism of Italian artisanal traditions, Rome had a long-standing tradition of dressmaking ateliers catering to the city's nobility, mostly specialized in adaptations and copies of Parisian couture.[67] Even if the Fascist government had been defeated and there was a Republic in the making, the centre of political power remained in Rome and with it persisted a lively society scene, populated by wives of politicians, diplomats, and aristocrats, enriched by the annual debutant season, and by several social engagements that demanded high fashion competence from the Rome-based dressmakers. For these and other reasons, Roman fashion names would contribute to the export of Italian fashion in the United States due to circumstances different from those experienced in the North. First, the developments of air travel and the celebrations of the Holy Year contributed to making Rome a palatable tourist destination between 1949 and 1950, especially considering that the airport of Rome Ciampino became the hub of Trans World Airlines (TWA) and its regular connections to the United States. Second, the US film productions of 'Hollywood on the Tiber' brought with them a so-called 'American colony' of actresses paying visits to Roman dressmaking ateliers, something that helped these firms acquire visibility in the highly coveted transatlantic market.

The celebrations for the Holy Year played a role in the representations of postwar, liberated Italy in the US press, with the developments of transatlantic air travel contributing to an increase in the flux of travellers to Rome. As soon as the outcome of the Second World War appeared to be in favour of the Allied Forces, the North American tourist industry and its representatives started planning the comeback of business activities.[68] Transatlantic travel to Europe experienced a boost in preparation for the Holy Year of 1950, with a significant increase in the airline traffic from the United States.[69] Thus the years between 1949 and 1950 represented a momentous shift in the flux of international travellers to Italy, and eventually a test of the country's transportation, lodging and entertainment standards. A dedicated column in the *New York Times* by foreign correspondent Paul Hofmann informed American tourists on the developments of Holy Year travel, warning them that the spring and summer of 1949 might have represented the last opportunity to enjoy Rome in relative quietness.[70] As the plane capacity of Ciampino reportedly totalled 400 flights per day in October 1949, Hofmann reported that a total of 300,000 Americans were expected to arrive in Rome for the celebrations.[71] Apart from information directed at pilgrims, Hofmann provided advice to more sophisticated travellers, as well as those willing to pursue more entertaining and leisurely aspects of travelling to Italy. He reported on how red tape had been eased on travellers coming from the coast of France to Italy, and how US citizens in particular did not require any visa for visits of up to three months.[72] Hofmann's columns, placed in the *New York Times'* Sunday travel section, were usually surrounded by a series of similar articles on other travel destinations and a considerable number of advertisements for dressmakers such as Biki in Milan, providing 'everything for the fashionable lady', and textile manufacturers; men's tailors in Naples; and glove factories, of which Barra seemed to be ever-present.[73] Besides families and groups of tourists, businessmen and businesswomen – since many fashion buyers were women – were the other main target category for transatlantic travel, with an increasing presence of middle-class travellers.[74] The series of articles written by Hofmann is interesting for grasping details that relate to the travel necessities of commercial buyers. In a profession where timing and efficiency were crucial, a transatlantic flight represented less time spent travelling compared to transatlantic liners. TWA promised an average of 19 hours on its flights from New York to Rome, while a cruise on either the Saturnia, the Vulcania or the Conte Biancamano transatlantic liners would last approximately fourteen days. The private letters of Giovanni Battista Giorgini to his family offer first-hand evidence of this: travelling back to Florence from the United States in January 1947, he boarded a liner in New York on Tuesday, 21 January, and arrived in Genoa on Monday, 3 February.[75] As liners were, however, less expensive, they were a palatable alternative when time was not a determining factor in the choice of transportation.

The experience of the Holy Year eventually endowed the major Italian cities (with the constant exception of the lower south) with a satisfying system of logistics and lodging that allowed them to handle future travellers with ease, especially in relation to other European countries. In an article published in February 1951, Hofmann stated that tourists were now finally able to 'find a commodity that tends to be scarce in West European holiday centres – plenty of elbow room. And almost uniquely on the Continent, the Italian tourist industry is also about to cut its rates'.[76] Additionally, there had been substantial easements in handling customs' red tape and in the requirements for travelling documentation, even if exchanging dollars for Italian lire on the free market had become less favourable; still, dollars could be imported in any amount, while gasoline was discounted for foreign travellers.[77] Earlier in 1950, Hofmann reported that Italian tourism officials were making sure to provide Holy Year tourists with a favourable impression, the utmost comfort, and planned assistance, as they were aware of the fact that efforts would be repaid with positive word-of-mouth and free publicity for the following seasons.[78] The message was clear: Italy was both charming and cheaper than other European countries. This same argument would be used plenty of times to promote the export segments of Italian fashion merchandising and couture.

The American colony in Rome

Italian fashion scholars have generally asserted, until recently, that the attractiveness of Rome, its monuments, its historically layered archaeological past, and its lush natural surroundings caused Hollywood to set some of its postwar productions in Cinecittà, starting the 'Hollywood on the Tiber' period. Specifically, the appearance of 'Hollywood on the Tiber' is, by and large, linked with three triggers: a pool of cheap film labourers, the exotic and historically rich scenery provided by the eternal city, and its emergent and convenient fashion scene.[79] In fact, 'Hollywood on the Tiber' and the ensuing upsurge of Rome-based dressmakers are closely related to the spread of postwar 'runaway productions', special Hollywood film productions operating in locations other than Southern California and particularly abroad.[80] In particular, US film production companies often decided to shoot on location in Rome, using the Cinecittà studios as headquarters, to recuperate the exhibition profits 'frozen' by the Italian protectionist monetary policies.[81] The so-called *legge Andreotti* (Andreotti law) of 1949 was partly responsible for the increasing number of US runaway productions in Rome's film studios of Cinecittà. The law encouraged the reinvestments of US funds, formerly blocked in Italy due to the war, in productions that virtually did not require the studios to spend any more money besides the sums owed to them by the Italian Government, as had happened with the movie *Quo Vadis?*.[82] This key economic factor contributed to keeping US productions, and the flock of celebrities that followed them, in the eternal city for many years to come. As pointed out by Robert S.C. Gordon, those years were

> not only characterized by collaborative, outsourced production, but by an entire subculture that grew up around it. Stars moved to Rome, renting villas on the via Appia; restaurants, bars and clubs sprouted to cater for them and their production crews and entourages. A local print and photo media developed and a culture of gossip, scandal and glamour – previously associated with far-off and exotic America – came to Italy.[83]

Eventually, as noticed by Elizabeth Castaldo Lundén, the reactivation of transatlantic trade made it possible for several international designers to even provide garments for the Hollywood actresses participating in the Academy Awards ceremony, among which many were Italians.[84] It was in this atmosphere that the dressmakers of Rome started to benefit from the visits of new, international patrons. While this book intentionally does not investigate the ways in which Roman dressmaking firms established relations with US actresses and film productions during the 'Hollywood on the Tiber' years, it acknowledges the connections that it established and their impact on the US press, which would be used by the Italian professionals seeking to promote Italian couture in the transatlantic trade.

The wedding of American actor Tyrone Power to Mexican actress Linda Christian, held in Rome in January 1949, is often quoted as the main trigger of the fruitful publicity relationships between American movie stars and Roman fashion houses.[85] Scholars Stephen Gundle and David Forgacs have pointed out that, despite the fact that the concept 'Hollywood on the Tiber' relates mainly to the 1950s and 1960s, the earliest US postwar production in Cinecittà was actually Twentieth Century Fox's *Prince of Foxes* (1949), starring Tyrone Power, during which the romance between Power and Christian reportedly bloomed.[86] Christian's wedding dress was commissioned to Rome-based dressmakers Sorelle Fontana, who would frequently recollect how this event officially launched their career with US customers. The Fontana atelier was located just across the street from posh via Veneto and the Doney, 'the most fashionable café in Rome' according to *Life* magazine.[87] While the wedding represented a publicity stunt of significant importance, it remains unclear how the association between Fontana and the actors materialized. Almost mythological qualities have been attributed to the Power–Christian wedding concerning the establishment of 'Hollywood on the Tiber' and its persistence in the conventional historiography of Italian fashion. This has in turn, for a long time, concealed the complex relations that link the emergence of Roman dressmakers in the US fashion press in the late 1940s, and the acknowledgement of their emancipation from French influences. The relationship between the Fontana sisters and their American representative Estelle Goldstein Stern, for instance, has only been recently pointed out by Ilaria A. De Pascalis.[88] While this association came into being in the 1950s, in the late 1940s the publicity-savvy Fontana sisters had already produced promotional photographs featuring US actresses wearing their creations, among which Linda Christian.[89] Photographing clients wearing their most prized couture models was a practice enacted by most dressmakers, and not just a prerogative of those specialized in reproductions of Parisian couture.[90] The photo shoots at Fontana's echoed a beautiful still taken by Clifford Coffin in Rome and featured in *Vogue* at the time of the wedding, in which Christian wore 'a sable-banded white ball gown of pleated chiffon over layers of net, which was made for her by the Italian designer [sic], Fontana'.[91] The Fontanas' propensity to cater to American actresses and the relevance gained with

American buyers became so established that in 1949 Gertrude Dinsmore of HIH contemplated the possibility of involving Fontana in a sponsored contest themed around the film *Prince of Foxes*.[92]

The Fontana atelier was also expressly chosen by the families of American diplomats and politicians, as shown by a portrait of Cynthia Cochrane Dunn, daughter of US Ambassador to Rome James Clement Dunn, executed by artist Federico Pallavicini and published in *Bellezza* (Figure 5.4). The firm Fontana would be associated with American actresses like Irene Dunne, Ava Gardner, and Audrey Hepburn, and the popularity of the sisters' dressmaking atelier in the United States would

5.4 Cynthia Cochrane Dunn wearing Sorelle Fontana, by Federico Pallavicini. *Bellezza*, May 1949. By permission of the Ministry of Culture – Pinacoteca di Brera – Biblioteca Braidense, Milan

only increase over time. Capitalizing on the international publicity brought by the Powers' wedding, CIMM held its inaugural collective fashion show in Rome. Linda Christian, now Mrs Tyrone Power, attended as a personal guest of Fontana.[93] *Bellezza* reported in the spring of 1949 that Italy was developing a reputation for being a country whose atmosphere fostered elegance. In this, it was aided at the time by 'the American actresses that "shoot" films here, who leave America for their vacations in Europe and lie over languorously, in Venice, in Rome, in Sicily'. This pool of international clientele included wives of diplomats, women employed in diplomatic offices, women in showbusiness, 'and all of them leave with suitcases full of clothes bought here, and all of them spread the tiding of what is our most astounding rebirth'.[94] The news resonated in the US specialized press, and in the summer of 1949 *Women's Wear Daily* announced that Roman dressmakers Simonetta Visconti, Fontana, Emilio Schuberth, Fernanda Gattinoni, and La Boutique had reportedly gained the interest of actresses, wives of diplomats and screenwriters, who were buying 'from one to 26 models from the top houses'.[95]

CIMM, an active and successful player in the promotion of Italian fashion abroad, managed to group those fashion houses that interested US consumers the most, among which Milan-based Marucelli emerged. As explained earlier, though, the council also recognized the popularity of Rome-based Fontana, 'currently one of the favorites of the visiting stars and wives of directors and script writers', and Simonetta Visconti, praised for young ideas and sportswear.[96] It is not a coincidence that Giorgini was in contact with CIMM staff in preparation for the *Italy at Work* fashion show and subsequently the First Italian High Fashion Show of 1951. CIMM was a leading intermediary in the fashion field and its staff had established a significant network of contacts with fruitful efforts. While the commercial and personal relationships established by Roman dressmakers with American movie stars, both on and off screen, represent a complex and rich matter of investigation, this section has barely scratched the surface of the issue, nevertheless suggesting that some of the most visible dressmakers involved with the 'Hollywood on the Tiber' phenomenon were offered the patronage of CIMM, as suggested by the pictures featured in *Women's Wear Daily* in connection to the 'emergent' Italian couture scene linked with the film industry and generally provided by CIMM.

J.L. Hudson's Italian couture, 1949

While the two main Italian fashion councils were particularly active in the organization of showings in Europe, they did not succeed in interesting US buyers with consistency. The war and immediate postwar years witnessed a resurgence of trade relationships mainly with European countries where Italian fashion makers had previously achieved success. In 1942, an Italian 'fashion gala' was held in Stockholm under the patronage of Madame Suzanne Renzetti, wife of the Italian Ambassador, and organized with the artistic direction of Vladimiro Rossini, director of ENM.[97] In the same year journalist Vera Rossi Lodomez described how Italian couture was steadily gaining foot in Europe, with foreign buyers appearing 'maybe a bit doubtful the first time on their arrival, but convinced and enthusiastic when back in their Countries' with a range of 'tastefully elegant models that are practical and in accordance with the new life rhythms of every country, even if neutral, of this period'.[98] Yet, while the first postwar Italian fashion show in Sweden happened in 1953, soon after the war Germany and Switzerland were considered interesting markets for Italian fashion products, and Italian fashion presentations were regularly organized there. Already in 1939 a collaboration between ENM and the Italian Chamber of Commerce organized a collective show of Italian models in Switzerland. An event was repeated in 1946 under the aegis of the newly formed EIM: the fashion show was held at the Hotel Dolder in Zurich and news of it reached the United States, demonstrating a fruitful circulation of news and an increasing interest towards Italian fashion.[99] Business historian Ivan Paris confirms that CIMM was active in the organization of collective shows of Italian houses abroad, such as the 1950 Zurich fashion show that included Fontana, Marucelli, and Simonetta Visconti, among others.[100] In the same year another fashion show was organized in München, in connection with the exhibition *Kultur und Mode* at the Haus der Kunst Museum.[101] According to *Women's Wear Daily* and a German newsreel of the event produced by USIS, Marucelli was the only Italian fashion house participating, together with textile manufacturer Visconti di Modrone, shoemaker Ferragamo, and the French houses of Rodier and Christian Dior.[102] These Italian fashion 'parades' abroad, as they would often be called, support the analysis of Emanuela Scarpellini according to which 'exports to the United States were always far behind the volume of trade with Europe' but, at the same time, the circulation of Italian fashion merchandise and couture in America functioned as an important springboard.[103]

The analysis of both Italian and US press, coupled with the private records examined so far have established that the immediate postwar years indeed experienced a flux of American buyers visiting Italy, more or less regularly depending on their stores' specialty and purchasing options, in search of different categories of fashion merchandise. The year 1949 saw a general opinion gaining foot in the specialized trade press, headed by *Women's Wear Daily*: Italian manufacturers were improving their technical skills and quality standards. Silks and light worsted fabrics were now qualitatively better and favourable in price, especially in comparison to England and the rest of Europe.[104] Fashion accessories, according to a stylist for

Macy & Co., sported traditional styles and were not particularly creative, but their workmanship was excellent and the producers were reportedly 'cooperative in matters of price'.[105] In this complex scenario, however, a steady feature was the fact that Italian couture remained generally overlooked until 1948. A tentative first introduction of Italian dress designs was tested by May's department store in Brooklyn, a large discount store known for its better-priced clothing. Original models from Milan-based Ventura, Vanna, and Noberasco inaugurated the store's 'new policy of selling authentic Italian dresses and suits': the collection was presented to the public and guest of honour Italian Consul-General Luigi Nardi, emphasizing how the event represented 'the first time an American store has promoted the prestige of Italian designs in fashion'.[106] May's buyer R. Best expected the arrival of copies of Italian designs, largely comprising 'soft jacket and dress costumes, smooth shouldered, full-skirted and intricately detailed', in about two weeks since the announcement, thus implying that the agreement concerned the reproduction of Italian designs with the formula of 'manufacturing couture' or *couture en gros*.[107] Nevertheless, the word couture was never used in the *Women's Wear Daily* announcement and the lower status of the department store makes it possible that additional promotions were not pursued further by the Italian designers, probably represented by CIMM. An ensuing systematic exploration of the Italian couture market, this time for the luxury segment, was made by Arthur Kaufmann of Gimbels, who visited Rome in May 1949 to 'study Italian developments in designing couture models with a view to the possibility of their promotion in the United States'.[108] The verdict was unfavourable to Italians, however, as their offerings were deemed too pricey to attract many American orders.[109]

The management of the Detroit department store J.L. Hudson seemed to be of a completely different opinion and set a significant precedent when it launched its first imported collection of Italian couture originals in September 1949 (Figures 5.5 and 5.6).[110] The promotion of Hudson's exclusive group of models was a crucial event as it contributed to demonstrating that the first attempts to import Italian couture in the United States clearly focused on establishing the notion of a collective 'Italian Look'. Reportedly displaying a new approach to merchandise strategies of imported designs, Hudson's head of foreign office John Millas had selected forty-nine original models from the houses of Biki, Vanna, Noberasco and Ventura, all from 'Milan, Italy, the city of the Italian Couture'.[111] The models were to be sold 'as they were' and not for reproduction or adaptation, introducing an innovative 'approach to the merchandising of imported fashions', as journalist Lois Barnes explained for *Women's Wear Daily*, thus seemingly repeating the formula of a manufacturing couture agreement proposed to

5.5 Advertisement for the J.L. Hudson Italian couture collection. *Detroit Free Press*, 18 September 1949

May's the previous year. Designs were specifically made for the American market, as Millas mediated with the Italian couturiers 'in having the fashions keyed to the way the American woman of discernment wants to look, and in having them made in accordance with the store's measurements'.[112] As this constituted a first-time business experiment for Hudson's in particular and for American upscale department stores in general, the Italian couture imports tested the market with a more economical formula that

Hudson's Launches Italian Couture Fashions in U.S.A.

At left, black silk faille short dinner dress by Ventura, with widened neckline, and wrapped skirt developed into asymmetric hip drape.

From the House of Vanna, a cape costume in oxford gray menswear woolen, with green silk satin blouse, price $295. This costume has already been sold in navy with burgundy.

5.6 *Women's Wear Daily*'s report of the Italian couture collection at J.L. Hudson, Detroit. 19 September 1949. Courtesy of Fairchild Archive

prevented the store from investing time and money in reproductions and in-store adaptations. By tweaking the designs at the source, J.L. Hudson took advantage of cheaper manufacturing costs, textile supplies, and accessories, creating original, imported designs that did not need to be modified or reproduced in the United States, where the costs would have been more significant. The fact that the models would be made with Italian textiles was particularly emphasized, as the advertising in the *Detroit Free Press* described the use of 'pure silks with so much body and drape they need no under-stiffening; wools so fine they have a silken feel, and tweeds that are feathery soft to touch'.[113]

Unfortunately, due to an overall failure of imports based on their high prices, Hudson's John Millas left his post of foreign representative soon after the Italian collection was promoted, while the store reportedly terminated his position permanently.[114] The promotional show might have played a part in this crisis, as an investment in designers largely unknown to the Midwest market would have likely crashed with the still costly price barriers of European fashion. The relative anonymity of designers, whose names were barely known to the more expert buyers but still not recognizable by final customers, was nonetheless a major issue for the promotion of Italian designers. Earlier that September, when the promotional campaign of Hudson's Italian couture had just launched, a *Women's Wear Daily* correspondent rhetorically asked: 'Is the Italian couture becoming a factor to be reckoned with by American retailers? ... high-fashion retailers in New York aren't so sure the Italians have "arrived" in the ready-to-wear field as yet.'[115] The authority of the New York fashion industry assessed the readiness of the market, however, as evolving, and a Fifth Avenue insider eventually affirmed: 'We are watching the Italian designers carefully, though ... and you can be sure that when and if we feel they're turning out things we can sell, we'll go right after it.'[116]

Nevertheless, *Women's Wear Daily* reported that the J.L. Hudson Italian collection had spurred interest in other US retailers and manufacturers, many of which had extensively travelled through Italy in the summer of 1949 and were ready to inquire of Italian dressmakers to explore business possibilities.[117] Among them was buyer Julia Trissell of Bergdorf Goodman, who had reportedly visited Rome on holiday and 'discovered' the dressmaking shop of Simonetta Visconti, recently featured in the *Vogue* article 'In Rome Now'. Trissell would later comment to fellow journalist Eugenia Sheppard that she remembered 'a busman's holiday in the late '40s, spent shopping in Rome. She spotted a little hole-in-the-wall shop run by some one named Simonetta, managed to get it opened up though it was siesta time, and came back to New York with goodies from a new designer'.[118] Italian correspondent Elisa Vittoria Massai wrote her first article for *Women's Wear Daily* right after the J.L. Hudson promotion, reporting on the increased interest of some American buyers in Italian couture:

> A colleague of mine, Antonio Giordano, was a correspondent for Fairchild, a famous American publishing group ... One day in October, the New York office of *Women's Wear Daily* called him up saying, 'We know that some American buyers are in Milan to buy outfits. Apparently, they are interested in Noberasco, Vanna, Fercioni, and Tizzoni'. They wanted an article telling what the buyers had purchased, what types of outfits and at what prices. Giordano had no idea where to begin ... he asked me to do the article. I went around to

the dressmakers' shops. I wrote the article, and it was published on the first page. Immediately afterwards, Giorgini called me up. He was already trying to organize his project, and the news of buyers in search of new Italian fashion proved that his idea was not entirely crazy.[119]

Following this and the popularity of Roman fashion houses visited by US actresses, the spring of 1950 saw an increase in the coverage of Italian couture activities. In Chicago, Marshall Fields' fashion coordinator featured Italian couturiers in the department store's seasonal presentation. No names were mentioned by *Women's Wear Daily*, but the article remarked that this was the first time that Italian designs were represented.[120] EIM attempted to capitalize on the interest demonstrated by US buyers, proposing to

> attract again the attention of the United States' market to the production of high fashion women's wear employing first of all the collaboration of commissionaire firms in Florence. For this reason, together with the firm Mario Ricci and others in Florence, we studied the possibility to recall American buyers to Italy and encouraging them to visit, in the different [fashion] centres of Italy, the main collections of models, with the assistance of both the Ente and the aforementioned commissionaires.[121]

The excerpt above is part of a report written by EIM's director Vladimiro Rossini in 1951 and uncovered by fashion historian Cinzia Capalbo. There Rossini explained how Giorgini's Italian High Fashion Shows were a copy of a project originally planned by EIM in 1950 and how, unfortunately, EIM was forced to abandon the project due to lack of funds. The report nevertheless supported the fact that Florence represented an important stop in the path of American fashion buyers at the time and, most of all, that many of the city's commissionaires were planning similar promotional strategies involving presentations of fashion merchandise exclusively Made in Italy for export.[122] Whether Rossini's account was truthful or not, there had been signals in the market that suggested the opportunity to try and export Italian designs to the United States. In particular, the purpose of Perkins' reporting on Italian dressmaking collections in the spring of 1950, discussed in the previous chapter, was to interest and inform American buyers by highlighting those dressmaking houses that were able to provide original, non-derivative designs.

In the first article of the series, for instance, Perkins concentrated on the houses of Germana Marucelli and Noberasco, as they were 'often named in answer to [her] question of where original Italian designs could be bought. Both houses have sold to American buyers'.[123] Mrs. Noberasco had a few Parisian models in her collection, although she claimed that her private customers liked the original creations better. Germana Marucelli, as it was reported, did not buy models nor toiles in Paris, and instead relied on simple silhouettes in which the emphasis was on embroidered *appliques* (cutout decorations) in contrasting fabrics. Subsequent articles continued to emphasize the embroidered work in her models. In particular, Marucelli reportedly proposed a plan to attract American buyers in a way that could cut the costs connected with importing her models. The idea was to sell embroideries and corsages separately from the skirts so that the final product could be assembled in the United States reducing costs and custom fees.[124] The practical solution devised by Marucelli exemplified how some fashion designers, more than others, understood the need for a certain degree of adaptation of what was perceived to be the artistic nature of their profession. This example additionally demonstrates how taste and style were often mediated in the first place by the designers themselves.

As Fairchild's foreign correspondent Giuseppe Ratti had predicted in 1949, the US market was ready to absorb Italian products, and it would have been unreasonable to just try and compete with Paris on the level of couture. The ideal category would have been *moda boutique*, the ready-made, quality clothing: knitwear, separates, play clothes that Ratti called 'an average production, of the finest taste and reasonably priced'.[125] A year later, the May issue of *Harper's Bazaar* was dedicated to summer and play clothes: on the cover, photographed by Richard Avedon, a model wears a wool sweater by Rome-based knitwear specialist Laura Aponte, worn with shorts by Carolyn Schnurer and a chiffon sash by Echo (Figure 5.7).[126] This can be considered one of the earliest covers of an American glossy magazine to feature Italian fashion merchandise; while neither the origin of the sweater nor the name of its designer are highlighted in the photo layout, they were mentioned in the cover page description.

Soon after, *Women's Wear Daily* described a selection of knitwear firms that had interested American buyers in Italy, among which were the firms Mirsa, by Olga di Gresy, and Adriana, by Maria Marzoli, both represented by Giorgini in the United States.[127] Mirsa models in particular (Figure 5.8) interested Italian and Parisian couturiers alike because they represented the perfect line of garments to be sold in the boutique, 'the waiting room of high fashion dressmaking ateliers'.[128] The versatility of knitwear manufacturing in creating shapes and patterns adapted to the requests of the buyers mirrored the flexibility of its production model,[129] traditionally based on subcontracting, characterized by hand-finished details, and sporting stylish designs.[130] This momentous popularity of knitwear would be later quoted by Italian journalist Elisa Massai as the founding introduction of Made in Italy recognition in this industry.[131] The practical garments seen in 1944 Rome by *Vogue* were thus

5.7 Cover of *Harper's Bazaar*, May 1950. Courtesy of *Harper's Bazaar*, Hearst Magazine Media, Inc. Photograph by Richard Avedon. © The Richard Avedon Foundation. Image published with permission of ProQuest LLC. Further reproduction is prohibited without permission

still interesting to the eyes of American commercial customers, and the Italian veteran fashion editor Elsa Robiola laid out clearly the strategy to follow in order to interest them. As the world of industrialized fashion was moving towards the triumph of 'easy fashion', Italian designers should face it as a unanimous front with a constant of simplified, streamlined collections, and a firm coordinating force. This, to Robiola, was only

Sweaters Made in Milan "Click" With Couturiers

Milan. — These are some of the types of sweaters shown at Maglificio Mirsa, of Galliate-Novara, which are reportedly interesting Parisian and Italian couturiers.

Left to right:

Striped sleeveless sports model in navy and white, with pointed trimming at front and armholes accentuating the V-neck.

Violet wool in ribbed stitch makes this blousy garment with attached scarf which can be draped in various ways across the front.

5.8 Italian knitwear by Mirsa. *Women's Wear Daily*, 2 January 1951. Courtesy of Fairchild Archive

possible if the Italian couturiers agreed to follow the guidance of CIMM, who seemed to deserve the lead, at least for the time being.[132]

Notes

1 C. Parisi, 'I Congresso Nazionale Della Moda: Atti Ufficiali'. In *Camera di Commercio Industria e Agricoltura Roma* (Rome: Tipografia Ugo Pinto, 1949) p. 12.

2 A thorough investigation of the role of Capri, its symbolic and manufacturing contribution to the Italian fashion industry, as well as the constitution of the council Centro di Moda Capri can be found in the works of Ornella Cirillo, and particularly in the article: O. Cirillo, 'Un "ambiente speciale" per la moda e il turismo: da Capri a Positano'. *ZoneModa Journal* 11(2), 2021, pp. 91–116.

3 G. Vergani, 'The Sala Bianca: The Birth of Italian Fashion'. In *The Sala Bianca: The Birth of Italian Fashion*, edited by Giannino Malossi (Milan: Electa, 1992), pp. 23–87; C.M. Belfanti, 'Renaissance and "Made in Italy": Marketing Italian

Fashion through History (1949–1952)'. *Journal of Modern Italian Studies* 20(1), 2015, pp. 53–66.

4 S. Colonna di Cesarò, *Una Vita al Limite* (Venice: Marsilio, 2008), p. 43; V.C. Caratozzolo, J. Clark, and M. Luisa Frisa eds. *Simonetta, La Prima Donna Della Moda Italiana* (Venice: Marsilio, 2008), p. 42.

5 Roberto Capucci to the author. Rome, 5 April 2017.

6 E. Celani, 'Bilancio delle attività della moda', *Bellezza* December 1943, p. 9.

7 Archivio Centrale dello Stato, Rome, Ministero dell'Industria, del Commercio e dell'Artigianato (hereafter ACS-MICA), Ente Moda. Manlio Sergenti, Draft of a Decree Concerning the Dissolution and Subsequent Controlled Administration of Ente Nazionale della Moda, 15 May 1944.

8 S. Gnoli, *La donna, l'eleganza, il fascismo: la moda italiana dalle origini all'Ente Nazionale della Moda* (Catania: Edizioni del Prisma, 2000); M. Lupano and A. Vaccari, *Fashion at the Time of Fascism: Italian Modernist Lifestyle 1922–1943* (Bologna: Damiani Editore, 2009); S. Gnoli, *Eleganza Fascista: La Moda Dagli Anni Venti Alla Fine Della Guerra* (Rome: Carocci Editore, 2017).

9 C. Rostagni, '"Bellezza" Della Vita Italiana. Moda e Costume Secondo Gio Ponti'. *La Rivista Di Engramma*, 175, September 2020, pp. 287–302.

10 S. Vacirca, *Fashioning Submission. Documenting Fashion, Taste and Identity in WWII Italy Through Bellezza Mensile Dell'alta Moda E Della Vita Italiana* (Milan: Mimesis International, 2023).

11 Celani, 'Bilancio delle attività della moda', 7.

12 Celani, 'Bilancio delle attività della moda', 8.

13 ACS-MICA, Ente Moda. EMSA Board Member Pacces to ENM, 9 February 1945.

14 ACS-MICA, Ente Moda. ENM commissioner Federico Leumann to EMSA, 5 March 1945.

15 Vacirca, *Fashioning Submission*, 112.

16 Vacirca, *Fashioning Submission*, 18.

17 V.C. Caratozzolo, *Irene Brin: Italian Style in Fashion* (Venice: Marsilio, 2006).

18 I. Brin, 'Il Nord e il Sud'. *Bellezza* November 1945.

19 ACS-MICA, Ente Moda. ENM commissioner Angiolina Richetti Cosmo to the Ministry of Industry and Commerce, 27 November 1945.

20 ACS-MICA, Ente Moda. Manlio Sergenti on behalf of Angelo Tarchi and Benito Mussolini, draft of a decree concerning the dissolution and subsequent controlled administration of Ente Nazionale della Moda, 15 May 1944.

21 ACS-MICA, Ente Moda. Ivan Matteo Lombardo to ENM, 18 September 1945.

22 ACS-MICA, Ente Moda. Angiolina Richetti Cosmo to the Ministry of Industry and Commerce, 27 November 1945.

23 In Italian: 'libera associazione riconosciuta dallo Stato'.

24 EIM's president Giordano delle Lanze confirmed in a press conference in 1951 that EIM had been functioning since 1945, G. delle Lanze, 'Trattative fra Torino e Milano per il nuovo Ente Italiano Moda'. *Nuova Stampa* (2 February 1950), p. 2.

25 ACS-MICA, Ente Moda. Carlo de Gaspari to the Ministry of Industry, Commerce and Labor, 18 June 1945. De Gaspari was president of Associazione Nazionale Produzione Artistica Abbigliamento, established in September 1944 in Rome; Confederazione generale dell'industria italiana, *Annuario 1950* (Rome: Studio Tipografico Failli, 1950), p. 686.

26 ACS-MICA, Ente Moda. Carlo de Gaspari to the Italian Ministries of Foreign Affairs and of Industry and Commerce, 20 February 1946.

27 ACS-MICA, Ente Moda. Carlo de Gaspari to the Ministry of Industry and Commerce, 27 September 1945; Ivan Paris, *Oggetti Cuciti: L'abbigliamento Pronto in Italia Dal Primo Dopoguerra Agli Anni Settanta* (Milan: F. Angeli, 2006), p. 233.

28 L. Savi, *A New History of 'Made in Italy'. Fashion and Textiles in Post-War Italy* (London: Bloomsbury Publishing, 2023), pp. 91–118.

29 'Ridare a Torino il primato della Moda', *Nuova Stampa* (29 September 1946), p. 2.

30 La Settimana Incom, n° 00028, 'Da Torino Arte della Moda', 17 October 1946, CinecittàLuce, 'Da Torino: arte della moda', video, 1:47, 15 June 2012, www.you tube.com/watch?v=vfSNmSFC3ic.

31 Original in Italian: 'Ma, a differenza del 1918, quando la moda doveva portare un cachet d'oltralpe, oggi sono Torino e Milano, Firenze, Bologna e Roma a inventare la figura, la sagoma della donna che ci piacerà nella prossima stagione.' *La Settimana Incom*, 'Da Torino Arte della Moda'.

32 'La Mostra "Arte-Moda" si inaugura stamane', *Nuova Stampa* (6 October 1946), p. 2.

33 'Torino Palazzo Reale', *Bellezza* October 1946, pp. 42–43.

34 Vacirca, *Fashioning Submission*, 131.

35 'Torino Palazzo Reale'.

36 'Ridare a Torino il primato della Moda'.

37 'Musiche e danze a conclusione di Arte-Moda', *Nuova Stampa* (17 October 1946), p. 2.

38 'Case italiane di Moda invitate a New York', *Nuova Stampa* (16 October 1946), p. 2.

39 '86 European Firms to Show at June 2 Textile Exhibit', *Women's Wear Daily* (12 May 1947), section II, p. 4. Among the exhibitors, the New York fair displayed samples from Terragni mills of Como, with whom Giorgini collaborated at the time.

40 'Stoffe, abiti e gioielli per 4 miliardi di lire', *Stampa Sera* (5–6 February 1949), p. 2.

41 'Stoffe, abiti e gioielli per 4 miliardi di lire'.

42 'Stoffe, abiti e gioielli per 4 miliardi di lire'.

43 E. Merlo, *Moda e Industria 1960–1980* (Milan: Biblioteca dell'economia d'azienda, EGEA, 2012), p. 74.

44 'A Roma si prepara un Congresso della moda', *Nuova Stampa Sera* (9–10 February 1949), p. 2.

45 G. Ratti, 'Esportare La Moda Italiana in America.' In *I Congresso Nazionale Della Moda: Atti Ufficiali*, edited by Camera di Commercio Industria e Agricoltura Roma (Rome: Tipografia Ugo Pinto, 1949), pp. 122–27, 123.

46 In later years Ratti would move on to managing roles in government-owned companies specialized in the production of textile fibres. An article in *Fortune* from 1978 reported that Ratti, a graduate of the University of Rome, started working in 1956 for the oil and gas company ENI under the mentorship of E. Mattei. 'In The News', *Fortune* 31 July 1978, p. 14.

47 Original in Italian: 'Voi non vedete in Italia una o due donne eleganti; ne vedete tante che non riuscite a contarle. Le italiane non vestono in modo esagerato e stravagante, ma hanno un'eleganza misurata e signorile.' Charles Armour, quoted in Ratti, 'Esportare La Moda Italiana in America,' 124. Original quote in English in 'Armour Joins In Praise of Italian Fashion', *Women's Wear Daily* (4 April 1949), p. 27.

48 Ratti, 'Esportare La Moda Italiana in America', 123.

49 Ratti, 'Esportare La Moda Italiana in America', 126.

50 'Suggests More Unification In Italy's Apparel Industry', *Women's Wear Daily* (6 June 1949), p. 10.

51 'Suggests More Unification In Italy's Apparel Industry'.

52 V. Vallonica, 'Dopo la distruzione dell'E.N.M. di Torino. La Moda Italiana e le Vicende Politiche', *Commercio d'Italia* (17 July 1950).

53 Vallonica, 'Dopo la distruzione dell'E.N.M. di Torino'.

54 C. Capalbo, *Storia Della Moda a Roma: Sarti, Culture e Stili Di Una Capitale Dal 1871 a Oggi* (Rome: Donzelli, 2012); A. Merlotti, 'I Percorsi Della Moda Made in Italy'. In *Enciclopedia Italiana Di Scienze, Lettere e Arti* (Istituto dell'Enciclopedia italiana, 2013), pp. 630–40; G. Di Giangirolamo, *Istituzioni per La Moda. Interventi Tra Pubblico e Privato in Italia e Francia (1945–1965)*. Collana Scientifica 'Culture, Moda e Società (Milan: Pearson-Bruno Mondadori, 2019), pp. 20–22; C. Faggella, '"Not So Simple": Reassessing 1951, G.B. Giorgini and the Launch of Italian Fashion' (PhD Dissertation, Stockholm University, 2019), pp. 199–200.

55 A. Fiorentini Capitani, *Moda Italiana Anni Cinquanta e Sessanta* (Florence: Cantini & C., 1991), pp. 8–9; Paris, *Oggetti Cuciti*, 187.

56 'Haute Couture of Italy Split by a Lively Feud', *Women's Wear Daily* (13 January 1950), p. 7.

57 Vallonica, 'Dopo la distruzione dell'E.N.M. di Torino'.

58 'Haute Couture of Italy Split by a Lively Feud', 7.

59 M. Pecorari, 'La Moda All'università: Una Ricostruzione Delle Prime Forme Di Studio e Ricerca in Ambito Accademico'. In *White Book. Imparare La Moda in Italia* (Venice: Marsilio, 2018), pp. 77–78.

60 I. Brin, 'Sfide a Venezia'. *Bellezza* October 1949, p. 44.

61 'Italian Couture Event Is Set for September', *Women's Wear Daily* (28 July 1950), p. 6.

62 'Abiti e indossatrici hanno diviso il trionfo', *Nuova Stampa Sera* (8–9 September 1950), p. 3; 'Sfilata di moda a Venezia', *Nuova Stampa Sera* (14 September 1950), p. 6. Archivio di Stato di Firenze, Archivio della Moda Italiana di Giovanni Battista Giorgini (hereafter ASF-AMIGBG), Album 2. G.B. Giorgini to Meyric R. Rogers, 15 September 1950.

63 I. Brin, 'Quattro giorni di moda a Venezia', *Bellezza* October 1950, p. 26.

64 'Italian Dressmakers: Selection of American Movie Stars', *Women's Wear Daily* (22 September 1950), p. 8.

65 Original in Italian: 'rappresentano a un tempo il banco di prova della produzione e la dimostrazione della sua armonia con i gusti del pubblico'. 'A Roma: Primi passi del "Centro Italiano della Moda"'. *Bellezza* May 1949, p. 88.

66 CinecittàLuce, 'Teatro dell'Opera: rassegna della moda italiana. La Settimana Incom 00275 (1949)', video, 1:41, 19 September 2011, www.youtube.com/watch?v=nUIE9SWtct8.

67 Capalbo, *Storia Della Moda a Roma*.

68 R.K. Popp, *The Holiday Makers: Magazines, Advertising, and Mass Tourism in Postwar America* (Baton Rouge: Louisiana State University Press, 2012), p. 32.

69 F. Graham, 'Best Year for the Airlines', *New York Times* (19 February 1950), international travel section, p. 7.

70 P. Hofmann, 'Rome Set for Big Travel Year', *New York Times* (6 March 1949), international travel section, p. XX 37.

71 P. Hofmann, 'Plans for the 1950 Holy Year', *New York Times* (23 October 1949), p. XX 1.

72 P. Hofmann, 'Italy's New Tourist Pattern', *New York Times* (17 June 1951), p. XX 25.

73 Advertisements, *New York Times* (23 October 1949), p. XX 25.

74 A.B. Van Riper, *Imagining Flight: Aviation and Popular Culture* (College Station: Texas A&M University Press, 2004), p. 99.

75 ASF-AMIGBG, Carteggio. G.B. Giorgini, Cable, 30 January 1947.

76 P. Hofmann, 'Rate Reductions and Plenty of Room in Italy', *New York Times* (18 February 1951), international travel section, p. 41.

77 Hofmann, 'Italy's New Tourist Pattern'.

78 P. Hofmann, 'All Roads Lead to Rome During the Holy Year', *New York Times* (19 February 1950), international travel section, p. 31.

79 S. Gnoli, 'Hollywood Sul Tevere'. In *Bellissima. L'Italia Dell'alta Moda 1945–1968*, edited by Maria Luisa Frisa, Anna Mattirolo, and Stefano Tonchi (Milan: Electa, 2014), pp. 362–65; Capalbo, *Storia Della Moda a Roma*, 131–35; E. Scarpellini, *La Stoffa Dell'Italia: Storia e Cultura Della Moda Dal 1945 a Oggi* (Bari: Laterza, 2017), pp. 52–54.

80 E. Hoyt, 'Asset or Liability? Hollywood and Tax Law'. In *Hollywood and the Law*, edited by Paul McDonald, Emily Carman, Eric Hoyt, and Philip Drake. London: BFI Palgrave, 2015), p. 193.

81 Ian C. Jarvie, 'The Postwar Economic Foreign Policy of the American Film Industry: Europe 1945–1950'. In *Hollywood in Europe: Experiences of a Cultural Hegemony*, edited by David W. Ellwood and Rob Kroes, pp. 155–75 (Amsterdam: VU

University Press, 1994), pp. 155–75, 171–72; R. Shandley, 'How Rome Saved Hollywood'. In *Cinematic Rome*, edited by Richard Wrigley (Leicester: Troubadour Publishing, 2008), p. 54.

82 D. Forgacs and S. Gundle. *Mass Culture and Italian Society from Fascism to the Cold War* (Bloomington: Indiana University Press, 2007), pp. 132–33.

83 Robert S.C. Gordon, 'Hollywood and Italy: Industries and Fantasies'. In *The Italian Cinema Book*, edited by Peter Bondanella (London: BFI Palgrave, 2014), p. 124.

84 E. Castaldo Lundén, 'Oscar Night in Hollywood: Fashioning the Red-Carpet from the Roosevelt Hotel to International Media' (PhD Dissertation, Stockholm University, 2018), pp. 170–90.

85 G. Bianchino and A.C. Quintavalle, *Moda Dalla Fiaba al Design: Italia 1951–1989* (Novara: DeAgostini, 1989), pp. 11–17; S. Gnoli, *Un Secolo Di Moda Italiana, 1900–2000* (Rome: Meltemi Editore srl., 2005), pp. 105–37.

86 Forgacs and Gundle, *Mass Culture and Italian Society*, 137.

87 'Rome'. *Life* 1 August 1949, p. 56.

88 I.A. De Pascalis, 'La Contessa Scalza e i suoi vestiti.' In *The Italian Presence In Post-War America, 1949–1972. Architecture, Design, Fashion. Volume 1, Architetture, Interni e Oggetti Nel Passaggio Attraverso l'atlantico*, edited by Marta Averna (Transatlantic Transfers. Studi e Ricerche Interdisciplinari 1 Milan: Mimesis edizioni, 2023), pp. 250–69, 257.

89 N. White, *Reconstructing Italian Fashion: America and the Development of the Italian Fashion Industry* (Oxford: Berg, 2000), pp. 136–37.

90 C. Faggella, 'Itinerari di moda fiorentina fra il dopoguerra e la fine degli anni sessanta: dal guardaroba alla memoria storica'. In *Moda, città e immaginari*, edited by Alessandra Vaccari (Milan: Mimesis edizioni, 2016), pp. 148–50.

91 'Linda Christian'. *Vogue* 1 January 1949, p. 124.

92 G. Pietrangeli, 'L'archivio della Compagnia nazionale artigiana (1947–1977)/ Inventario', 2021, p. 24.

93 CinecittàLuce, 'Teatro dell'Opera: rassegna della moda italiana. La Settimana Incom 00275 (1949)'. Mrs. Power (Linda Christian) is shown in attendance.

94 E. Robiola, 'Pausa Estiva'. *Bellezza* June 1949, p. 28.

95 'American Film Stars Are Buying Wardrobes at Italian Dressmakers', *Women's Wear Daily* (22 July 1949), p. 4.

96 'American Film Stars Are Buying Wardrobes at Italian Dressmakers'.

97 This and other promotions of Italian fashion in Sweden and in Scandinavia are under investigation in the author's research project '*Italiana* on tour. Fashion Made in Italy in Postwar Scandinavia', generously supported by the C.M. Lerici Foundation of Stockholm, Sweden.

98 V. Rossi Lodomez, 'Ritorno degli ospiti: collezioni preparate per gli stranieri'. *Bellezza* September 1942, p. 22.

99 ACS-MICA, Ente Moda. Report of the Consul General of Italy in Zurich, 29 April 1946.

100 Paris, *Oggetti Cuciti*, 189.

101 'Italian, French Styles to Show at Munich', *Women's Wear Daily* (9 May 1950), p. 4.

102 Filmothek, Bundesarchiv, 'Wet im film nr. 264', video, 0:56. 22 June 1950, Accessed 3 March 2018. www.filmothek.bundesarchiv.de/video/583696.

103 E. Scarpellini, *Italian Fashion since 1945: A Cultural History* (London: Palgrave Macmillan, 2019), p. 128.

104 'Conditions in Italy Favor American Fabric Buyer, M. Goodman Reports', *Women's Wear Daily* (1 September 1949), p. 30.

105 'Italy, Switzerland Now Better Sources, Macy Stylist Finds', *Women's Wear Daily* (17 June 1949), p. 18.

106 'Mays of Brooklyn Introduces Italian Design Group', *Women's Wear Daily* (27 September 1948), p. 3.

107 L. Tregenza, *Wholesale Couture. London and Beyond, 1930–1970* (London: Bloomsbury Publishing, 2023), pp. 56–57.
108 'Kaufmann Sees Paris Mayor', *Women's Wear Daily* (17 May 1949), p. 6.
109 'Prices in Italy Held Too High for American Stores', *Women's Wear Daily* (3 June 1949), p. 2.
110 L. Barnes, 'Hudson's Launches Italian Couture Fashions in U.S.A.', *Women's Wear Daily* (19 September 1949), p. 1.
111 Hudson's Advertisement, *Detroit Free Press* (18 September 1949).
112 Barnes, 'Hudson's Launches Italian Couture Fashions in U.S.A.'.
113 Hudson's Advertisement.
114 'Report Millas Will Leave Hudson Post', *Women's Wear Daily* (16 November 1949), p. 1.
115 G. Fowler, 'Second Thoughts Around Gotham', *Women's Wear Daily* (23 September 1949), p. 2.
116 Fowler, 'Second Thoughts Around Gotham'.
117 E. Massai, 'Italy Promotes Couture Styles, Tie-Ups in U.S.', *Women's Wear Daily* (25 October 1949), p. 1.
118 E. Sheppard, 'How Italy Was Discovered', *New York Herald Tribune* (23 June 1961), p. 15.
119 Vergani, 'The Sala Bianca', 41. The article in question, unspecified by Massai, is 'Italy Promotes Couture Style, Tie-Ups in the US'.
120 'Marshall Field Imports Point To Straighter Lines', *Women's Wear Daily* (15 March 1950), p. 3.
121 Capalbo, *Storia Della Moda a Roma*, 143.
122 Mario Ricci, head of the European buying office in Florence of Chicago department store Marshall Field & Co, would later collaborate with CNA and be involved with the last vicissitudes of the traveling exhibition *Italy at Work*.
123 A.K. Perkins, 'Report From Italy on Dressmaker Showings', *Women's Wear Daily* (21 March 1950), p. 3.
124 Perkins, 'Report From Italy on Dressmaker Showings'.
125 Ratti, 'Esportare La Moda Italiana in America,' 126.
126 Cover. *Harper's Bazaar* May 1950.
127 'Knitwear News From Europe: Novelties Attract Buyers to Italian Quality Knits', *Women's Wear Daily* (27 September 1950), p. 42.
128 'Successo delle "boutiques"'. *Bellezza* April 1950, p. 76.
129 C. Faggella, 'Dietro Le Quinte Alla G.B. Giorgini. Le Assistant Buyers e l'esportazione Di Moda Italiana Negli Stati Uniti, 1946–1956'. In *Un Oceano Di Stile. Produzione e Consumo Di Made in Italy Negli Stati Uniti Del Dopoguerra*, edited by Simone Cinotto and Giulia Crisanti (Milan: Mimesis edizioni, 2023), p. 177.
130 E. Currie, 'Knitwear'. In *The Glamour of Italian Fashion Since 1945*, edited by Sonnet Stanfill (London: V&A Publishing, 2014), pp. 115–20, 116.
131 E. Massai and P. Lombardi, 'The Knitting Industry in High-Fashion and Ready-Made Knitwear 1950–1980'. In *Italian Fashion: The Origins of High Fashion and Knitwear*, edited by Gloria Bianchino, Grazietta Butazzi, Alessandra Mottola Molfino, and Arturo Carlo Quintavalle (Milan: Electa, 1985), pp. 260–75.
132 E. Robiola, 'Compiti Difficili della Moda Facile'. *Bellezza* April 1950, pp. 25–26.

6

Florence: a new experience of couture

The book has so far outlined the process through which Italian fashion exports in the postwar years originally concerned handcrafted fashion merchandise, and eventually came to encompass high-end dressmaking specifically developed for international customers. Chapter 5 demonstrated that, by the late 1940s, American commercial buyers started expanding their European seasonal purchases to include the new Italian couture and established agreements for introducing some of these designs in their domestic market. The touring exhibition *Italy at Work: Her Renaissance in Design Today* was about to showcase a highly representative selection of handcrafted Italian fashion merchandise in twelve museums of eleven states in America and establish collaborations with department stores in each one of the cities in which the exhibition was due to open. This chapter contextualizes these developments with the first five Italian High Fashion Shows organized by Giorgini and the cultural and commercial scenarios outlined in the previous chapters. The themes highlighted by the promotional activities that had taken place before 1951, including the recent *Italy at Work*, are here examined from the perspective of Giorgini's first five Shows: the establishment of Italian couture and fashion merchandise exports; the inputs injected by the Shows in the definition of an 'Italian Look' and an identity for Italian fashion with the focus on *moda boutique*; the difficulties encountered by Giorgini in the supervision of the Shows; and the supposed rivalry with the Parisian fashion industry. From the point of view of the chronology adopted, the chapter considers the earliest Shows, the First through to the Fifth, from February 1951 to January 1953. By that last date, the Shows would become a fixed date in the transatlantic fashion calendar of seasonal presentations, and Italian fashion and couture exports would firmly set foot in the American market.

Participants and attendees at the
First Italian High Fashion Show

The promotion envisioned by Rogers and Giorgini in connection with the opening of *Italy at Work* at the Brooklyn Museum aligned with the proposal of Fairchild's correspondent Giuseppe Ratti at *Primo Congress Nazionale della Moda* in Rome in 1949. Italian efforts to promote Italian fashion exports should prioritize events and exhibitions in the United States, according to Ratti.[1] For this reason, given his collaboration with B. Altman, Giorgini attempted to have the Fifth Avenue luxury store sponsor the first *Italy at Work* fashion show in New York. As the exhibition's second stop was in Chicago, Giorgini planned to rely there on a possible sponsorship from department store Carson Pirie & Scott, a client of his since the 1930s.[2] Yet, once it became clear that B. Altman would not grant its sponsorship to the first fashion event, the plan of having commercial shows of Italian fashion in connection with the exhibition was never accomplished by Giorgini and instead, in the following years until the last stop of *Italy at Work*, various department stores organized their own.

Given what has been outlined in the previous chapters, the concern expressed by the management at B. Altman towards what they considered an undeveloped fashion scene is an expression of the prevalent sentiment at the time towards Italian couture. The two department stores in the United States that had attempted to promote their own selections of Italian couture had not been successful, as discussed in Chapter 5, and the general feeling expressed by buyers was that the American market was not ready to endorse a fashion scene that still appeared to owe much to Parisian collections. Moreover, the push imprinted by HDI and its subsidiary activities to the handicraft industry had left a mark toward the recognition of Italy as a reputable 'country of origin' mainly for fashion merchandise, dress textiles, and some novelty ready-made garments.[3] The monopoly of Paris as a source of ideas for the international fashion trade was still, by and large, undisputable and thus the rebuttal of B. Altman's endorsement of Giorgini's show is to be understood according to this mindset. The sponsorship of a potentially derivative show in connection to such a highly advertised exhibition as *Italy at Work* could have exposed B. Altman to a fiasco in terms of publicity and investments.[4]

As B. Altman communicated their negative response by mid-October, Giorgini was left with less than four months to think of an alternative. The archival sources transmit a feeling of rushing around towards the final goal, as letters and cables are dated quite closely to one another and to the ultimate date of 12 February 1951, the first day of the First Italian High Fashion Show. Parisian *haute couture* houses were showing at the beginning of February and, ideally, the Italian collections should have been presented roughly at the same time, to avoid accusations of derivativeness.

This had been suggested by other fashion professionals, for instance Carla Guido of the renowned Milanese model house Villa, whose point of view was introduced in Chapter 5. Giorgini announced his decision to host an independent show featuring multiple dressmakers and fashion merchandise in Florence before the end of 1950, relieving B. Altman from any concrete commitment and making it clear that the burden of a possible publicity backlash relied on Giorgini and the fashion houses only.[5] In a clever move of reciprocation, Giorgini negotiated with B. Altman to have a dedicated buyer from the store in Florence, pointing out that he had organized the Italian Show expressly for the benefit of Violet Meison, Altman's merchandising manager of ready-to-wear. 'As per the enclosed card, you will see', he wrote to Keillor, 'that I have organized this Fashion Show in Florence for you'.[6] According to *Women's Wear Daily*, Meison had already visited Italy in the summer of 1950 and joined other department store buyers in affirming that Italy was increasing its importance in the international fashion market.[7]

Since B. Altman communicated that Meison was unable to attend the Show, Giorgini requested permission to invite other buyers from the department stores Saks and Lord & Taylor.[8] These two major players in the US department stores' scenario had a reputation for their taste and authority in fashion, and therefore represented an audience to yearn for. Both stores had their own representatives in Florence and, as pointed out in Chapters 3 and 4, their seasonal collections often incorporated Florentine luxury accessories such as Ferragamo shoes and ready-made garments by Emilio Pucci.[9] The strategy of pressing with the threat of competitors eventually worked, because after some consideration the management at B. Altman sent Gertrude Ziminsky, buyer of coats and dresses, to Florence, but asked Giorgini to avoid inviting other buyers, a condition that seemingly indicates a will from B. Altman to keep the Show confidential.[10] Ensuing developments demonstrate that Giorgini obtained the participation of other department stores as well. New York luxury store Bergdorf Goodman sent Julia Trissell, coat and suit buyer, and couture veteran buyer Ethel Frankau.[11] For the west coast, I. Magnin sent Stella Hanania, head of the couture department of the San Francisco store. Records in the Giorgini archive do not clarify if Giorgini's acquaintance with I. Magnin dated before 1951, but the European fashion coordinator of I. Magnin at the time was Odette Tedesco, who collaborated with commissionaire Lucien Schloss in Paris, as it was outlined in the discussion of Giorgini's Parisian showroom in Chapter 3. Tedesco started working with Schloss in 1928 and, after the end of the Second World War, she became 'a "liaison officer" between the California stores and Paris couture'.[12] Thanks to their link with Schloss, contacts between Giorgini and Tedesco might have resulted in Hanania attending the First Show.

Not only department store buyers were in attendance. Specialty shops and manufacturers would become an increasingly large pool of clients for the Giorgini Shows. Together with department stores, specialty shops represented a crucial retailer category for Italian fashion merchandise in the 1950s. An advice book on fashion careers identified the main characteristic of a specialty shop to be 'standing for something' and thus filling a perceived necessity in the community where it was to be opened.[13] Importer Ann Roberts, the former employee of HDI in New York and now the owner of a specialty shop, read in *Women's Wear Daily* news of the First Show and announced her participation to Giorgini via cable.[14] Roberts explained there that she aimed to select Italian designs for an International Fashion Show in Atlantic City organized by the Fashion Group, of which she was a member. The attendance of New York manufacturers Martin Cole and Hannah Troy reportedly happened accidentally, while strolling around Florence together on an antique shopping spree and running into the other guests near Florence's Grand Hotel.[15] New York-based designer Hannah Troy would later be credited for being the one who 'literally discovered Italy as a fashion center' and 'introduced modern Italian styles to the United States'.[16] Martin Cole was one of the two founding members of the 'better coats and suits' manufacturing firm Leto, Cohn & LoBalbo of New York.[17] The firm was already purchasing fabrics in Italy, some of which they had recently used in evening coats for the fall/winter collection of 1950.[18]

Throughout his career and up until that point too, Giorgini demonstrated the ability to access relevant information that could guide his business in what could potentially interest the average US buyer of his time. Yet, as the date of the event approached, the negotiations with the American stores affected those with the Italian fashion houses. Dressmakers Sorelle Fontana were hesitant to accept Giorgini's invitation without knowing the names of the buyers in attendance and eventually accepted only if Giorgini confirmed there would be at least seven or eight US buyers willing to make purchases. This condition was compatible with their role in the Italian couture scenario at the time. Speaking also on behalf of dressmakers Carosa and Schuberth in a prizeworthy front of Roman ateliers, the request was an attempt to protect the reputation gained with US buyers with their previous promotions. In connection to the requirements expressed by Fontana, who wanted to be sure that there would be a reputable audience interested in buying their creations, Giorgini pressed his client Morgan's in Canada to send fashion merchandising manager John Nixon, whose attendance was 'most important'.[19] Nixon did not plan to visit Italy that spring since he had no buying allowance for such a trip, but was willing to make a stopover in Florence after Paris if that could have aided Giorgini 'in any way with the Italian manufacturers'.[20] This was an important result since specialty shop Henry Morgan was the most prestigious fashion store in Montreal,[21] especially considering that the store eventually purchased 'a big cape coat in a nubby tweed, a navy cocktail dress and an out of this world evening dress, in pink net embroidered in wide bands of sequins and pearls, from Fontana'.[22] The group of Rome-based couturiers, besides Fontana, Carosa and Schuberth, included Simonetta Visconti, the noblewoman previously introduced in Chapter 1 among the many 'sophisticated Italian women' described by journalists Mannes and Keene. Visconti was praised by *Women's Wear Daily* who included her among the most successful dressmakers frequently catering to American film stars in Rome: the 'beautiful young Countess Di Modrone', explained the trade journal, 'acts as her own designer. Her clothes, which have been chosen by Jennifer Jones and others of the Hollywood colony, are young in idea, with many sportswear pieces shown'.[23]

CIMM's protegé fashion houses Germana Marucelli, Noberasco, Vanna, and Jole Veneziani joined the Show as well, a collaboration probably spurred by a meeting between Giorgini and a representative of CIMM a year before the First Show.[24] A few weeks before the First Show, Giorgini met with dressmaker Jole Veneziani to discuss the possibility of her participation. There they were joined by Marzio Simonetto, public relations manager at SNIA Viscosa and director of Centro Sviluppo Tessile (Textile Development Centre) of Milan.[25] Simonetto was also the editor-in-chief of the fashion/textile magazine *I Tessili Nuovi*, the former in-house publication of SNIA Viscosa turned high fashion magazine.[26] A key professional in the Milanese fashion scene of the time, Simonetto was involved with CIMM, the fashion council created by SNIA's president Franco Marinotti.[27] Giorgini tried to obtain the participation of dressmakers from Turin as well and he was reportedly interested in obtaining the participation of San Lorenzo, a dressmaking house established in 1945, but was advised by an associate of the Cerruti textile group to contact instead Longo e Comollo, stressing the fact that the owner was not reproducing nor adapting Parisian models:

> It is not true that Longo copies and exploits French models only. The clothes that brought her the most success are all clothes created entirely by her. Bista, if you listen to me, leave aside San Lorenzo that is tacky and is not worth half of Longo … With all my pride as an Italian, beating in my heart, I tell you that, with Longo and her models, Turin and Italian fashion have an 'X MAS' … The harbours might not be those of Alexandria or Gibraltar, but the harbours of Christian Dior and Jacques Fath, etc … will get some good old punches.[28]

While the collaboration never materialized, despite the fervent letter (and its not-so-subtle Fascist references), Giorgini was actively seeking dressmakers and fashion merchandising firms that were as original as possible, to avoid any claim of derivativeness from US buyers and manufacturers alike. Eventually, however, the final roster consisted only of Roman and Milanese couture names, plus fashion accessories and knitwear since most of the fashion-related business that Giorgini had done until then consisted of these merchandise categories.

The finalized roster of couture houses reveals the absence of many famous Italian dressmakers who regularly catered for the local clientele, and the inclusion of independent dressmakers already known in the United States, such as the Roman couture house Fontana and the Milanese Vanna, Marucelli, and Jole Veneziani. It would have been pointless and dangerous to try and involve dressmakers who based their business on reproducing and adapting Parisian models. Despite the considerable coverage already obtained in the US press, for instance, neither Irene Galitzine nor Gabriellasport participated in the First Show, as they regularly included copies and adaptations in their collections. Because of this, no Florentine dressmakers were included as well.

The format of the Italian Shows

A series of seemingly small details allows us to reconstruct how the earliest Fashion Shows of Florence took inspiration, at the same time, both from the format of Parisian collection showings and those organized in-house by US department stores. Showing models in a *salon*-like environment was common practice for Parisian couture houses. Caroline Evans has retraced the origins of fashion shows in both couture houses and department stores since the nineteenth century, pointing out how in the 1950s the shows usually took place 'in the couturier's salon, or some other space decorated in *ancien régime* style'.[29] This has also been pointed out by dress historian Bonizza Giordani Aragno in her analysis of the spatial configuration of Italian dressmakers' ateliers and how they both resembled and differed from Parisian *haute couture* ones.[30]

Even though Giorgini had never been directly involved with fashion houses and their promotion before embarking on the project, he had done some research in 1950 to prepare for his possible involvement with the *Italy at Work* show. When he reprised his travelling routine to the United States, visits to Paris became occasions to rekindle his collaboration with Parisian commissionaire Schloss. He additionally attended the collection shows of several Italian couture houses in preparation for the Italian fashion show at the Brooklyn Museum: at Emilio Schuberth in Rome he saw

> three or four hundred people: the ladies in lavish daytime dresses, loaded with jewelry; the men … I found myself to be the only one with a tuxedo! During the intermission between daytime and evening wear trays of liquors, whisky, champagne, and cookies were passed. An orchestra [was playing] the whole evening.[31]

The same format was used for the First Show, during which guests enjoyed breaks with refreshments, a small orchestra playing and, at the end of the event, a farewell ball.

With the Second Show the Grand Hotel in Florence became the stage and the 1952 move to Palazzo Pitti's Sala Bianca further enhanced similarity of the Shows with the commercial fashion events organized by US department stores. For Canadian and US stores, the biannual shows that followed the presentations in Paris were a significant promotional vehicle, collecting all the purchases made during the buyers' expeditions and showcasing the store's role as a tastemaker in the diffusion of new trends within its community.[32] Stanfill details the preparation for the seasonal shows held at the I. Magnin stores in California following the return of buyers from Italy and France, a promotional feast that enticed customers and displayed the 'buying acumen' of the staff.[33] On those occasions, all Europeans models bought were generally presented at the same event and announced by a speaker. Giorgini decided to proceed in the same way, so models were grouped and presented according to their sub-categories: evening wear, day wear, cocktail gowns, sportswear, and so on, as confirmed by the typed programmes of the Shows found in the Giorgini archive and those published by the press.

Nevertheless, the Italian Shows shared a similarity with the Parisian couture showings that concerned the way in which models paraded the garments: many photographs taken during the earliest Shows depict buyers examining the models from close range, a situation quite different from fashion shows of contemporary times. This mirrored the features of commercial couture shows in Paris, where buyers were allowed to examine and touch the garments, as can be inferred from press articles and photographs. Already in 1933, *Harper's Bazaar* reported on the hectic days of the international fashion buyers in Paris in an article aptly called 'Ten Days in the Paris Madhouse': in an accompanying photograph buyers strike the fabric of a Schiaparelli model purchased by many: 'they are all there – Mr. and Mrs. Adam Gimbel, of Saks; Miss Frankau of Bergdorf Goodman … – more than a hundred buyers from all the big American cities'.[34] The model shown in the picture, carrying a number in her right hand, pauses in front of two women looking at the details of her dress, reaching for the fabric and the decorative elements that embellish the cut. In 1951, only a few days before Giorgini's First Show, *Life* photographed commercial buyers at the spring/summer collections in Paris, while lifting and spreading the hem of a Jacques Fath gown, while the model, dressed in a light-flecked fabric, stood by.[35]

Similarly, the models employed in the Florentine Shows were instructed to pause in front of the buyers and to take their time, so that, if interested, the buyers could ask them to take a better look at the dresses (Figure 6.1). Clelia Bruno Marzili, who worked as an assistant buyer at G.B. Giorgini in the mid-1950s, remembers that the Fashion Shows in Florence

> were very quiet because the buyers needed to observe every detail of the dress showing. [The models] would stop in front of the buyers, they would turn once,

6.1 Andrew Goodman of Bergdorf Goodman at the Second Italian High Fashion Show, July 1951. Cameraphoto Epoche/©Vittorio Pavan

> they would turn twice … it was quite a slow thing, the runway. The models could not be distracted by other things because the buyers were there in front of them. [The buyers] had catalogues and all, but they also needed to see the details, because, if they needed to, they would ask for modifications in the original model … Perhaps a buyer would gesture to [the model], and she would stop longer, they were all at the disposal of the buyers.[36]

In her recollection of the everyday tasks required from assistant buyers employed at the G.B. Giorgini office, Marzili offers a glimpse into the organization of one of the most prestigious intermediaries in the city of Florence.[37] Her reconstruction of the modelling performance identifies the practical functions ascribed to it with the specific aim of simplifying and facilitating the work of the buyers. The description suggests a much quieter environment than those in contemporary fashion shows, especially concerning the press photographers involved. The main job of a model during the show was to move as slowly as possible in a way that would be both informative and entertaining for the buyers, while press photos were usually taken after the Shows, in a separate situation, in which the models could be instructed to pose against specifically selected backdrops.

Press and publicity of the earlier Shows

Before accepting the invitation to participate in the First Italian High Fashion Show, Sorelle Fontana requested also to Giorgini to exclude Italian journalists from the show.[38] Either Giorgini evaded the latter condition or the issue was resolved eventually, since the few journalists present at the First Show were all Italian and included Elisa Massai for *Women's Wear Daily*, Vera Rossi Lodomez, *Bellezza*'s Elsa Robiola, and Misia Armani. Sofia Gnoli and Ivan Paris report that Sandra Bartolomei Corsi, writer for the Genoese newspaper *Il Secolo XIX*, was also in attendance together with Gemma Vitti of *Il Corriere Lombardo*.[39] Since the condition posed by the Fontanas on fashion journalists specifically referred to Italians only, Giorgini took into consideration the presence of foreign press and sent an invitation to Bettina Ballard, one of the earliest commentators of the 'Italian Look' among US fashion reporters.[40] Ballard could not be present, but nevertheless noted later to Giorgini:

> I have had very good reports of your show from Miss Jessica [Daube] and Miss Franco [sic] of Bergdorf Goodman and from Mr. Cole of Leto Cohn Lo Balbo. Everyone seems very interested in Italy. *Vogue* is too, and I am sure we can do something in the near future. One of our editors may be in Florence this spring and if so I will let you know.[41]

There is no further correspondence in the Giorgini archive following this letter. Whether or not one of the *Vogue* editors indeed went to Florence, the magazine did not cover the First Show, nor is there any mention of the appearance of Italian collections in the purchases made by US buyers for the spring/summer of 1951. Until August 1951, when it published the photographs of two coats from the autumn/winter collection of Simonetta Visconti, *Vogue* did not report on the Florentine Shows.

Given the investment operated by Giorgini in terms of his own reputation as commissionaire, it is important to consider also the perspective of confidentiality. The limited attendance of buyers during the First Show was not coincidental. When the Paris showings ended in the second week of February 1951, several of the manufacturers and commercial buyers that attended there from North America were on route to Italy, many reportedly to visit the textile market.[42] Despite this, the number of guests attending the Show was restricted a priori in order to keep the news conveniently confined within friendly walls:

There were five or six buyers, not many, but every one of them had a significant buying appropriation. There were two or three journalists, because they were family friends, trusted people, because the outcome was not taken for granted. Indeed, it was a, let's say, 'intimate' event, among people that he knew and whom he trusted, with whom he had a personal relationship. Because he could not risk organizing something big that would then be a fiasco: the repercussions would have been terrible.[43]

Furthermore, as outlined in previous paragraphs, the specialized US press had generally expressed a lack of confidence towards Italian couturiers. These are significant circumstances contributing to explaining how only a handful of buyers and journalists eventually attended the First Italian High Fashion Show. The intimate and confidential tone of the event was set to protect the privacy of all participants, in case the response from North American buyers would have been negative, or even moderately positive. With Massai on his side, Giorgini could module the outcome of the Show for the specialized press. The presence of the 'Italian' voice of *Women's Wear Daily* signals a very precise publicity strategy, which forecasted the possibility of needing some form of 'damage control'. The intimacy of the First Show might have also contributed to injecting some curiosity in those who did not manage to attend, as, for instance, *Vogue*'s Bettina Ballard. As the Second Italian Fashion Show attracted a large group of international buyers and journalists, the highly controlled first event paved the way for the following ones.

As the response from the First Show appeared favourable, the organization of the Second Show counted on a much more substantial presence of buyers and press. The buyers became 300, according to Giorgini, and this time the event was covered by *Vogue*, *Life* and many fashion columns across the United States.[44] Pictures of the Show, which took place in the main hall of the Grand Hotel in Florence in July 1951, show journalists such as *Harper's Bazaar*'s Carmel Snow and Italian correspondent Irene Brin, *Vogue*'s Bettina Ballard, *Life*'s Sally Kirkland, and many more. Yet, the publicity aggravated disagreements between Giorgini and some of the Roman designers, who would later decide to skip the Florentine events and show in their own ateliers. Among them, Simonetta Visconti recounted in her memoir that one of the reasons for her departure was that travelling to Florence for the Shows required long, expensive and exhausting preparations, not to mention a heavy load of work to coordinate models, baggage, business meetings, and public relations with the press and buyers.[45] Additionally, the constitution of a competing fashion council, the Italian Fashion Service, complicated an already crowded picture that the buying audiences failed to understand.

The Italian Fashion Service was sponsored by the Italian Government, and it had been jointly established by EIM of Turin and CIMM of Milan, who formed an alliance 'for the promotion of fashions and textiles in general …

backed by interest closely connected with the textile industry'.[46] Italian journalist Irene Brin, then Rome correspondent for *Harper's Bazaar*, would later comment on the Italian Fashion Service and its sudden appearance:

> in January 1952, when we were certain that *an avalanche* of buyers would come from America, Italians divided themselves in Medieval Factions, or Constitutional Regions, which is almost the same thing. Every city raised its flag, boasted its ancestors, listed fictional clients such as Elisabetta of Este or Lucrezia Borgia, and sent out invitations. Even a special organization was born out of it, the Italian Fashion Information [sic], aiming to help possible buyers: 'For knitwear you could go to Trepuzzi [small village in Apulia], there is a skillful elementary school teacher who instructs pupils' ... 'Would you prefer Taranto or Turin?' ... 'Do you like traveling by plain, or by direct local train?', 'Are you interested in handicrafts, in historical monuments?'[47]

In her witty style, Brin remarked on the awkwardness of an organization that seemed to be tied to the many interests of small dressmaking shops and manufacturers that had little if no experience in exporting and coordinating buyers. Some firms decided to participate in both initiatives, those sponsored by the Italian Fashion Service and those in Florence with Giorgini. One of them, the Milanese manufacturer Valstar that specialized in luxury ready-to-wear, did not have the opportunity to conclude any business transaction in Florence. Its management praised the G.B. Giorgini organization anyway for exposing Valstar to a significant public of foreign buyers and for giving them the opportunity to 'tune' their image in order to attract more customers.[48] Nevertheless, the chaotic effect caused by the establishment of the Italian Fashion Service, argued the Italian press, ignited controversies and rumours, since publicity generated by the Giorgini Shows had aroused rivalries among cities and designers. The complicated internal matters of supposed jealousy, pointed out by journalist Misia Armani, emphasized a provincialism that could potentially endanger the reputation of Italy in the eyes of foreign buyers, 'for whom rigor is the thing that matters most in business'.[49] Armani's accusation was echoed by fellow journalist Vera Rossi Lodomez, who specifically pointed her finger towards the newly launched Italian Fashion Service and the divisive impact that it had on the experiences of foreign buyers.[50]

Among the visible effects of the quarrels, the defection of Carmel Snow from the Third Show was particularly significant for Giorgini. As the Third Show was set for 18–22 January 1952, Snow wrote to Giorgini in December, announcing that, since she had to be in Paris after a few days, she preferred to fly to Rome and skip Florence, 'especially as practically all houses showing [in] Florence will show [in] Rome'.[51] The importance of this event is emphasized by the fact that the Giorgini archive contains messages from different people informing, or rather warning, Giorgini about Snow's plans. Specifically, it includes a letter that Snow sent to socialite Lanfranco Rasponi to inform him about her plans, and a letter from journalist Irene Brin who urged Giorgini to contact her if he wanted to meet with Snow in private. In connection to the issues that arose with Roman dressmakers, the fact that Snow preferred to visit solely Rome was linked to the possibility of having a short-timed stopover. As explained in Chapter 5, Rome was efficiently served by transatlantic air flights, while Florence was poorly equipped in this sense. The transportation of foreign visitors to Florence was complicated by the fact that the small airport there, the 'Amerigo Vespucci' in the Peretola area, was not a hub for transatlantic flights, as Ciampino in Rome was. Giorgini tried to prevent critiques for the lack of convenient transportation by organizing a connection by train from Rome to Florence, reserving some of the cars expressly for the buyers.[52] Still, this did not seem to help Carmel Snow change her mind and visit both cities. For the following Show of July 1952, Giorgini reported to *Women's Wear Daily* that the increasing organization costs forced his firm to introduce an entrance fee of $100 for buyers.[53] The additional money, in turn, allowed him to plan a special return flight from Florence to Milan, in addition to the reserved train cars from Rome.[54]

Perceived adaptability of Italian fashion

Besides the matter of transportation, which would trouble the Florentine Shows and personally worry Giorgini until his retirement, further issues were rising. A reputation for creating overstated, lavish evening gowns began circulating at the time concerning some Italian couturiers, something that would linger for a few years more. After the Fourth Italian High Fashion Show of 1952, columnist Dorothy L. Wallis reported that 'nothing is too extreme, sweeping, exaggerated for the Italians'. Comparing the most recent British collections with the Italian ones shown in Florence (and presumably Rome), Wallis emphasized in her article how Italian designs tended to appear overstated, especially if put side by side with British subtle tones, flowing silhouettes and 'no nonsense' clothes.[55] Claims of derivativeness, too, were highly frequent in the US press: a 1953 article in *Vogue* declared that, in the spring/summer Italian collections of that year, 'dresses still tend to be too French in manner'.[56] Eveningwear did not meet the favours of all US buyers at the outset of the Florentine showings. A press agency photo found in the Giorgini archive and dating back to the summer of 1951 shows a dark-haired model wearing a richly embroidered evening gown, illustrated by the caption as:

> NOT SO SIMPLE – A mannequin models a white organdy lace evening gown with mother-of-pearl decorations. One of the criticisms leveled at the Italian creations by American buyers was that their evening styles were a bit too elaborate to be practical.[57]

Interestingly enough, the Italian press was at the same time proposing the opposite argument, often by saying that Italian designers needed to create extravagant clothes to catch the attention of US buyers. For instance, following the First Show, *Bellezza* published the sketch of an evening gown by Simonetta Visconti (Figure 6.2), who reportedly 'knows the American taste oriented towards evening gowns, extremely rich'.[58] The same penchant for decorated garments that had its exquisite peak in French fashion, continued the article, was often at the request of US buyers, who were nonetheless starting to grow weary of it. New York designer and manufacturer Hannah Troy had expressed the same type of criticisms towards the elaborateness of evening gowns, when she affirmed in *Women's Wear Daily* that she only bought a few 'show pieces' following the First Italian High Fashion Show. The garments' detailed decorations, in Troy's opinion,

6.2 Evening gown by Simonetta Visconti. *Bellezza*, April 1951. By permission of the Ministry of Culture – Pinacoteca di Brera – Biblioteca Braidense, Milan

would have made them too expensive to be reproduced in the US: 'Labor is cheaper in Italy than it is in France', she added, 'and [Italian dressmakers] are able to turn out some elaborate garments with a great deal of trimmings that it would be difficult to duplicate'.[59] Russel Carpenter, general manager at I. Magnin Beverly Hills, chimed in and lamented to Giorgini that there were

> many things shown that are too extreme for the American customer, and ... many beautiful clothes are lost because of the presentation of extreme, unsalable models. As you know I suggested that a committee could pass on the models to be presented so that anything that was freakish could be eliminated from the showings.[60]

In the press, Carpenter praised the workmanship and the sensibility for colour of Italian designers, denying that they were 'French copyists' and instead mentioning their preference for simple designs in which 'they expend their creative energies on superb fabrics and beautiful ornamentation'.[61] Paris designs, continued Carpenter, were more sober, but the value for money was higher in Italian evening gowns due to the amount of workmanship that went into these 'spectacular' creations.[62] In private, Carpenter had a series of requests for Giorgini and the improvement of the Shows: more transportation options; easier connections between the Shows and the airport, whether in Florence or Rome; and stricter control on the fashion houses, reserving more space to the 'better' ones and concentrating newcomers and smaller firms in the latter days of the Shows.[63]

The overview of the US press' opinions regarding Italian fashion merchandise and couture presented so far throughout the book highlights how, from the earliest appearances, the 'uncomplicated' Italian styles seemed to match particularly well the average US female consumer. Fairchild correspondent Giuseppe Ratti had said it in 1949: the moment was right to try and captivate US fashion buyers, for their opinion of Italian styles was that they suited American women better than French products. When, in the same year, department store J.L. Hudson had presented the first collection of Italian couture models in the United States, the specialized press stressed how the models were created keeping in mind the taste of American women, their lifestyle, and their measurements.[64] Starting with the First Show of February 1951, the US fashion press reported that the most interesting items from the new Italian collections were to be found in the category of 'play clothes', embodied by *moda boutique*. A category of garments destined for leisure settings and informal occasions, play clothes were particularly popular for summer holidays, which explains the use of the alternate term 'resort wear'. In the United States, play clothes and resort wear represented a segment of the fashion market that particularly interested American women. In 1947, $200 million was expected to be spent on summer garments, focusing on colourful, practical fabrics, 'flattering to tan and functional in action'.[65] As discussed by fashion scholar Rebecca Arnold, the years preceding the Second World War were crucial in the establishment of the sportswear segment as representing American fashion's own sense of identity.[66] When Italian *moda boutique* started to appear more consistently on the pages of US fashion magazines and newspapers, the selective eye of the press chose to focus on those characteristics – streamlined designs, smart fabrics, colourful separates – that more seemingly matched the American taste and the ready-to-wear industry.

Such a tendency started from the very First Italian High Fashion Show, when journalist Elisa Massai focused her *Women's Wear Daily* article mainly on coats and *moda boutique*. According to Massai, 'the development of Italian tweeds and fleeces was interesting. One tweed capecoat … sold to three firms. Two loose silk toppers embroidered with mother of pearl on gilded straw appliques … were listed among the successes'.[67] The creations mentioned in detail are those of Simonetta Visconti, an 'amusing' selection of resort wear; the handweaves of Tessitrice dell'Isola for Emilio Pucci, a collaboration identified as the House of Capri; simply cut resort ensembles from Noberasco; and knitwear from Mirsa. Besides an initial mention of the 'embroidered formal gowns [that] especially interested the audience', Massai emphasized the less expensive and freshest items, positioning the offer of Italian houses in a different segment in comparison to French ones. The ready-made garments of *moda boutique* became the asset that differentiated and characterized the Italian designers for transatlantic customers.

Even if Parisian couture houses produced their own ready-to-wear lines, and Italians were well aware of them since they often appeared in *Bellezza* (Figure 6.3), the prestige of French *couture creation* towered over these lower-status collections and thus allowed Italian ready-made garments to fit with more distinction in the mix and differentiate the Italian offering by grounding its identity in the transatlantic marketplace.[68]

Weaving the Renaissance thread in

Scholar Carlo Marco Belfanti argues that the innovation introduced by Giorgini in 1951 was the adoption of a revival of the Renaissance to promote Italian fashion internationally and solve both the lack of a homogeneous cultural identity among designers and the absence of international recognition for Italian fashion.[69] To Belfanti the Renaissance, intended by historian Jacob Burckhardt's definition of it as the period in which Italian civilization(s) represented the pinnacle that steered European culture, has been used as the argument to support the continuity of artisanal, high-level craftsmanship until today.[70] In particular, this book shares Belfanti's concern towards 'the consistent rhetorical sedimentation with which [the appropriation of the Renaissance as an intangible asset in the promotion

6.3 French 'boutique' fashions. *Bellezza*, July 1950. By permission of the Ministry of Culture – Pinacoteca di Brera – Biblioteca Braidense, Milan

of Italian fashion on the international market] is encrusted'.[71] As discussed earlier, the Renaissance lay as the main promotional backdrop to the postwar exports of Italian handicrafts, and thus fashion merchandise and, later, couture. However, the Renaissance, both as a cultural validation and as a reflection of contemporary times, was referenced in different ways in postwar years as the interest towards Italian fashion started to grow.

In the late 1940s, several US fashion magazines and newspapers expressed enthusiasm for Italian handicrafts, calling the period a 'new Renaissance' and praising the vigour of the Italian artisans who were rebuilding, through their skills, the reputation of Italy in the postwar configuration of the Western world. As a result, Italian designers, journalists, and professionals reprised the use of the Renaissance for promotion, mostly on the weight of the cultural heritage that it represented and making it an intangible seal of approval to guarantee for the skills of the designers and the quality of the materials used. The advent of the Holy Year in 1950 added the presence of a trans-European Renaissance trend that was confirmed by *Women's Wear Daily*, which forecasted the trends that would be adopted by Parisian fashion in the spring of 1950 and included 'Italian Renaissance because of the Holy Year pilgrimage putting Italy very much in the public eye and exposing thousands of travelers to Italian art'.[72] Renaissance trends in millinery and coiffures were already announced through the pages of *Women's Wear Daily*, as well as a similar one for coiffures.[73] In cinema, the Machiavelli-inspired film *Prince of Foxes* (directed by Henry King for Twentieth Century Fox, 1949), reportedly shot entirely in Italy, contributed to reinforcing the Renaissance trend in the United States, while in Italy it made the popularity of Tyrone Power explode.[74] Corresponding from the opening of the film, *Women's Wear Daily* stressed that its 'costume designs have special interest this coming year when Italy will be the mecca in Holy Year, and Renaissance art is expected to be one of the leading influences in fashion'.[75] The film featured Renaissance costumes made in Florence, using 'the laces from Venice, the shoes from Rome, the swords and belts from Genoa and the beautiful brocades and velvets from all over Italy'.[76] The appearance of *Prince of Foxes* in *Women's Wear Daily* is particularly significant as the trade journal specified that the costumes were serving as inspiration to contemporary designers, while some of them had participated by 'designing merchandise in connection with this picture'.[77] The Renaissance trend reportedly did not interest French fashion creators, with the president of Paris' Chambre Syndicale Jean Gaumont Lanvin admonishing the audiences that this was not the first time that designers turned to the Renaissance for inspiration:

> they can hardly go further than this, and I would consider it a sacrilege if the Haute Couture should base its advertising on finding new selling arguments in the publicity given to the Holy Year and launch a religious fashion. Let us not confuse religious pomp in all its beauty and splendor with the modest pursuit of the fashion designers, which is that of adorning woman [sic].[78]

As affirmed by Lanvin, this was hardly the first time that Renaissance paintings had served as inspiration for the applied arts in general, and for fashion trends in particular. In the early years of the twentieth century, Italian dressmaker and social activist Rosa Genoni promoted the affirmation of an Italian aesthetic in fashion based on the cultural prestige of the Renaissance. In 1908, Genoni participated in the First National Congress of Italian Women and delivered the speech 'Per Una Moda Italiana' (for an Italian fashion), which championed the vision of a non-derivative fashion scene in Italy.[79] In her speech, Genoni encouraged Italian women to insist their dressmakers shy away from copying Parisian models, and instead asked them to endure the exertion and the labour required by creating original models.[80] Foreign artists celebrate Italian women, argued Genoni, for their intuitive disposition towards art and beauty, of which these women could become active propagandists if they only responded to the aforementioned appeal.[81] Genoni explained that, once King Francis I (1494–1547) and the Italian noblewomen of his court introduced Italian fashion styles in France, it was not until after Queen Catherine (de' Medici, reigning between 1547–59) that France 'emancipated' itself from Italian fashions, thus slowly forgetting 'that the first cradle of good taste and of classic lines in art and clothing had been Italy'.[82] In her work as dressmaker, Genoni created sumptuous gowns inspired by different historical periods and dressed influential celebrities of the time, such as actress Lyda Borelli.

Nevertheless, the Renaissance was not just a historical backdrop from which it was possible to draw and provide a cultural legitimation. The idea of an *esprit de retour* applied particularly well to the image of postwar Italy that was presented by the US fashion press. Since the Liberation, cultural correspondents writing from Italy for *Vogue*, its sister publications at Condé Nast, and *Harper's Bazaar* highlighted the energetic Italian arts and crafts scene, marking the shift from the harshness of the regime to the newly acquired freedoms of speech and expression granted by the Allies. Frances Keene, corresponding for *Harper's Bazaar* from Rome in 1947, emphasized that, even though the war bled Italy white, the country nevertheless displayed an amazing vigour that largely stemmed from 'her creative artists and her little people, artisans, designers, weavers'.[83] To Keene, it was these creative people's persistence and imagination that led to the revival of individualities after nearly twenty years of totalitarianism and allowed for the set-up of numerous creative little businesses whose ingenuity was especially evident in the fashion accessories available in many shops (Figure 6.4). This same narrative reverberated from the series of articles resulting from Marya Mannes' trip to Italy in 1946. Mannes' constant praise of Italian vitality was directed mainly to the creative minds of Milan, such as architect Gio Ponti, credited for reviving the artisanal tradition of the Renaissance in 'the great anonymous Army of Italian artisans [that] produce decorative and useful objects'.[84] In the field of fashion merchandise and couture, it was that 'apparently inexhaustible pool of hand-labour' that represented one of the two advantages of Italian women (the other being 'wonderful materials').[85] Contrasting the harshness of war experienced until recently (however self-imposed, she noted), Mannes stressed the bustle and the excitement of the Italian artisans:

> In spite of this [past war], Italy is at work. Her people are not only rebuilding towns and bridges; they are looking forward creatively. They are making new things with new ideas. With every material obstruction, they are laying cornerstones of a new and better Italy.[86]

Not coincidentally, Mannes concluded the article by pointing out the efforts of 'Handicraft Development, Inc. ... an organization responsible for the first

6.4 'Marvelous' Italian leather handbags, *Harper's Bazaar*, July 1947. Courtesy of *Harper's Bazaar*, Hearst Magazine Media, Inc. Image published with permission of ProQuest LLC. Further reproduction is prohibited without permission

postwar *resumption* of Italy's export trade with America'.[87] This representation of the Italian design and handicraft scene in its resumption, following the moral resurgence that the Italian people were experiencing through their hard work, is a direct reminder of Max Ascoli's conceptualization of work as a propeller of freedom and an antidote against totalitarianism (at this point, Bolshevism).

Furthermore, the network of professionals and intermediaries that worked on the organization of *Italy at Work* was strongly connected to the cultural events taking place in Florence in the postwar years. In 1949, a year considered to be Florence's own Holy Year, the celebrations for the anniversary of Lorenzo de' Medici's birth in 1449 brought a similar spirit of rebirth and revival after the despair brought by the war. Scholars Cristelle Baskins and Silvia Bottinelli remark how Lorenzo de' Medici's own motto, *le temps revient*, meaning that a prosperous time is about to return, permeated the celebrations and the art exhibition mounted for the occasion with the curatorial direction of Ragghianti, implying a strong symbolism with the theme of restoration and rebirth – a new Renaissance of Florence and

Italian arts.[88] It is only appropriate, then, that the Renaissance became the main theme around which *Italy at Work* revolved, as recalled by selection committee member Walter Dorwin Teague:

> I think it was in Milan that our experience found expression in a name for the show. It was Meyric's [R. Rogers] suggestion, and we all recognized its right-ness immediately: 'Italy at Work'; and we added a subtitle, 'Its Renaissance in Design Today.' This phrase is a clue to the recurrent thrills we were getting from what we saw: everywhere we felt an upsurge of creative energy, of great power and vigor.[89]

As discussed earlier, the possibility of having a fashion show in connection with and as a complement to the exhibition was discussed by Giorgini and Meyric R. Rogers, curator of *Italy at Work*. The two had outlined a pres-entation of both historical costumes and contemporary designs, planning for its development in the summer of 1950. The original plan, according to Giorgini, would have also included 'costumes which were made for some of the best-known films, by Italian dressmakers. All this would have as a background a presentation of old Italian dresses throughout the past cen-turies'.[90] *Italy at Work* can be then considered the setting that contributes to merging the two interpretations of Renaissance used up to that point. As the original location was forcibly moved from the Brooklyn Museum to Florence, the references to the Renaissance as a cultural legitimiza-tion of the Shows appeared more than fitting, and Giorgini was keen to make it very visible to those who would participate. This is supported, for instance, by the fact that the invitation cards for the First Italian Fashion Show sent to both Italian guests and US commercial buyers reproduced the painting *Young Woman with Unicorn* (*Dama con liocorno*) by Raffaello Sanzio on the cover.[91] The habit of reproducing a famous painting would continue through the years and become a trademark of Giorgini's Shows.[92] As demonstrated earlier, Giorgini constantly reworked and re-used his business proposals and ideas according to the occasion. This could be seen, for instance, in the correspondence from the late 1930s in which he explained to potential associates his attempt to reopen the shop Le Tre Stanze and make it a store chain with retailers all over Italy.[93] After the experience of the Allied Forces Gift Shop, he drafted a new project based on its same format: a small department store-like space, featuring Florentine handicrafts, dressmakers' ateliers and home décor, which was in turn derivative of the idea at the foundation of Le Tre Stanze. Because of this seriality highlighted in Giorgini's correspondence and business papers, among the reasons why the theme of the Renaissance was heavily present in the First Italian High Fashion Show was the fact that it derived from the project created with Rogers in connection to *Italy at Work*. The idea was to structure the fashion show in accordance with the themes of an exhibition of Italian goods specifically designed for the United States, to present to 'the American public ... a field which *supplements rather than competes* with our own production'.[94] The exhibition, presenting real, commercial objects, contextualized the interest of US buyers in a production 'that Italy offers us today out of the vitality of her present, resting, but not relying, on the greatness of her past'.[95]

As for the reliance on the historical prestige of the Italian Renaissance, this thread would also be largely exploited in the many references to paintings, sculpture, architecture, and costume history dispersed by Giorgini during the fourteen years of his Florentine Shows. Already during the planning stage of the show in New York, Giorgini was reminding Rogers that it was important to demonstrate, by showing historical costumes as a small backdrop to the contemporary ones, 'how Italy has always been important through the centuries in this field. The splendour of the Medici family is well-known, as is that Catherine [de Medici, queen of France] brought it to the Paris court and that the men's fashions were brought to Paris by the Venetians'.[96] The argument presented in this letter by Giorgini, albeit historically patchy, is similar to the one proposed by Rosa Genoni almost half a century earlier, though slightly different in terms of protagonists: for Genoni it was King Francis I who introduced the Italian style of dress to France. Furthermore, besides the earlier example of the invitation cards featuring famous Renaissance paintings, historical reenactments became part of the official entertainment organized by the G.B. Giorgini offices in connection to the Shows.

In July 1952, as the number of guests invited to the Fourth Show had increased and the need to entertain them pressured him, Giorgini obtained the permit to use the Sala Bianca in Palazzo Pitti. Situated on the other side of the river Arno from Piazza della Signoria and across the Ponte Vecchio, the colossal palace was initially built by the Florentine banker Luca Pitti in the fifteenth century, to be later owned by the Medici family and the grand duke of Tuscany. Representing the archetypal *reggia* of the Italian Renaissance, the location provided the historical prestige already suggested by Giorgini with his constant references to the glorious past of Italian fashion. The mid-week reception was organized at Boboli, the magnificent garden that extends itself from Pitti up to the outskirts of the city centre. With the sumptuous 'Boboli Ball', Giorgini recreated the glory of the Florentine past, in the 'primary locus of representation of the grand duke as the divinely authorized dispenser of justice and mercy, as ruler and protector of the state, and as assurer of prosperity and peace – *quietus* as the Medici traditionally termed it – of the Tuscan state and its people'.[97]

The luscious greenery and the amphitheatre of the Boboli Gardens were often in photoshoots featuring Florentine dressmakers: in the spring of 1947, for instance, a *Bellezza* issue featured models from the collections of Florentine dressmakers made for their most prestigious foreign customers (Figure 6.5), while a few pages earlier journalist Emilia Kuster Rosselli quipped that, unconsciously, 'Florence offers a fashion of

its own that travels around the world through its century-old export channels. Such fashion adheres to current taste because of the international
community that lives here, but it is sparked by a local vein of instinctive
taste imbued with instinctive civilisation', somehow anticipating the primitive qualities attributed to Italian artisans by Rogers.[98] The impact of such
stunning architecture was historically guaranteed to impress Giorgini's
guests, and the first ball at Boboli was commented enthusiastically on by
Giorgini's trusted acquaintance Fay Hammond, fashion editor for the *Los
Angeles Times*:

> Only incomparable Florence could offer such a setting for a party. This beauti-
> ful city seems carved out of the ancient hills of Tuscany. It's a flower bowl –
> edged in living obelisks of black-green cypresses and age-old olive trees. To
> brush aside a few centuries and view the patina of the Middle Ages or the
> Renaissance seemed a simple and natural thing here. And it was done, just
> like that, to transport a thousand guests to this fabulous fete. G.B. Giorgini,
> impresario of the Italian high-fashion showings recently concluded, made the
> arrangements with history.[99]

At the end of January 1953, as the Fifth Show was taking place during the
Carnival season, the main salon of Palazzo Vecchio hosted the re-enactment
of the wedding between Eleonora de Medici and Vincenzo I Gonzaga, which
originally occurred in 1584. The descendants of the most important aristocratic families in Italy were asked to participate and impersonate their
ancestors.[100] Embarking on the organization of such events allowed Giorgini
to establish a common theme for the entertainment planned for his foreign

6.5 Boboli garden fashion shoot. *Bellezza*, May–June 1947. By permission of the
Ministry of Culture – Pinacoteca di Brera – Biblioteca Braidense, Milan

visitors and solidify the influence of the Renaissance in the Shows' organization. Together with the balls at Boboli, the opera nights, or the fancy 'cold suppers' in the courtyards that once hosted the Medici family, the historical garments in the paintings reproduced on the Shows' invitations were a constant reminder, year by year, that Italy had something to offer to contemporary women, as much as it had centuries ago with Queen Catherine.

'France's enemy number one'

From Catherine de Medici onwards, then, the general opinion was that French couture had steered the business of fashion ideas, and that its creations still represented mandatory reference. The export trade of Italian couture and fashion merchandise needed a promotion adequate to its emerging status. Individual names of couturiers or fashion houses did not mean much to the majority of American final consumers, despite the few who had previously gained traction in the United States. They also did very little to suggest anything to most buyers, manufacturers, and designers who were looking for inspiration and new merchandise. As fashion historians Aurora Fiorentini and Stefania Ricci point out, the postwar present of Italy as a fashion centre was not conditioned by grand designer names of its past.[101] Thus, its reputation and identity had to be started anew. As has been discussed so far, a commercially palatable narrative on Italian fashion started to appear in the postwar years, way before the promotions done by Giorgini in connection to the Shows. With the advent of the Florentine Shows, the reputation of Italian designs and merchandise was modelled in opposition to French ones, since it was still Paris that led the business of fashion ideas. Nevertheless, the quarrel between Italy and France was presumably a means to characterize Italian products for the US market as exotic insofar as they were European, even if not French. Press articles of the time addressing the quarrel as non-existent or insignificant have been overlooked by previous research, which has largely maintained that there existed a genuine clash between Italian and Parisian collection showings.

The opinion according to which Giorgini's 'battle' for the recognition of Italian fashion in the transatlantic market was exclusively motivated by a patriotic feeling has been advocated mostly by previous research belonging to the 'celebratory' wave and by members of his family.[102] Italian weekly L'Europeo described the personality of Giorgini in early 1953 as, it claimed, American reporters saw it at the time: a highly popular, hardworking man with a commanding presence.[103] This tireless Florentine with such unflappable cool looks, continued the article, boasted an illustrious lineage, impeccable manners and was convinced that aristocratic snobbism was the best Italian asset when dealing with US businessmen: 'he thinks that … it always impresses people who have very little past and recent traditions'.[104] The presence of Giorgini in media discourses of the time represents an exception to the traditional model in which the fashion houses occupied the spotlight. The most prestigious stores' buyers enjoyed a certain degree of fame in the specialized press, and their travelling habits would be largely featured in *Women's Wear Daily*, but this had a mere practical relevance: competitors and collaborators needed access to that information for their own business interests. The 'anonymity of buyers', as discussed by Stanfill, is a phenomenon of our time, if considering how little is known and researched on their profession within the fashion history community.[105] Instead, postwar and 1950s press articles emphasized how the presence of buyers and journalists at a fashion show would make or break a collection, as one would look at the others' reaction for confirmation as a model passed by. The status of the press had only been elevated quite recently, since before the early 1920s the presence of journalists at fashion shows would be seen as a piracy threat to designers.[106] In the case of Giorgini, the share of publicity and press coverage that he received represented a different type of contribution within the traditional patterns of fashion history, where fashion houses or designers enjoyed most of the attention. By carving a role for himself as an 'impresario' of Italian fashion, his name acquired a significance in the market that increased the value of his firm and its intermediary qualities. His archive is rich in both Italian, American, and European press clippings that celebrate his illustrious ancestors, comparing the family's patriotic lineage with his diplomatic skills in transatlantic trade, and celebrating his own devotedness to the quest for the transatlantic recognition of Italian fashion. An analysis of such clippings and their collation with the promotional brochure printed by G.B. Giorgini for the Second Italian High Fashion Show revealed that the latter was used as a press release to promote such a narrative.[107] There it was described how:

> [b]rought up in an atmosphere of fervent family patriotism, Signor Giorgini has always kept alive that spirit of national feeling, and his efforts have always been directed towards the appreciation of Italian products. He has spent the greater part of his life among the artisans, giving them advice, helping them, passing on ideas to them which he had brought back from his numerous visits to the United States.[108]

The quest for Italian fashion's independence depended upon the ability to attract foreign buyers. It was not a matter of the establishment of a cultural superiority of one fashion industry over the other, as was affirmed by different journalists of the time. Giorgini himself, when dubbed 'France's enemy number one' by French magazine *Paris Match*, was quick to reassure the press that it was never his aim to start an unfruitful battle for supremacy.[109] Journalist Gilbert Graziani authored the infamous article that has been frequently referenced as an attack of the French press towards the emergent Italian couture scene, yet the article appears in line with other contemporary Italian and American reports.[110] It is an article very considerate of the reputation of the firm G.B. Giorgini and its founder: it opens with the history of Giorgini's business and his ancestors as laid out in the Second Italian High Fashion Show brochure, reaffirms the historically inaccurate notion that it was indeed Giorgini who organized the exhibition *Italy at Work*, and faithfully explains that the seven buyers that visited Florence for the First Show did it merely out of courtesy towards Giorgini, whom they knew personally. The article represented indeed an interesting platform for Giorgini to express his feelings towards Paris:

> Paris remains the city of fashion. Attacking it would be stupid. We have more than admiration for your great designers. Next to them, we are pygmies. That you are upset by our creations is surprising to us: it is as if an Army of giants was frightened at the sight of an infant. But we are working as well and want to launch our haute couture and our textiles on the world market. We have many assets and we will take advantage of them. We also want to have a bite of the American cake. What could be more normal?[111]

The last two sentences of the statement above condense the mission statement of G.B. Giorgini. The firm expressed its will to become an integral part of the fashion circuit, and bite into the opportunities offered by the United States, but at the same time carving out a permanent place for itself in the transatlantic fashion market.[112]

By and large, the article was a clever instance of promotion done at a moment in which Giorgini's Third Show suffered the first drawbacks. As previously mentioned, some fashion creators were already abandoning the platform of Florence, preferring to host buyers in their ateliers; competitor organizations attempted to set up alternative collective showings and services; and the number of North American buyers had decreased in comparison to the last Show of July 1951, when the publicity buzz had been at its utmost. With the *Paris Match* article, Giorgini managed to make a diplomatic statement on Florence's relationship with Paris, acknowledging the supremacy of the French capital and, at the same time, winking at US clients, both established and potential ones, by having a French journalist confirming that Florence had indeed something different to offer than Paris. Prices were more affordable in Italy because taxes were lower and workmanship cheaper, and that alone was a significant element that Graziani deemed 'the bottom of the problem', especially considering that Giorgini did not start to charge buyers and manufacturers an entrance fee until the Fourth Show, in July 1952.[113] Together with simplicity, price repeatedly appeared in the examined primary sources as a discriminatory element that contributed to the creation of interest towards Italian fashion merchandise and ideas in the reprise of postwar transatlantic commerce.

Specifically, as was the case with the idea of 'simplicity', price was an element of differentiation in opposition to Parisian couture and accessories.

As previously discussed, the perceived quality of Italian goods in the eye of the average North American consumer undoubtedly influenced the fluctuation of prices. Perceived lower quality would have cost less, especially if the geographical connotation of the goods was not significant. In other words, anything that was not French or Parisian did not have a sufficiently appealing allure. Additionally, Parisian prices were not favourable to US business, and a frequent opinion expressed by US buyers and manufacturers to *Women's Wear Daily* in the early postwar years was that French prices appeared too high for the American fashion market.[114] Already in the summer of 1947, buyers returning from Europe after the presentation of autumn/winter Parisian collections lamented high prices, although the majority of them generally praised the quality of the styles seen: the clothes 'were very rich and the fabrics "fabulous"'. Prices of models had reportedly gone up in comparison to the February collections, and the high living costs for buyers abroad were adding a hefty toll on stores and manufacturers' travel budgets. Ethel Frankau, veteran manager of the Bergdorf Goodman's Custom Salon, noted that both designs and fabrics seemed to her astonishingly beautiful, although she was unable to make significant purchases due to the scarcity of textiles for exports. Moreover, she estimated a 30 per cent increase in the prices of models, which compromised her buying appropriation.[115] By guaranteeing lower prices than Paris and, at the outset, no entrance fee, Giorgini's Shows represented a convenient fallback for those buyers who wanted to differentiate and enlarge the range of their European seasonal purchases.

In the *Paris Match* article, Graziani explained also how the Florentine Shows provided a way for buyers to save time, assembling a large number of fashion houses and manufacturers together, which Americans appreciated. As many had outlined before, styles and fabrics suited the transatlantic market, a factor that should not come as a surprise to French couturiers since they sold the same Italian boutique lines and accessories in their Parisian shops, teased Graziani.[116] Additionally, hospitality represented a key component of the Florentine offer, which pleased the transatlantic guests: 'Every evening, there [were] galas and theatrical performances. The show concluded with a grand soirée in the royal-like villa of Giorgini. The Americans complain about the cost of living [when paying in] Francs and the expensiveness of hotels.'[117] As it emerges from his personal archive, the attention that Giorgini himself paid to the organization of his Shows was among the elements that he cared about the most, in a way that would reflect his reputation and that of his firm. In this perspective, the many letters that he meticulously kept of the international, mostly American clients are a testament to the opinion that he wanted posterity to form about him.

Some of these, in addition, support the fact that good business relations were immensely important to Giorgini and his firm, opposing the notion that it was merely a 'patriotic spirit' that animated his business activities. It is undoubtedly accurate to say that both his family background and socio-political formation pushed Giorgini towards the nationalistic celebration of Made in Italy. However, Giorgini was first and foremost a businessman who constantly strived to pursue a career in trade, notwithstanding the many difficulties encountered in this profession: insolvency, controlled administration of his firms, insufficient funds, and so forth.[118] In this perspective, it was desirable for G.B. Giorgini to secure as many opportunities as possible to obtain friendly relationships with European retailers as well, including French ones. Indeed, the management of Parisian department store Aux Galeries Lafayette wrote to Giorgini after the Fifth Show of 1953, inquiring about the possibility of a joint collaboration for an 'Italian show' in Paris later that same year. The new fashion of straw hats introduced as an accessory to evening wear had caught the attention of the store managers, who asked if it was possible to introduce this trend, still unexploited in France, in their promotions.[119] The proposal by Aux Galeries Lafayette represents the intention to do business with Italian designers in France, highlighting the importance of commercial relationships even with those countries that the press had dubbed the country's 'number one enemy'.

All-Italian rivalries

Even if the Third Show had suffered what Graziani called a potential half-failure, the culprit was decidedly not Giorgini. The alliance of CIMM and EIM, organizing the (short-lived) contender Italian Fashion Service, was with those Italian couturiers who forfeited Florence to present their new collections in their own ateliers, thus dispersing the flux of both European and transatlantic buyers and dissolving what Graziani called 'the unity of Italian *haute couture*, a reality six months ago, [which] is no more than a memory for foreign buyers'.[120] This might have come as a surprise to Giorgini. Correspondence found in the Giorgini archive demonstrates that in the years immediately following the end of the Second World War Giorgini was in contact with at least one person at CIMM, someone who would have provided him with valuable information on fashion buying trends, yet there is no indication of official collaborations with the Milanese council.[121] To contrast this new competitor, Graziani explained how Giorgini grouped more than twenty fashion houses and manufacturers and convinced them to keep showing in Florence, the city that represented the 'ideally neutral place that would spare all the transalpine sensibilities and rivalries'.[122] The Italian press seemed also critical towards this new organization. According to journalist Elsa Robiola, writing for the Italian women's magazine *Marie Claire*, Giorgini had tried to mend the strained relationships between EIM and CIMM in the past, but with no luck. The two organizations overcame their rivalry and joined forces only once the flux of export dollars became steadier. The Italian Fashion Service, an effort to surpass their previous disagreements, was thus called by Robiola a 'propaganda' agency, aiming to promote several fashion showings in different Italian cities in competition with Giorgini.[123]

Representing Turin's EIM, Vladimiro Rossini had attended the Second Italian High Fashion Show in Florence on 19–21 July 1951. When interviewed about it for an Italian radio broadcast, Rossini affirmed that his response to the Show was

> excellent, I dare to say enthusiastic. We are in the atmosphere of an event of the outmost moral and economical importance. All our expectations have been widely exceeded ... And since you are asking for a genuine statement, I will tell you that truly all this result is due to the really brave and timely initiative of our good friend Giorgini ... I firmly believed [that the future is full of promises] because, after all, today was just the first step. The organization of these conventions will be surely developed and fine-tuned season after season.[124]

Rossini's comments, broadcasted on the radio programme *Voci dal mondo* on 22 July, sounded quite enthusiastic and celebratory, in contrast to the reportedly bitter rivalry that would characterize the relationship between Turin and Florence in the span of a few months. The establishment of the Italian Fashion Service was advertised by both EIM and CIMM, the latter scheduling the showing of Milanese fashion creators from 7 February and advertising it in American newspapers.[125] The director of CIMM at the time was Carmine Cialfi, the former secretary of the Federazione Nazionale Fascista dell'Abbigliamento (National Fascist Clothing Federation), who had since 1945 occupied the same position within the newly formed Associazione Italiana degli Industriali dell'Abbigliamento.[126] During Fascism, Cialfi had been chief editor of the Federation's official publication, the monthly *L'Industria della Moda*, later renamed simply *Moda*, where he authored educational articles on the nature of fashion.[127] When he died in 1954, *Women's Wear Daily* remembered him as well-known to many United States fabric and clothing buyers, and as someone who 'played a major part in building up the prestige of Italian fashions. He organized many of Italy's biggest fashion shows and taught export "know-how" to boutiques that had previously concentrated solely on the domestic market'.[128] Not long before, Giorgini, Rossini, and Cialfi held professional positions and business relationships with the Fascist government. It is noteworthy that these men were responsible for promoting Italian fashion abroad for several years. This is particularly significant since the president of CIMM was Dino Alfieri, a former head of the Ministry of Popular Culture under the Fascist regime and Italian Ambassador to Berlin from 1940 to 1943.

This internal rivalry among Italian committees displayed a certain animosity, as it had been pointed out by *Women's Wear Daily* in 1950. Obtaining control of the main fashion events in Italy was so valuable that, following Giorgini's Second Show of 1951, Rossini sent an embittered report to the Ministry of Industry and Foreign Commerce lamenting the inappropriateness of Giorgini's leadership in the Italian High Fashion Shows:

> In February of this year, a Florentine commissionaire firm, Soc. G.B. Giorgini, piazza Santa Trinità 1, imitating the aforementioned original project, invited some of its American clients to take a look, in Florence, at some high fashion models created by a selected group of Italian firms … [It] was held in Italy, so to speak, on the sly, but it was represented abroad with the title 'Second Italian High Fashion Show', which created the wrong impression that [the Show] was to be considered an official event and organized with the cooperation of all the best Italian high fashion enterprises.

As previously discussed in Chapter 5, EIM had originally planned an Italian fashion show for international buyers in 1950, the 'aforementioned original project' cited by Rossini whose plans fell through due to lack of funds.[129] The fact that the Shows were carried out by a private organization was not appreciated by the two main fashion agencies, EIM and CIMM, active since the end of the war with the same purpose of promoting Italian fashion merchandise and couture abroad. Even if EIM and CIMM received some financial support and patronage from the government, their Italian Fashion Service and collective showings were short-lived, since by early 1952 their efforts had 'collapsed'.[130] In just two years, EIM would eventually join forces with Giorgini and jointly assume the patronage of the Italian High Fashion Shows, while Giorgini would become vice-president of EIM and serve on the board of CIMM.[131]

Strategical alliances with textile manufacturers, plus the moral and financial support of acquaintances in Florence greatly aided Giorgini in establishing a new council, the Centro di Firenze per la Moda Italiana (Florence Centre for Italian Fashion). As explained in detail by business historian Valeria Pinchera, the Centro was established in 1954 to join private and public forces in the enhancement and preservation of the Shows in Florence.[132] As stockholders were, besides Giorgini, various local public administration bodies, it is not surprising that Mario Vannini Parenti was elected as the Centro's president in 1954 and remained linked to its promotional activities until the beginning of the 1960s.[133] Further proof of this eventual fashion connection between the two intermediaries is a photo shoot, taken during the Thirteenth Italian High Fashion Show of 1957, in which Giorgini and Vannini Parenti hosted the First Lady of Italy Carla Gronchi (Figure 6.6).

The need to find unity in the fragmented scenario of the Italian fashion councils prevailed, at least on paper, but critiques of Giorgini had hardly been spared. To those critiques he often replied through the press, to keep a firm grasp on his US clients. Graziani's article in *Paris Match* was a benevolent instance of publicity that was reportedly read by all American buyers in Paris who had just come back from Florence. It significantly helped Giorgini reaffirm that his Shows were the most convenient way to tour the Italian fashion market of the time.[134] The letter sent by Graziani to Giorgini after the Third Show demonstrates that the French journalist had been welcomed by Giorgini, his family, and his associates with the courtesies extended *de ritu* to the most important visitors. Yet, the opening picture of the article emphasized the hype surrounding Giorgini's Shows: it depicted a photographer lying down on the ground facing Florence's cathedral while taking a picture of a model, as several onlookers surround the scene at due distance.

Commenting on Graziani's review in *Women's Wear Daily*, veteran fashion correspondent B.J. Perkins defined Graziani's piece as 'analytical, not unfriendly' and quoted his mention of Giorgini being 'the Christopher Columbus of the Italian couturiers. For them, he discovered America and its markets. Yet, he ignores everything about fashion'.[135] While the book has clearly established that Giorgini was acquainted with the trends of the international fashion scene, it is important to notice that such a statement added a fortuitous character to his intuition. And while this addendum contributed to the mythical characterization of Giorgini through time, Graziani impartially praised the strategic organization of his clients' stayings while in Florence. In so doing, his article claimed that the problem for French couture professionals was that Italians could offer better value for money to American buyers.[136]

6.6 Mario Vannini Parenti, First Lady of Italy Donna Carla Gronchi, and Giovanni Battista Giorgini. Thirteenth Italian High Fashion Show, 23 January 1957.
© Archivio Foto Locchi Firenze

The war between Italian and French couturiers seemed, however, to have been constructed for the sake of keeping alive an already stagnating market. Previous literature has largely missed the fictitious nature of the quarrel and instead misinterpreted the sources to produce a hagiographic narrative of the 'birth' of Italian fashion. This celebratory discourse was significantly promoted by journalist Guido Vergani in the exhibition catalogue *The Sala Bianca*. In the catalogue, the commendable purpose of merging primary sources with oral histories resulted in some occasional misrepresentations, as in the case of a *New York Times* article from 1952 that reportedly stated how there was 'no doubt that Florence is about to take the place of Paris'.[137] In fact, the original article had a completely different tone and instead reassured that 'Paris is still the style center'.[138] While it was titled 'Italian [read: Giorgini] is Praised for High Fashion', the byline stated: 'Florentine Exporter's Third Show a Success, but Paris is Still the Style Center.' Published in the business section of the newspaper, and not in the fashion pages, the article quoted Carmel Snow as saying that, despite the superlative fabrics, a marvellous sense of colour, and freshness of styles, 'for real creativity, we must still look to Paris'.[139]

French fashion creators weighed in on the supposed battle. On one hand, Elsa Schiaparelli was among those who denounced the clash as a move created by US buyers.[140] Such competition with Paris had 'been put in the Italian's mouth by someone else', she argued, hinting at the fact that American clients had all the interest to fuel a dispute that would stimulate the market.[141] The interview hints at how, to Schiaparelli, the appearance of foreign competitors in the already threatened Parisian market of *haute couture* contributed to making smaller fashion houses weaker and weaker.[142] On the other hand, Christian Dior would later point out in his biography how his trade relationships with Italy were fruitful and amicable. His friendship with Salvatore Ferragamo, which apparently started aboard the transatlantic that brought them to the United States in 1947 to receive the Neiman Marcus Award, reinforced this vision. In his biography, Dior confirmed his popularity among Italians as well: 'a world-wide public was marching in my direction, following the vanguard of the critics. The English followed the Americans; then came the Italians, who were excellent clients, giving the lie to the absurd myth of a Franco-Italian fashion war'.[143]

Notes

1 See page 138.
2 Archivio di Stato di Firenze, Archivio della Moda Italiana di Giovanni Battista Giorgini (hereafter ASF-AMIGBG), Album 2. G.B. Giorgini to Meyric R. Rogers, 29 August 1950.
3 See Chapter 2.
4 ASF-AMIGBG, Album 2. B. Altman (presumably James A. Keillor) to G.B. Giorgini, 11 October 1950.

5 ASF-AMIGBG, Album 2. G.B. Giorgini to B. Altman, 27 November 1950; ASF-AMIGBG, Album 2. G.B. Giorgini to James A. Keillor, 9 January 1951.

6 ASF-AMIGBG, Album 2. G.B. Giorgini to James A. Keillor, 9 January 1951.

7 'Italy's Growth as Source of Fashion Noted', *Women's Wear Daily* (23 August 1950), p. 2.

8 ASF-AMIGBG, Album 2. G.B. Giorgini to James A. Keillor, 9 January 1951.

9 E. Merlo and M. Perugini, 'The revival of fashion brands between marketing and history: The case of the Italian fashion company Pucci'. *Journal of Historical Research in Marketing* 7(1), 2015, pp. 91–112, 96; C. Faggella, 'Il nuovo Rinascimento della moda italiana: Ferragamo e il dopoguerra'. In *Salvatore Ferragamo 1898–1960*, edited by Stefania Ricci (Milan: Skira, 2023), pp. 482–89.

10 ASF-AMIGBG, Album 2. B. Altman & Co. to G.B. Giorgini, 15 January 1951. The letter is, interestingly, cut in half and its bottom part is missing.

11 ASF-AMIGBG, Album 2. G.B. Giorgini to Bartlett Morgan, 15 January 1951.

12 'Behind the Paris-California Entente Cordiale', *Women's Wear Daily* (9 January 1959), p. 18.

13 F. Steinmann Curtis, *Careers in the World of Fashion* (New York: Woman's Press, 1953), p. 238.

14 ASF-AMIGBG, Album 2. Ann Roberts to G.B. Giorgini, undated; 'Intl. Fashion Show Represents Eleven Nations', *Women's Wear Daily* (5 March 1951), p. 3.

15 G. Chesne Dauphiné Griffo, 'G.B. Giorgini: The Rise of Italian Fashion'. In *Italian Fashion: The Origins of High Fashion and Knitwear*, edited by Gloria Bianchino, Grazietta Butazzi, Alessandra Mottola Molfino, and Arturo Carlo Quintavalle (Milan: Electa, 1985), p. 67; G. Vergani, 'The Sala Bianca: The Birth of Italian Fashion'. In *The Sala Bianca: The Birth of Italian Fashion*, edited by Giannino Malossi (Milan: Electa, 1992), p. 47.

16 A. Friedman, 'Designer Hannah Troy Dead at 93', *Women's Wear Daily* (25 June 1993), p. 11.

17 'Coats and Suits: Leto, Cohn Join in New Concern', *Women's Wear Daily* (25 May 1939), p. 28.

18 'New York Fall Openings: Velvet Coats for New Fashion', *Women's Wear Daily* (7 June 1950), p. 3; 'Evening Wraps Again – Three Lengths for the Important Dress Types', *Women's Wear Daily* (21 September 1950), p. 3; 'New York Spring Openings: Fabrics Enhance Silhouettes', *Women's Wear Daily* (15 November 1950), p. 3.

19 ASF-AMIGBG, Album 2. G.B. Giorgini to John Nixon, undated [February 1951].

20 ASF-AMIGBG, Album 2. John Nixon to G.B. Giorgini, 2 February 1951.

21 A. Palmer, *Couture & Commerce: The Transatlantic Fashion Trade in the 1950s* (Vancouver: UBC Press, 2001), p. 72.

22 M. Cragg, 'Top Imported Fashions Feature of Morgan Show', *Globe and Mail* (15 March 1951), p. 15.

23 'American Film Stars Are Buying Wardrobes at Italian Dressmakers', *Women's Wear Daily* (22 July 1949), p. 4.

24 ASF-AMIGBG, Carteggio. G.B. Giorgini to Nella Giorgini, undated [2 February 1950].

25 G. Monti, 'Attraverso Uno Specchio Di Carta'. In *Bellissima. L'Italia Dell'Alta Moda 1945–1968*, edited by Maria Luisa Frisa, Anna Mattirolo, and Stefano Tonchi (Milan: Electa, 2014), pp. 34–39.

26 S. Cagol, 'Towards a Genealogy of the Thematic Contemporary Art Exhibition: Italian Exhibition Culture from the Mostra Della Rivoluzione Fascista (1932) to the Palazzo Grassi's Ciclo Della Vitalità (1959–1961)' (PhD Dissertation, Royal College of Art, 2013), p. 147.

27 The correspondence preserved in his personal archive proves that Giorgini had 'his own contact' in Milan within CIMM, though it is unclear who the person was and which position they had within CIMM.

28 Original in Italian: 'Non è vero che la Longo copi e sfrutti solo modelli francesi. I suoi abiti che hanno ottenuto il successo maggiore sono tutti abiti creati completamente da lei. Bista, se mi ascolti, lascia da una parte la San Lorenzo che è pacchiana e non vale la metà della Longo. Con tutto l'orgoglio di Italiano che mi batte col cuore, ti dico che con la Longo e con i Suoi modelli Torino e la moda Italiana hanno una "X MAS" ... I porti non saranno quelli di Alessandria o Gibilterra, ma i porti di Christian Dior e Jacques Fath, etc. ... riceveranno dei bravi duri colpi.' ASF-AMIGBG, Correspondence, Unknown sender to G.B. Giorgini, 11 May 1951. The Decima Flottiglia MAS or X MAS was a flotilla of the Italian Navy. After the armistice, its captain Junio Valerio Borghese and part of his sailors continued fighting with the Italian Social Republic (RSI). In the post-war years, the X MAS became a symbol of opposition to the Allies. Even today, it is an unmistakable sign of support for neo-fascism.
29 C. Evans, 'The Enchanted Spectacle'. *Fashion Theory* 5(3), 2001, pp. 271–310, 295.
30 B. Giordani Aragno, 'The Mirror's Role in the Atelier'. In *Italian Fashion: The Origins of High Fashion and Knitwear*, edited by Gloria Bianchino, Grazietta Butazzi, Alessandra Mottola Molfino, and Arturo Carlo Quintavalle (Milan: Electa, 1985), pp. 90–105.
31 ASF-AMIGBG, Carteggio. G.B. Giorgini to Nella Giorgini, undated [19 October 1950].
32 Palmer, *Couture & Commerce*, 123–24.
33 S. Stanfill, 'Anonymous Tastemakers: The Role of American Buyers in Establishing an Italian Fashion Industry, 1950–55'. In *European Fashion. The Creation of a Global Industry*, edited by Regina Lee Blaszczyk and Veronique Pouillard (Manchester: Manchester University Press, 2018), pp. 160–65.
34 Stanfill, 'Anonymous Tastemakers', 160–65.
35 'A Hectic Week of Paris Showings', *Life* 5 March 1951, p. 101.
36 Clelia Bruno Marzili to the author, 15 January 2018, Florence.
37 C. Faggella, 'Dietro Le Quinte Alla G.B. Giorgini. Le Assistant Buyers e l'esportazione Di Moda Italiana Negli Stati Uniti, 1946–1956'. In *Un Oceano Di Stile. Produzione e Consumo Di Made in Italy Negli Stati Uniti Del Dopoguerra*, edited by Simone Cinotto and Giulia Crisanti (Milan: Mimesis edizioni, 2023), pp. 163–80.
38 ASF-AMIGBG, Album 2. Sorelle Fontana to G.B. Giorgini, 13 January 1951.
39 S. Gnoli, *Un Secolo Di Moda Italiana, 1900–2000* (Rome: Meltemi Editore srl., 2005), pp. 141; Ivan Paris, *Oggetti Cuciti: L'abbigliamento Pronto in Italia Dal Primo Dopoguerra Agli Anni Settanta* (Milan: F. Angeli, 2006), p. 94; L. Settembrini, ed., *1951–2001 Made in Italy?* (Milan: Skira, 2001), p. 130.
40 As discussed in Chapter 1.
41 ASF-AMIGBG, Album 2. Bettina Ballard to G.B. Giorgini, 1 March 1951.
42 'Prices Higher, Buying Declines On Paris Styles', *Women's Wear Daily* (9 February 1951), pp. 1, 41.
43 Neri Fadigati to the author, 11 January 2018, Florence.
44 'From the Italian collections, casual clothes'. *Vogue* 1 September 1951; 'Italy Gets Dressed Up'. *Life* 20 August 1951, pp. 104–12.
45 S. Colonna di Cesarò, *Una Vita al Limite* (Venezia: Marsilio, 2008), pp. 51, 62.
46 'More Houses in Italian Showings in Milan, Rome', *Women's Wear Daily* (11 January 1952), p. 50.
47 I. Brin, *L'Italia Esplode. Diario Dell'anno 1952*. Edited by Claudia Palma (Rome: Viella, 2014), p. 54.
48 ASF-AMIGBG, Album 4. Valstar to G.B. Giorgini, 26 January 1952.
49 M. Armani, 'Moda e baruffe di casa nostra'. *La Scala* 15 February 1952.
50 V. Rossi Lodomez, 'La moda italiana precede le collezioni parigine'. *Grazia* 26 January 1952.
51 ASF-AMIGBG, Album 4. Carmel Snow to G.B. Giorgini, 18 January 1952.
52 'Special Train to Florence', *Women's Wear Daily* (11 January 1952), p. 50.

53 '$100 Admission Fee for Fashion Show in Florence Is Set', *Women's Wear Daily* (17 June 1952), p. 56.

54 '$100 Admission Fee for Fashion Show in Florence Is Set'.

55 D.L. Wallis, 'No Nonsense – By D.L.W.', *Women's Wear Daily* (29 July 1952), p. 1.

56 'Italy. Collections Bubbling With Ideas'. *Vogue* 15 March 1953, p. 77.

57 ASF-AMIGBG, Album 3. International News Photos picture, original with byline, undated.

58 M. Cattaneo, 'Da Firenze la Moda Trova la Via dell'America'. *Bellezza* April 1951, p. 49.

59 F. Engle, 'More Return From Visit to Paris Openings', *Women's Wear Daily* (1 March 1951), p. 14.

60 ASF-AMIGBG, Album 5. Russel D. Carpenter to G.B. Giorgini, 26 September 1952.

61 M. Barnett, 'Spectacular Italian Clothes Rely on Fabric, Ornamentation', *Los Angeles Mirror* (4 September 1952).

62 Specific examples included gowns by Emilio Schuberth and Carosa.

63 ASF-AMIGBG, Album 5. Russel D. Carpenter to G.B. Giorgini, 26 September 1952.

64 L. Barnes, 'Hudson's Launches Italian Couture Fashions in U.S.A.', *Women's Wear Daily* (19 September 1949), p. 1.

65 'Play Clothes'. *Life* 7 July 1947, pp. 43–45.

66 R. Arnold, *The American Look: Fashion, Sportswear and the Image of Women in 1930s and 1940s* (New York: I.B. Tauris, 2009), pp. 75–103.

67 E. Massai, 'Italian Styles Gain Approval of U.S. Buyers', *Women's Wear Daily* (15 February 1951), p. 1.

68 Palmer, *Couture & Commerce*, 15–16.

69 C.M. Belfanti, 'Renaissance and "Made in Italy": Marketing Italian Fashion through History (1949–1952)'. *Journal of Modern Italian Studies* 20(1), 2015, pp. 53–66; C.M. Belfanti, 'History as an Intangible Asset for the Italian Fashion Business (1950–1954)'. *Journal of Historical Research in Marketing* 7(1), 2015, pp. 74–90.

70 J. Burckhardt, 1937. *The Civilization of the Renaissance in Italy* (London: Routledge, 2019).

71 Belfanti, 'History as an Intangible Asset for the Italian Fashion Business (1950–1954)', 76.

72 'Fashion Group Hears New York-Paris Trends', *Women's Wear Daily* (15 December 1949), p. 3.

73 'Baroque Sculpture Theme of Pauline's Fall Collection', *Women's Wear Daily* (14 July 1949), p. 3; 'Fashion Significances', *Women's Wear Daily* (23 December 1949), p. 3.

74 Stephen Gundle has discussed at large the popularity of film star Tyrone Power in Italy: see D. Forgacs and S. Gundle. *Mass Culture and Italian Society from Fascism to the Cold War* (Bloomington: Indiana University Press, 2007), pp. 163–64; S. Gundle, *Glamour: A History* (Oxford: Oxford University Press, 2008), pp. 204–05. According to Gundle, though, the popularity of Tyrone Power declined drastically after his 1949 wedding to Linda Christian: Stephen Gundle, 'Memory and Identity: Popular Culture in Postwar Italy'. In *Italy since 1945*, ed. Patrick McCarthy (Oxford: Oxford University Press, 2000), pp. 183–96.

75 'Slim Black at Film Premiere', *Women's Wear Daily* (27 December 1949), p. 3.

76 'Designers Develop Adaptations of Italian Styles in New Movie', *Women's Wear Daily* (5 October 1949), p. 3. Costume designer Vittorio Nino Novarese was nominated for an Academy Award in 1950 for his work on this movie.

77 'Designers Develop Adaptations of Italian Styles in New Movie'.

78 'Holy Year Will Not Influence Fashion Design Says Lanvin', *Women's Wear Daily* (31 January 1950), p. 3.

79 R.L. Pisetzky, *Il Costume e La Moda Nella Società Italiana* (Torino: G. Einaudi, 1978), p. 356; E. Paulicelli, *Rosa Genoni, La Moda è Una Cosa Seria: Milano, Expo 1906 e La Grande Guerra* (Rome: Deleyva editore, 2015).

80 R. Genoni, *Per Una Moda Italiana. Relazione al I° Congresso Nazionale Delle Donne Italiane in Roma* (Milan: Tipografia Ercole Balzaretti, 1908), p. 12.

81 Genoni, *Per Una Moda Italiana*, 12.

82 Genoni, *Per Una Moda Italiana*, 12.

83 Frances Keene, 'The New Italy'. *Harper's Bazaar* July 1947, p. 31.

84 Marya Mannes, 'Italy Looks Ahead'. *House & Garden* June 1947, p. 92. For an interesting study on the role of Gio Ponti in creating the commercial image of Italian design in the United States see Dellapiana, 'Italy Creates'.

85 Marya Mannes, 'The Fine Italian Hand'. *Vogue UK* September 1946, p. 45.

86 Mannes, 'Italy Looks Ahead', 92.

87 Mannes, 'Italy Looks Ahead', 141.

88 C. Baskins and S. Bottinelli, '"La Casa va Con La Città": Lorenzo the Magnificent and the Arts, 1949'. *California Italian Studies* 7(1), 2017, p. 4.

89 W. Dorwin Teague, 'Italy at work: record of a journey'. *Interiors* November 1950, p. 198.

90 ASF-AMIGBG, Album 2. G.B. Giorgini to Charles Nagel, 5 October 1950.

91 The invitation card refers to it as *Maddalena Strozzi*, according to an attribution later disputed.

92 The cover of the invitation cards for the Second Show featured Raffaello Sanzio's *Portrait of Doña Isabel de Requesens y Enríquez de Cardona-Anglesola*; for the Third Show, Sandro Botticelli's depiction of Giovanna Tornabuoni in *Venus and the Three Graces Presenting Gifts to a Young Woman* from the Villa Lemmi frescoes.

93 For a more detailed investigation of this aspect of Giorgini's professional biography, see C. Faggella, 'Before 1951: Setting up the Network of G.B. Giorgini and the Launch of Made in Italy'. *Italian American Review*, 14(1), 2024, pp. 95–109.

94 Meyric R. Rogers, *Italy at Work. Her Renaissance in Design Today* (Rome: Compagnia Nazionale Artigiana, 1950), p. 18. Emphasis mine.

95 Rogers, *Italy at Work*, 62.

96 ASF-AMIGBG, Album 2. G.B. Giorgini to Meyric R. Rogers, 15 September 1950.

97 M. Campbell, 'Hard Times in Baroque Florence: The Boboli Garden and the Grand Ducal Public Works Administration'. In *The Italian Garden: Art, Design and Culture*, edited by John Dixon Hunt (Cambridge: Cambridge University Press, 1996), pp.160–201, 162.

98 E. Kuster Rosselli, 'Alle sorgenti dell'artigianato fiorentino'. *Bellezza* May 1947, p. 4.

99 F. Hammond, 'Boboli Ball Attracts Fashion Press, Buyers and Society', *Los Angeles Times* (4 September 1952), part III, p. 1.

100 S. Bernasconi, 'Antico e Nuovo a Firenze'. *Arbiter* 163, 1953, pp. 38–40.

101 A. Fiorentini Capitani and S. Ricci, 'The Winning Card of Italian Fashion'. In *The Sala Bianca: The Birth of Italian Fashion* (Milan: Electa, 1992), pp. 91–130, 96.

102 G. Vergani, 'February 1951. Italian Fashion Is Born. Not Even Mussolini Succeeded in Accomplishing as Much'. In *1951–2001: Made in Italy?*, edited by Luigi Settembrini (Milan: Skira, 2001), pp. 130–41; N. Fadigati, 'Giovanni Battista Giorgini, La Famiglia, Il Contributo Alla Nascita Del Made in Italy, Le Fonti Archivistiche'. *ZoneModa Journal* 8(1), 2018, pp. 1–15.

103 G.C. Fusco, 'Dietro Tante Donne C'è Quest'Uomo', *Europeo* 5 February 1953.

104 Fusco, 'Dietro Tante Donne C'è Quest'Uomo'.

105 Stanfill, 'Anonymous Tastemakers'.

106 C. Evans, *The Mechanical Smile: Modernism and the First Fashion Shows in France and America, 1900–1929* (New Haven: Yale University Press, 2013), p. 165.

107 ASF-AMIGBG, Album 3. Brochure for the Second Italian High Fashion Show, 19–21 July 1951.

108 ASF-AMIGBG, Album 3. Brochure for the Second Italian High Fashion Show.

109 B.J. Perkins, 'Interest Lag At Showings in Italy Claimed', *Women's Wear Daily* (30 January 1952), p. 21.

110 Gilbert Graziani, 'Voici les premiers modèles de la mode nouvelle'. *Paris Match* 2 February 1952, pp. 35–37.

111 Original in French: 'Paris reste la citadelle de la mode. L'attaquer serait stupide. Nous avons plus que de l'admiration pour vos grands couturiers. A côte d'eux, nous sommes des pygmées. Que l'on s'émeuve de nos créations nous étonne: c'est comme si une armée de géants prenait peur à la vue d'un nourrisson. Mais, nous aussi, nous travaillons et voulons lancer notre haute couture et nos textiles sur le marché mondial. Nous avons beaucoup d'atouts en main et nous en profiterons. Nous voulons mordre aussi au gâteau américain. Quoi de plus normal?'

112 The verb 'mordre au' connotes the further meaning of 'becoming an expert of', 'getting interested in'.

113 Simonetta Visconti and Alberto Fabiani, who deserted the Florentine Show of January 1952, had reportedly requested an entrance fee the see their collections in Rome. The showings were held simultaneously and in competition with the Third Italian High Fashion Show. While buyers did not pay to attend the first three Italian High Fashion Shows, the fashion houses and manufacturers that participated as exhibitors did pay a commission to Giorgini, which in 1951 amounted to 25,000 lire. The fee requested by G.B. Giorgini to buyers in July 1952 was $100.

114 B.J. Perkins, 'Buying Conservative, Prices High as Paris Openings Start', *Women's Wear Daily* (6 August 1947), pp. 1, 3.

115 'Offering by Couture Not Due to Revive Second Lines', *Women's Wear Daily* (26 August 1947), p. 8.

116 Original in French: 'La couture sport et le genre « boutique »: les petites robes pratiques, les pull-overs, les jupes, les imperméables et les accessoires: gants, sacs et chaussures, sont les atouts de la suprématie italienne dans ce domaine. Les grands couturiers le savent bien, qui vendent ces créations à Paris même, dans leurs boutiques.' Graziani, 'Voici les premiers modèles de la mode nouvelle', 36.

117 Graziani, 'Voici les premiers modèles de la mode nouvelle', 36.

118 See Chapter 3.

119 Original in French: 'Cette tendance de la haute mode n'étant pas exploitée en France, je souhaiterais, pour une exposition italienne que nus préparons au mois de mai, étudier s'il ne serait pas possible de faire rentrer des marchandises de cette conception.' ASF-AMIGBG, Album 6. J. d'Allens to G.B. Giorgini, 7 February 1953. D'Allens and a representative for Au Bon Marché had visited Florence during the Fifth Italian High Fashion Show of January 1953.

120 Graziani, 'Voici les premiers modèles de la mode nouvelle', 36.

121 At the beginning of 1950, the branch office was in via Ugo Foscolo, close to Galleria Vittorio Emanuele and the Duomo, while in 1952 the office had moved to via Cerva, near Piazza San Babila. ASF-AMIGBG, Carteggio. Head letter G.B. Giorgini, 3 February 1950.

122 ASF-AMIGBG, Carteggio. Head Letter G.B. Giorgini.

123 E. Robiola (uncredited), 'Ogni passione spenta'. *Marie Claire* 16 February 1952.

124 ASF-AMIGBG, Album 3. Unspecified transcript of radio broadcast, 22 July 1951.

125 'Italian Stylists Get Spring Jump', *Chicago Daily News* (16 January 1952).

126 Decreto Ministeriale 17 gennaio, 1920, 'Approvazione della nomina del segretario della Federazione nazionale fascista dell'abbigliamento', *Gazzetta Ufficiale del Regno d'Italia* (parte prima) (22 January 1929), p. 367.

127 R. Carrarini and M. Giordano, *Bibliografia Dei Periodici Femminili Lombardi (1786– 1945)* (Milan: Lampi di stampa, 2003), p. 191; M. Lupano and A. Vaccari, *Fashion at the Time of Fascism: Italian Modernist Lifestyle 1922–1943* (Bologna: Damiani Editore, 2009), p. 382.

128 'Carmine Cialfi', *Women's Wear Daily* (19 October 1954), p. 22.

129 See page 153.

130 B.J. Perkins, 'Milan Showing of Fashions Is Abandoned', *Women's Wear Daily* (17 January 1952), p. 4.

131 'Dr. Furio Cicogna Named Head of Ente della Moda', *Women's Wear Daily* (22 January 1953), p. 2.
132 V. Pinchera, 'I provvedimenti per la ripresa economica nel secondo dopoguerra. Promozione e sostegno della moda italiana (1945–1970)'. In *L'intervento dello Stato nell'Economia Italiana: continuità e cambiamenti (1922–1956)*, edited by Alberto Cova and Gianpiero Fumi (Milan: FrancoAngeli, 2011), pp. 485–514, 500.
133 E. Greco, 'L'Attività Culturale di Mario Vannini Parenti (1887–1983)' (Research paper, Università di Firenze, 2010–11), p. 98.
134 B.J. Perkins, 'Interest Lag At Showings in Italy Claimed', *Women's Wear Daily* (30 January 1952), p. 21.
135 Perkins, 'Interest Lag At Showings in Italy Claimed'; Graziani, 'Voici les premiers modèles de la mode nouvelle'.
136 Graziani, 'Voici les premiers modèles de la mode nouvelle'.
137 Vergani, 'The Sala Bianca', 43; Vergani, 'February 1951. Italian Fashion Is Born', 138.
138 'Italian is Praised for High Fashions', *New York Times* (29 January 1952), p. 28.
139 'Italian is Praised for High Fashions'.
140 'Schiaparelli Charges That Italian Fashions Hitting Hard-up Paris Below Belt', *Daily Argus Leader* (28 January 1952), p. 3.
141 'Schiaparelli Charges That Italian Fashions Hitting Hard-up Paris Below Belt'.
142 J. Zanon, 'The 'Sleeping Beauties' of Haute Couture: Jean Patou, Elsa Schiaparelli, Madeleine Vionnet' (PhD Dissertation, University of Oslo, 2017), p. 138.
143 C. Dior, *Christian Dior and I* (New York: E.P. Dutton & Company, 1957), p. 50.

Conclusion

The year 1953 ended with the announcement by *Women's Wear Daily* that, at the request of American buyers and by the Italian Ministry of Foreign Commerce, the individual shows of Roman dressmakers and couturiers for the 1954 spring–summer collections would anticipate the Florentine Shows.[1] That same year *Italy at Work* came to an end, having inspired similar travelling exhibitions in the United States[2] and in the rest of Europe.[3] While the Florentine Shows had undoubtedly established a successful practice of collective exhibitions and a recurring date for the benefit of international buyers, they certainly suffered from several drawbacks from the beginning. In 1955 the American market recognized the existence of two systematized showings, the Florentine ones and those organized in Rome by the Sindacato Italiano Alta Moda, founded by the Roman couturiers who forfeited the Florence circuit of promotion.[4] In the same year, the firm G.B. Giorgini printed a special calendar of 1956 to be distributed as a Christmas gift to clients and collaborators. Designed as a booklet, each month contains a short text telling the story of eleven elegant Italian women (and one man) through the centuries. From Camisene, 'The Etruscan Bride' whose comfortable and elegant dress became the traditional costume adopted by the ancient Romans, to a celebration of 'Amaranta' and the demure elegance of Giuseppina Giorgi Mancini as portrayed by her lover Gabriele D'Annunzio, this little *Calendario Giorgini* offers another example of the persistent rhetoric that celebrates the innate, timeless elegance that has been the prerogative of Italians for centuries. The booklet concludes with a quip on the key role of the Shows in Palazzo Pitti, which stimulated and preserved the same tradition with which '[i]nspiration from art, the study of silhouettes, harmony, taste, and refinement continue – in Florence, of Florence, the glorious past in the history of fashion'.[5] From today's point of view, and especially after the contextualization of the many issues encountered by Giorgini in organizing the Shows, the *Calendario* acquires a deeper historiographical meaning.

The years that followed were complicated by quarrels among designers, councils, and promoters, which deeply affected Giorgini's management of the Shows and his own health, and eventually led him to resign in 1965, sensing that the couture market was heading into its final throes.[6] The engraving of a sundial on the first page of the *Calendario* and the accompanying Latin motto 'horas non numero nisi serenas' (I only count the serene hours, Figure 7.1), then, evoke the success obtained with the Shows through the years and the will to remember the positive aspects associated with a business initiative that was nonetheless consuming. In hindsight, the sundial foreshadows also the formation of what would become Giorgini's scrapbooks and private archive, constructed event after event by Giorgini himself and his collaborators with at least two specific goals: to emphasize his vast network of connections with international personalities, firms, and businesses, and to memorialize his biographical details and activities, both personal and work-related, 'to have an all-around picture, projected over time'.[7] By selecting the documents to be preserved and, later, used to reconstruct the story of his success to posterity, the reluctance displayed by his daughter Matilde in allowing his private archive to be openly accessible is understandable, as she was supposedly afraid of external judgement over a complex archival source that encompasses successes and controversies alike, as in every business.[8] Concerning this aspect, this book has analyzed Giorgini's involvement with *Italy at Work* from the point of view of the exhibition's organizers and reframed it accordingly, making the Giorgini archive a relevant case study to demonstrate the need for the historical criticism advocated by Marc Bloch and the use of multiple sources, since '[d]espite what beginners sometimes seem to imagine, documents do not suddenly materialize, in one place or another, as if by some mysterious decree of the gods. Their presence or absence in the depths of this archive or that library are due to human causes which by no means elude analysis'.[9]

At the same time, the meaning of the Latin motto found in the *Calendario* mirrors the early historiographical attitude demonstrated towards Giorgini's pioneering role that, as has been the case with other exceptional figures such as Emilio Pucci, followed 'the approach centered on the outstanding founder' and overlooked for too long the usefulness of the Giorgini archive in the study of the Italian fashion industry as a whole.[10] Therefore, Giorgini's role is uniquely fascinating as he was not a fashion designer, the professionals whose biographies have long been the focus within fashion history. It is only since the past two decades or so that studies on the designers' roles have been integrated with those 'retailers, buyers, commissionaires, forecasters, photographers, sketchers, and journalists' who took part in the transatlantic circuits of exchanges between Europe

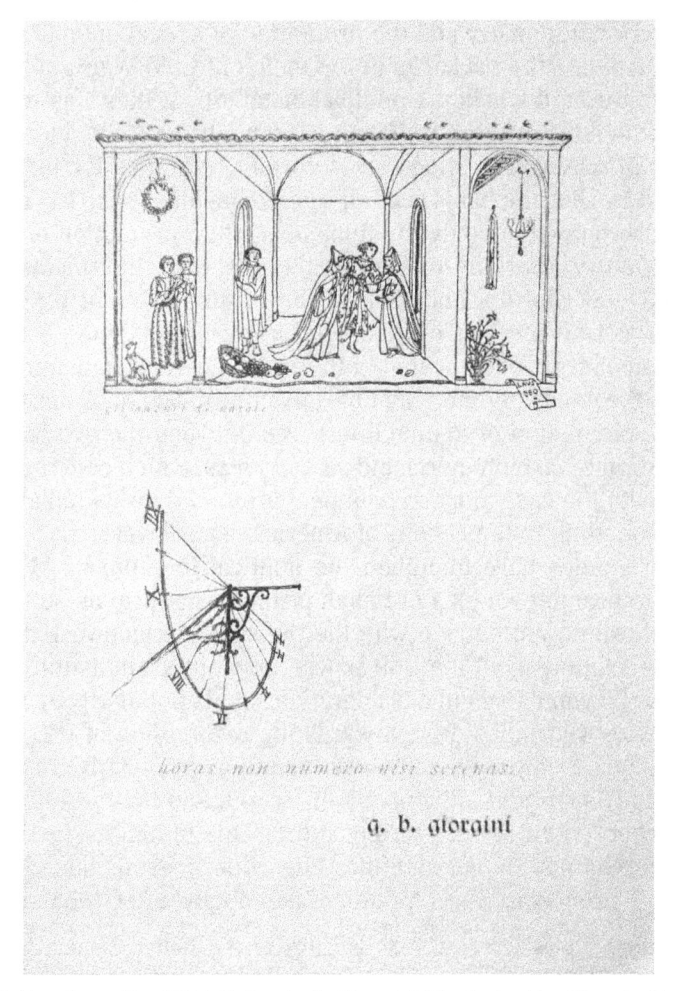

7.1 Inscription from the 1956 *Calendario Giorgini*. Illustrated by Giorgio Perfetti

and the United States.[11] With the establishment of the Italian High Fashion Shows, the G.B. Giorgini firm started to be recognized as a brand that, thanks to the publicity and press exposure it received, would later venture into manufacturing partnerships as the 1960s Japanese-Italian company Lucrezia.[12] Following the examples and the approaches of previous scholarship in the new business history of fashion, this book has thus historicized, as intended by historian Pierre-Yves Saunier, Giovanni Battista Giorgini's contribution in the larger context of all the transatlantic actors that, immediately after the Second World War, were striving to promote and export Italian fashion merchandise first and Italian couture later.

The efforts of many other private groups of professionals such as the HDI–CADMA–CNA conglomerate outline the connections between the

Italian handicraft industry and the promotion of a local independent fashion scene. Against the backdrop of the incipient Cold War and the fear of Bolshevism through which the political instability of Italy was seen by the US press, the advancement of Italian artisans through the agencies kickstarted by Max Ascoli provides an important reference for the narrative established by Giorgini in his fashion-related business post-1951, of which *Italy at Work* represents only the final step in the promotion of Italy as a valuable country of origin for fashion merchandise. Intermediaries such as CADMA and Giorgini emphasized the critical value of direction and feedback received by their clients, used in the production of items that, through constant practice, would both reflect a certain Italianness and be suitable to the needs of American final customers. The book has thus highlighted the circulation of mutual influences between the two countries in the circulation of fashion merchandise and ideas, which concretized more evidently with the case of *moda boutique*, promoted for its Italianness and still corresponding to the canons of American sportswear.

Recent studies have identified the political intentions of Giorgini in its efforts to promote an idea of Italian fashion as a form of 'soft power',[13] although these do not engage with the theoretical framework that comes with the developments of the 'soft power' concept, from its introduction[14] to David W. Ellwood's recent considerations on its popularity in contemporary debates.[15] Giorgini's drive towards the recognition of Italian fashion abroad can be considered a 'soft power ambition' in an early era of the projection of Italy's cultural influence in the world, and therefore the concept of 'soft power' might not be entirely appropriate in his case.[16] Within this perspective, Sonnet Stanfill identifies one of the reasons that contributed to electing Florence as Italy's 'premier fashion city' after 1951 as

> the United States Government's support of the Italian fashion industry; in diplomatic circles, encouraging a flourishing fashion sector was part of an American political strategy to deter communism in Italy. Members of the United States Foreign Service advocated on behalf of the Florence fashion events as part of a wider effort to re-establish Italy as an American economic and political ally.[17]

The representations of Italy as a fashionable and independent player that circulated in the American fashion press undoubtedly helped the cause of the United States in its international battle against Communism. This aspect was nevertheless of the utmost importance for other organizations, besides and before Giorgini's, who sought after the patronage of influential American citizens and members of the diplomatic community in the promotion of their fashion events. One example is the fashion show organized by CIMM during the Venice Film Festival of 1949, during which the Ambassador of the United States to Italy James C. Dunn and his wife were photographed while enjoying the reception and attending the show (Figure 7.2). Dunn was often photographed for the society column of the

Italian magazine *Bellezza*: in that same year, for instance, he had been a guest in Cortina and photographed with the PR manager of the Cortina municipality, Romeo Manaigo.[18] At the same time, the efforts of Carlo Ludovico Ragghianti and Mario Vannini Parenti for CADMA and the HDI and HIH staff in New York systematically included ways of reaching out to politicians and diplomats whose presence could hallmark the worthiness and the quality of the proposed events, an attitude chiefly represented by the repeated involvement of Ivan Matteo Lombardo, Carlo Sforza, and Alberto Tarchiani.

In this and other instances, the book has highlighted a series of continuities. By mapping out several of the professional intermediaries that contributed to the legitimization of Italian fashion designs as couture, the book has demonstrated that the postwar years provide a vantage point to spot the continuity between professional appointments in important roles and individuals formerly associated with Fascism, as seen with Mario Vannini Parenti of CADMA; Giorgini himself, a former active member of the National Fascist Party; of Vladimiro Rossini and Dino Alfieri of EIM; and Carmine Cialfi of CIMM and Italian Fashion Service. Historian Claudio Fogu has argued that if 'Italians in the postwar era were successful at reinventing themselves as anti-fascist, it was not only by forgetting that

7.2 Ambassador of the United States to Italy James C. Dunn and his wife (on the left) photographed at the Venice Film Festival. *Bellezza*, October 1949. By permission of the Ministry of Culture – Pinacoteca di Brera – Biblioteca Braidense, Milan

they (or a majority of them) *ever were* fascist but also by transfiguring the historical imaginary they had absorbed under the regime'.[19] Flipping Ascoli's 1944 observation according to which '[t]he Allies thought that they could rely, at least for a while, on the civil and the local administration, or on those people who may be called civic or business leaders. They found themselves faced with a situation where Fascism was everywhere and the Fascists were nowhere',[20] we might say that, by the mid-1950s, Fascism might have been overruled, but 'Fascists' were still around and often in pivotal roles, and that former affiliations with the Fascist regime and its apparatuses were more common than we might expect.

Outlining the earliest appearances of discourses surrounding an 'Italian fashion scene' in US magazines *Vogue* and *Harper's Bazaar*, the book has charted the attributes describing a collective identity of Italian fashion exports and highlighting the attention on discourses over simplicity and ingenuity. With the early instances of the Florence Shows, on the other hand, several press reports of the time emphasized the elaborateness of Italian designs as something peculiar to certain designers, privately discouraged by American buyers. The 1954 autumn-winter Roman fashion showings were commented on in a special fashion column for the *New York Times*, noticing that '[w]ith the notable but hardly unexpected exception of Schuberth, the trend here is much more toward simplicity. Beading, fringes, tassels, and appliqués that once characterized Italian fashion have been dispensed with in favor of new richly woven tweeds and woolens and glorious autumn color'.[21] In fact, while the opinions of the US press on the stylistic qualities of Italian couture creations were mixed, the idea of a simple Italian elegance was a discourse that had originated in the late 1940s, exemplified by the reports by Bettina Ballard, Marya Mannes, and Frances Keene, whose circulation in connection with the Italian High Fashion Shows was mainly linked to the sports-, resort-, and knitwear shown in the *moda boutique* collections. Here the reception of mutual influences between American buyers and Italian designers and manufacturers concretized with a considerable commercial success, as the garments embodied the required exotic feeling of a European luxury import but corresponded nonetheless to the canons of US sportswear and the 'uncluttered' style of the American look, detailed by Rebecca Arnold, so adamantly promoted by Lord & Taylor's Dorothy Shaver.[22] In relation to this, *moda boutique* highlighted an additional element of continuity between Fascism and democracy that impacted on the fashion merchandise exported, especially visible in the selection presented during *Italy at Work* and demonstrating a similar penchant for transformability as the practical, transformable garments often seen in *Bellezza* during the last years of the Second World War and evoking the modernity of late 1930s clothing. The *Italy at Work* exhibition aimed to convey an experience to American visitors, modelled to resemble a tour of the numerous artisan workshops found throughout Italy. The curators and the organizers systematically utilized symbols and signs to construct a representation believed to align with the average American tourist gaze while visiting Italy.[23]

Keeping in mind the quote from Arturo Carlo Quintavalle cited in the Introduction, this book demonstrates that the Italian High Fashion Shows were not so much an ingenious intuition but rather the consolidation of trends and sentiments that invested several Italian intermediaries and trade professionals at the time. Correspondence and business documents separated from the Shows' scrapbooks in the Giorgini archive provided several insights into the trademarks of the Tuscan commissionaire. His connections with the United States were built through years of continuous contact with the overseas market, but also through a network of acquaintances developed through his family and his religious affiliation with the Protestant communities. In Italy, his contacts with both the local Florentine artisans and those in other districts, such as the glass and lace ones in Veneto or the silk manufacturers in Como, constituted the basis of his offer for US buyers. Most of all, the trait that comes out most vividly is his will to pursue business opportunities despite adverse economic configurations, as had been the case with Le Tre Stanze. The bankruptcy did not stop Giorgini from continuing to ask for loans (quite the contrary) and attempting to resurrect his original retail concept of a mini department store chain based on the finest, and thus the most expensive, handicrafts of Italy. A similar enterprise was made possible in the aftermath of the Second World War. With the presence of the Allied Forces in Florence since the summer of 1944, the possibility of resuming trade was presented to Giorgini through his management of the Allied Gift Shop, a retail space dedicated exclusively to the US military troops and their allies. This case history of such specific fashion-related shopping is a complex and unexplored theme peculiar to wartime, a practice largely destined to what Giorgini had called the 'kind custom of the gift' from soldiers to wives, girlfriends, mother and sisters, and a largely ignored vehicle for Italian fashion merchandise to reach the United States. Most importantly, the Gift Shop allowed Giorgini to set aside the capital needed to resume his commissionaire duties and his travels to the United States, at a moment in which several other notable import–export firms were also reprising their activities. In the late 1940s, the acquisition of Henry Morgan in Canada and B. Altman in New York brought two significantly fashion-savvy clients into Giorgini's portfolio, while the brokering of textiles put him and his buyers in contact with fashion designers, as in the case of Adele Simpson. Eventually, the circumstances that brought Giorgini to cross paths with Meyric R. Rogers and the organization of *Italy at Work* provided an interesting occasion to gather all his contacts in Italy, establish new ones, and put to use his expertise in the transatlantic trade, becoming the leading firm in the brokerage of Northern Italy's fashion-related merchandise to the United States and Canada. By collating the available sources in the Giorgini archive and further references found in newspapers, magazines, and other institutions' archives, the book explains that Giorgini's claim of his involvement with *Italy at Work* was not so much a forgery or a fabrication, but rather represented a key narrative element used in promotions that contextualized his firm's up-to-date monitoring of the cultural and commercial influences within the transatlantic market.

However, Giorgini was not the only one interested in the promotion of Italian couture and fashion merchandise after the Second World War. Up until 1950, it was CIMM that was in charge of most of the events that promoted Italian couture internationally and, specifically with the Venice Film Festival fashion showings, in attempts to reach the United States. Collective fashion shows were thus not so uncommon in Italy before 1951, and neither were those catering to foreign markets. Additionally, US department stores seemed to gradually accept the idea of an 'Italian couture', spearheaded by J.L. Hudson's Italian collection of 1949, an instance which contributed to increasing the interest of both retailers and manufacturers towards Italian dressmakers. The legitimacy was eventually sealed with the publication of an advertisement (Figure 7.3) by ENIT, the Italian State Tourist Office, in glossy American magazines, officially promoting '[a] reason in itself for visiting Italy ... the exciting new Italian couture'. Spurred by the interesting opportunities created by the textile industry as had been the case of Hudson's Italian couture collection of 1949, arguably modelled against the French model of *couture en gros*, more and more department stores, specialty stores, and fashion manufacturers tapped the dense Italian map of suppliers. The acknowledgement of the 'Italian couture' in the United States resulted in Italian fashion houses' sartorial productions getting purchased by specialty shops, replicated in the garment industry, and having journalists and trendsetters promoting their creativity and independent design. Italian fashion houses became analogous to Parisians such as the emerging Christian Dior and Balmain or the more established Lelong and Balenciaga, in that they shared: the creative purpose of producing original designs for clothes and accessories; the commercial distribution, with foreign markets as the main destination; and the organization of work, structured according to a hierarchy at the head of which stood a creator.

The Florentine Shows materialized the tendencies of their time towards the export of Italian fashion merchandise and couture in the United States. The innovation brought by the First Show of 1951, the establishment of an international attendance of buyers registered with the Second Show, plus the consequent improvements in logistics and presentation brought on by the following three Shows represented a relevant two-year span of Italian fashion history, in which the different inputs and multiple experiences finally merged. Here Giorgini's capitalization on the Renaissance as a rhetorical trope and a key theme in the celebrations and social events that accompanied the Shows condensed three different traditions: the magnificence of the historical past of Florence as an element of awe, recently revived by the circulation of news and photoshoots on the celebrations for the Holy Year; the re-enactment of historical events for the entertainment of the foreign guests, adopted and enhanced during Fascism and still quite present in the Florentine tradition of celebrations,[24] reprised with the 1948 exhibition *La casa italiana nei secoli* and the 1949 anniversary of the birth of Lorenzo de Medici;[25] and, finally, the trope of Italian creativity dating back to ancient times, a theme dear to Rosa Genoni at the outset of the twentieth century and, for different reasons, to the propaganda machine of the Fascist regime in its project for a national style.

The clash between Italian and French fashion in their competition for the US market that is found in Italian press reports during the early 1950s had an illustrious precedent at the beginning of the twentieth century, as an argument used to create a nationalist market for Italian fashion exports. The contrast was taken up again with the Italian High Fashion Shows as it served the purpose of defining Italian fashion merchandise and couture in opposition to the French, especially in the case of *moda boutique*. In fact, correspondence between Giorgini and French journalist Gilbert Graziani demonstrates that there was a willingness to cooperate, confirming that the rivalry between Italian and Parisian collection shows was largely a publicity device, while US press articles of the time that treated the quarrel as

7.3 ENIT advertisement promoting the 'new exciting' Italian couture. *Harper's Bazaar*, January 1952. Courtesy of *Harper's Bazaar*, Hearst Magazine Media, Inc. and ENIT Spa. Image published with permission of ProQuest LLC. Further reproduction is prohibited without permission

non-existent or insignificant have been overlooked in the earliest reconstructions of the Shows. The correspondence between Giorgini and the management of Aux Galeries Lafayette and Au Bon Marché shows that the French retailers supported the introduction of Italian fashion goods, and thus it was possible to promote Italy as a complementary fashion market for international buyers, much as it had happened a few years earlier with the establishment of the London couture scene, as Michelle Jones cleverly explains.[26]

As French fashion creators weighed in on the supposed battle to agree that it was largely a publicity move to revitalize the international market, *Women's Wear Daily* columnist Dorothy L. Wallis voiced a similar concern after the Second Italian High Fashion Show of July 1951.[27] The quarrelling between Italian and Parisian fashion houses, she argued, recalled the same stubbornness that American producers displayed when refusing to import French fashion again after 1945. According to Wallis, fashion professionals 'interested in new styles are going to go anywhere in the world to inspect them. Where the creative impulse throbs, there the seekers of fashion news flock. It's not necessarily a case of off with the old love-there's room for all, as in a mother's heart'. The introduction of more competition in the market of fashion ideas, according to Wallis, was a development that improved products, as stimulation caused by challenge 'has frequently brought out latent and unsuspected abilities'. Indeed, Wallis' comment can also be understood as referring to the absence of a ground for dispute. As childish as the belittling of Italian designers was, she stated, the same applied to those who exaggerated praises of something that did not deserve it. 'I hold no brief for either side,' she continued, 'but surely in the world of fashion creation we can draw on every new talent which can be cultivated'.

Indeed, as American commercial buyers initially flocked to the Shows, Italian couture designers seized the opportunity to expand their market and establish their brands in the United States. The Shows not only provided a space to present their collections, but also facilitated business deals and collaborations with American department stores and manufacturing firms. Through these partnerships, Italian fashion gained a foothold in the American market and laid the foundation for additional visibility and future success. The work of the many intermediaries had thus a significant impact, not only in terms of economic growth and international trade but also in shaping the image and identity of Italian fashion. The efforts of the many councils, the press coverage, and the resonance of the exhibitions organized after the Second World War marked the starting point of a process of transformation in the industry, as Italian fashion shifted from being an exotic handcrafted merchandise, almost souvenir-like in its connotation, to an authoritative source of inspiration and, eventually, 'a fashion system characterized by the vertical integration of production, from the fibre to the finished product'.[28] The later emergence of a new 'Italian Look' associated with the ready-to-wear industry of the late 1970s, fostered within conglomerates such as Gruppo Finanziario Tessile and Marzotto, ended up symbolizing a stylistic appearance identified as typically Italian.[29] While fashion journalist Adriana Mulassano's *I Mass Moda* traces the origins of the 'Italian Look' back to Giorgini and the Florentine Shows, outlining the developments of the Italian fashion industry's promotional circuits,[30] Silvia Giacomoni asserts that the 'Italian Look' is a phenomenon specifically born in the middle of the 1970s.

> It is thus to see why intelligent observers of fashion, such as the American publisher Fairchild, deny that there is any specific Italian Look and feel that it's a waste of time to get involved in definitions regarding the differences between what is produced in Paris, Milan, New York or Tokyo. There is only one sort of fashion, as they see it, and it's international. Good clothes are like good wines: you can judge them on the basis of their ability to stand up to transport. If Krizia sells well in Washington it's because her clothes, like those of Saint-Laurent or Issey Miyake, are completely free of limiting local features. Fairchild is doubtless right, but this doesn't detract from the interest of a study of how Italians 'lost their accent' and how what was once made in Italy is now the Italian look.[31]

Giacomoni grounds the reasons for this development, from the postwar Made in Italy fashion to the 'Italian Look', of the 1970s in observations of a sociological nature that are specifically related to Italian society. When the economic boom of the early 1960s deflated and wealth became more evenly distributed among the population, she argues, the emerging classes of Italian society did not show the yearning to identify with the upper classes of foreign countries. As the French couture collections in particular no longer met the needs of these informed customers, creating a gap that was temporarily filled by the rediscovery of vintage clothing, Giacomoni states that Italian manufacturers were quick to recognize this trend, born out of the market's inability to satisfy its national clientele, which led to the reinterpretation of clothing categories such as sportswear and knitwear that Giacomoni deems as 'foreign'.[32] While the prestige of couture declined internationally and Italian institutions failed to act accordingly, as pointed out by Ivan Paris and Lucia Savi,[33] the postwar period had already consolidated the Italian production of sportswear and knitwear created specifically to meet the demands of foreign buyers and retailers, thus laying the foundations for that 'loss of local accent' that Giacomoni speaks of and that will eventually help Italian brands move away from the equation that associated representations of Italian fashion with a transatlantic tourist gaze.

Notes

1 W. Fairchild News Service, 'Revised Dates Set For Italian Showings', *Women's Wear Daily* (15 December 1953), p. 1.

2 P. Cordera, 'Molto più di una mostra d'arte'. In *L'Italia al Lavoro. Un Lifestyle da Esportazione*, edited by Paola Cordera and Chiara Faggella (Bologna: Bologna University Press, 2023), pp. 77–84.

3 C. Faggella, '*Nutida Italiensk konst/Italiana* (1953). Popularizing Italian Fashion Through Art'. Conference *Art Exhibitions as Intersections in Post War Europe*: Stockholm, Royal Academy of Arts and Moderna Museet (May 2022).

4 I. Paris, 'Le Istituzioni Della Moda. Uno Sguardo al Caso Italiano Nel Secondo Dopoguerra'. In *La Formazione Del Sistema Moda Italiano. Industria, Istituzioni, Innocazioni e Family Business*, edited by Cinzia Capalbo. Collana Di Scienze Della Moda e Del Costume (Rome: Edizioni Nuova Cultura, 2020), pp. 19–40, 20.

5 From the author's private collection.

6 V. Pinchera, *La Moda in Italia e in Toscana: Dalle Origini Alla Globalizzazione* (Venice: Marsilio, 2009), pp. 39–43.

7 N. Fadigati, 'Giovanni Battista Giorgini, La Famiglia, Il Contributo Alla Nascita Del Made in Italy, Le Fonti Archivistiche'. *ZoneModa Journal* 8(1), 2018, p. 13.

8 'Serenas' can be translated as either serene or sunny, fair; a sundial cannot tell the time when the weather is cloudy, hence the double entendre.

9 M. Bloch, *The Historian's Craft* (Manchester: Manchester University Press, 1992), p. 59.

10 E. Merlo and M. Perugini, 'The Revival of Fashion Brands between Marketing and History: The Case of the Italian fashion company Pucci'. *Journal of Historical Research in Marketing* 7(1), 2015, p. 108.

11 V. Pouillard, 'Keeping Designs and Brands Authentic: The Resurgence of the Post-War French Fashion Business under the Challenge of US Mass Production'. In *Made in Europe: The Production of Popular Culture in the Twentieth Century*, edited by Klaus Nathaus (London: Routledge, 2015), p. 237.

12 L. Savi, *A New History of 'Made in Italy'. Fashion and Textiles in Post-War Italy* (London: Bloomsbury Publishing, 2023), pp. 86–88.

13 D. Calanca, 'Fashion in Italy (1951–1965). Consenso e Opinione Pubblica Tra Europa e Stati Uniti: Un'introduzione'. *Dimensioni e Problemi Della Ricerca Storica* 2 (2021): 121–38; D. Calanca and N. Fadigati, 'Introduction'. *ZoneModa Journal* 11(15), 2021: iii–v.

14 J.S. Nye, *Bound to Lead: The Changing Nature of American Power* (New York: Basic Books 1990).

15 D.W. Ellwood, 'Taking Soft Power Seriously: Power and Prestige in International Relations Today'. *Annals of the Fondazione Luigi Einaudi*, LV, December 2021, pp. 305–326.

16 My infinite gratitude goes to David W. Ellwood for his guidance in the framework of 'soft power' studies and his generosity in suggesting this perspective of interpretation.

17 S. Stanfill, 'G.B. Giorgini: Fashion, Florence and Diplomacy, 1950–55'. *ZoneModa Journal* 11(15), 2021, p. 29.

18 'Cortina Inverno 1949'. *Bellezza* February 1949, p. 100.

19 C. Fogu, 'Italiani Brava Gente. The Legacy of Fascist Historical Culture on Italian Politics of Memory.' In *The Politics of Memory in Postwar Europe*, edited by Richard Ned Lebow, Wulf Kansteiner, and Claudio Fogu (Durham: Duke University Press, 2006), p. 150.

20 M. Ascoli, 'Italy, an Experiment in Reconstruction'. *The Annals of the American Academy of Political and Social Science* 234 (July 1944), pp. 36–41, 38.

21 'Italian Fashions Enter World Competition With Rome Show', *New York Times* (21 July 1953), p. 20.

22 R. Arnold, *The American Look: Fashion, Sportswear and the Image of Women in 1930s and 1940s* (New York: I.B. Tauris, 2009), p. 169.

23 J. Urry, *The Tourist Gaze* (second edition) (London: Sage Publications, 2002), pp. 12–13.

24 D.M. Lasansky, *The Renaissance Perfected. Architecture, Spectacle & Tourism in Fascist Italy* (University Park: The Pennsylvania State University Press, 2004).

25 C. Baskins and S. Bottinelli, '"La Casa va Con La Città": Lorenzo the Magnificent and the Arts, 1949'. *California Italian Studies* 7(1), 2017, pp. 1–30. See also C. Faggella, 'Il Rinascimento nel dopoguerra: un fil rouge nella trama della nascente moda italiana'. *RIHA Journal of the International Association of Research Institutes in the History of Art* (forthcoming).

26 M. Jones, *London Couture and the Making of a Fashion Centre* (Cambridge: MIT Press, 2022), p. 145.

27 D.L. Wallis, 'Room for all', *Women's Wear Daily* (22 August 1951), p. 1.

28 L. Fortunati and E. Danese, *Manuale Di Comunicazione, Sociologia e Cultura Della Moda. Volume III: Il Made in Italy* (Rome: Meltemi Editore srl, 2005), p. 7.

29 E. Merlo and M. Perugini, 'Making Italian Fashion Global: Brand Building and Management at Gruppo Finanziario Tessile (1950s–1990s)'. *Business History* 62(1), 2017, pp. 1–28.

30 A. Mulassano, *I Mass Moda: Fatti e Personaggi Dell'Italian Look* (Florence: G. Spinelli & C., 1979), pp. 13–22.

31 S. Giacomoni and A. Castaldi, *The Italian Look Reflected.* (Milan: Mazzotta, 1984), pp. 9–10.

32 Giacomoni and Castaldi, *The Italian Look Reflected*, 10–11.

33 I. Paris, 'Fashion as a System: Changes in Demand as the Basis for the Establishment of the Italian Fashion System (1960–1970)'. *Enterprise and Society* 11(3), 2010, pp. 524–559, 539; Savi, *A New History of 'Made in Italy'*, 79.

Bibliography

Alhaique, Claudio. 1948. 'Problemi attuali del credito all'artigianato'. *Moneta e Credito*, 1(3): 327–33.

Alhaique, Claudio. 1950. *Le esportazioni dei prodotti artigiani e la Compagnia Nazionale Artigiana nel suo primo anno di attività*. Rome: Scuola Tipografica 'Don Luigi Guanella'.

Arnold, Rebecca. 2009. *The American Look: Fashion, Sportswear and the Image of Women in 1930s and 1940s*. New York: I.B. Tauris.

Aschengreen Piacenti, Kirsten, Stefania Ricci, and Guido Vergani, eds. 1985. *I Protagonisti Della Moda. Salvatore Ferragamo (1898–1960)*. Florence: Centro Di.

Ascoli, Max. 1944. 'Italy, an Experiment in Reconstruction'. *The Annals of the American Academy of Political and Social Science* 234 (July 1944): 36–41.

Ascoli, Max. 1949. *The Power of Freedom*. New York: Farrar, Straus and Company.

Barrese, Manuel. 2023. 'Il dialogo Roma-Stati Uniti per la promozione dell'artigianato artistico italiano'. In *L'Italia al Lavoro. Un Lifestyle da Esportazione*, edited by Paola Cordera and Chiara Faggella, 193–202. Bologna: Bologna University Press.

Baskins, Cristelle, and Silvia Bottinelli. 2017. ' "La Casa va Con La Città": Lorenzo the Magnificent and the Arts, 1949'. *California Italian Studies* 7(1): 1–30.

Battisti, Danielle. 2014. 'Italian Americans, Consumerism, and The Cold War in Transnational Perspective'. In *Making Italian America: Consumer Culture and the Production of Ethnic Identities*, edited by Simone Cinotto, 148–62. New York: Fordham University Press.

Bedarida, Raffaele. 2012. 'Operation Renaissance: Italian Art at MoMa, 1940–1949'. *Oxford Art Journal* 35(2): 147–69.

Bedarida, Raffaele. 2016. 'Export/Import: The Promotion of Contemporary Italian Art in the United States, 1935–1969' (PhD Dissertation, Graduate Center, City University of New York).

Bedarida, Raffaele. 2023. 'Ceramiche per ricostruire l'Italia: Lucio Fontana nelle mostre americane del dopoguerra'. In *L'Italia al Lavoro. Un Lifestyle da esportazione*, edited by Paola Cordera and Chiara Faggella, 107–15. Bologna: Bologna University Press.

Belfanti, Carlo Marco. 2015. 'Renaissance and "Made in Italy": Marketing Italian Fashion through History (1949–1952)'. *Journal of Modern Italian Studies* 20(1): 53–66.

Belfanti, Carlo Marco. 2015b. 'History as an Intangible Asset for the Italian Fashion Business (1950–1954)'. *Journal of Historical Research in Marketing* 7(1): 74–90.

Belfanti, Carlo Marco. 2019. *Storia culturale del Made in Italy*. Bologna: Il Mulino.

Belfanti, Carlo Marco and Elisabetta Merlo. 2016. 'Patenting Fashion: Salvatore Ferragamo Between Craftmanship and Industry'. *Investigaciones de Historia Económica – Economic History Research*, 12(2): 109–19.

Beyerle, Tulga, and Karin Hirschberger, eds. 2006. *A Century of Austrian Design 1900–2005*. Basel: Birkhäuser.

Bianchino, Gloria, and Arturo Carlo Quintavalle. 1989. *Moda Dalla Fiaba al Design: Italia 1951–1989*. Novara: DeAgostini.

Bianchino, Gloria, Grazietta Butazzi, Alessandra Mottola Molfino, and Arturo Carlo Quintavalle, eds. 1985. *Italian Fashion; the Origins of High Fashion and Knitwear*. Milan: Electa.

Blaszczyk, Regina Lee. 2000. *Imagining Consumers: Design and Innovation from Wegwood to Corning*. Baltimore: JHU Press.

Blaszczyk, Regina Lee. 2012. *The Color Revolution*. Cambridge: MIT Press.

Blaszczyk, Regina Lee. 2013. 'The Hidden Spaces of Fashion Production'. In *The Handbook of Fashion Studies*, edited by Sandy Black, Amy de la Haye, Joanne Entwistle, Agnès Rocamora, Regina A. Root and Helen Thomas, 181–97. London: Bloomsbury.

Bloch, Marc. 1992. *The Historian's Craft*. Manchester: Manchester University Press.

Bosoni, Giampiero. 2008. *Italian Design. MoMA Design Series*. New York: The Museum of Modern Art.

Brin, Irene. 2014. *L'Italia Esplode. Diario Dell'anno 1952*. Edited by Claudia Palma. Rome: Viella.

Buckley, Réka. 2014. 'Costume and Couture Italian Style: From Hollywood on the Tiber to the Italian Screen'. In *The Italian Cinema Book*, edited by Peter Bondanella, 133–41. London: BFI Palgrave.

Burckhardt, Jacob. 1937. *The Civilization of the Renaissance in Italy*. Reprint, London: Routledge, 2019.

Cagol, Stefano. 2013. 'Towards a Genealogy of the Thematic Contemporary Art Exhibition: Italian Exhibition Culture from the Mostra Della Rivoluzione Fascista (1932) to the Palazzo Grassi's Ciclo Della Vitalità (1959–1961)' (PhD Dissertation, Royal College of Art).

Calanca, Daniela. 2021. 'Fashion in Italy (1951–1965). Consenso e Opinione Pubblica Tra Europa e Stati Uniti: Un'introduzione'. *Dimensioni e Problemi Della Ricerca Storica* 2(2021): 121–38.

Calanca, Daniela. 2023. '*Italy at Work*, From Craftmanship to Fashion, 1923–1950/*Italy at Work*, dall'artigianato alla moda, 1923–1950'. In *G.B. Giorgini and the Origins of Made in Italy*, curated by Neri Fadigati, 40–54. Florence: Gruppo Editoriale.

Calanca, Daniela, and Neri Fadigati. 2021. 'Introduction'. *ZoneModa Journal* 11(15): iii–v.

Campbell, Malcolm. 1996. 'Hard Times in Baroque Florence: The Boboli Garden and the Grand Ducal Public Works Administration'. In *The Italian Garden: Art, Design and Culture*, edited by John Dixon Hunt, 160–201. Cambridge: Cambridge University Press.

Camurri, Renato. 2012. 'Introduzione. Il Liberale Gentiluomo'. In *Max Ascoli: Antifascista, Intellettuale, Giornalista*, edited by Renato Camurri, 9–24. Milan: FrancoAngeli.

Capalbo, Cinzia. 2012. *Storia Della Moda a Roma: Sarti, Culture e Stili Di Una Capitale Dal 1871 a Oggi*. Rome: Donzelli.

Caratozzolo, Vittoria Caterina. 2006. *Irene Brin: Italian Style in Fashion*. Venice: Marsilio.

Caratozzolo, Vittoria Caterina. 2011. 'Enchanted Sandals. Italian Shoes And The Post-World War II International Scene'. In *Accessorizing the Body: Habits of Being I*, edited by Cristina Giorcelli and Paula Rabinowitz, 220–36. Minneapolis: University of Minnesota Press.

Caratozzolo, Vittoria Caterina. 2014a. 'Reorienting Fashion: Italy's Wayfinding after the Second World War'. In *The Glamour of Italian Fashion Since 1945*, edited by Sonnet Stanfill, 46–57. London: V&A Publishing.

Caratozzolo, Vittoria Caterina. 2014b. '1952–1968: *L'Italia esplode*. Considerazioni sull'inedito di Irene Brin'. In Irene Brin, *L'Italia esplode. Diario dell'anno 1952*, edited by Claudia Palma, 191–208. Rome: Viella.

Caratozzolo, Vittoria Caterina, Judith Clark, and Maria Luisa Frisa (eds.). 2008. *Simonetta, La Prima Donna Della Moda Italiana*. Venice: Marsilio.

Carotti, Lisa. 2020. *Del disegno e dell'architettura: il pensiero di Carlo Ludovico Ragghianti. Analisi critica delle mostre di Wright, Le Corbusier e Aalto a Palazzo Strozzi*. Lucca: Edizioni Fondazione Ragghianti Studi sull'arte.

Carrarini, R., and M. Giordano. 2003. *Bibliografia Dei Periodici Femminili Lombardi (1786–1945)*. Milan: Lampi di stampa.

Casciato, Maristella. 2006. 'Between Craftmanship and Design: Italy at Work'. In *La Arquitectura Norteamericana, Motor y Espejo de La Arquitectura Espanola En El Arranque de La Modernidad (1940–1965)*, 9–18. Pamplona: T6 Ediciones.

Castaldo Lundén, Elizabeth. 2018. 'Oscar Night in Hollywood: Fashioning the Red-Carpet from the Roosevelt Hotel to International Media' (PhD Dissertation, Stockholm University).

Castaldo Lundén, Elizabeth. 2020. 'Exploring Fashion as Communication: The Search for a New Fashion History against the Grain'. *Popular Communication* 18(4): 249–58.

Castaldo Lundén, Elizabeth. 2021. *Fashion on the Red Carpet. A History of the Oscars®, Fashion and Globalisation*. Edinburgh: Edinburgh University Press.

Cavarocchi, Francesca, and Valeria Galimi, eds. *Firenze in Guerra, 1940–1944: Catalogo Della Mostra Storico-Documentaria*. Florence: Firenze University Press.

Chesne Dauphiné Griffo, Giuliana. 1985. 'G.B. Giorgini: The Rise of Italian Fashion'. In *Italian Fashion: The Origins of High Fashion and Knitwear*, edited by Gloria Bianchino, Grazietta Butazzi, Alessandra Mottola Molfino, and Arturo Carlo Quintavalle, 66–71. Milan: Electa.

Cirillo, Ornella. 2018. 'Fashion and Tourism in Campania in the Middle of the Twentieth Century: a Story with Many Protagonists'. In *Almatourism. Journal of Tourism, Culture and Territorial Development* 9(9): 23–46.

Cirillo, Ornella. 2012. 'Un "ambiente speciale" per la moda e il turismo: da Capri a Positano'. *ZoneModa Journal* 11(2): 91–116.

Colonna di Cesarò, Simonetta. 2008. *Una Vita al Limite*. Venice: Marsilio.

Confederazione generale dell'industria italiana. 1950. *Annuario 1950*. Rome: Studio Tipografico Failli.

Cook, Richard M. 2007. *Alfred Kazin: A Biography*. New Haven: Yale University Press.

Cooke, James J. 2009. *Chewing Gum, Candy Bars, and Beer: The Army PX in World War II*. Columbia: University of Missouri Press.

Coppedè, Giovanna. 2009. 'La Promozione Dell'artigianato Artistico Italiano Negli Stati Uniti d'America (1945–1953): Il Contributo Di Max Ascoli e Carlo Ludovico Ragghianti' (Dissertation, Università degli Studi di Pisa).

Cordera, Paola. 2022. 'L'incantesimo Della Casa. L'arte e l'industria in Vetrina'. In *Storytelling. Esperienze e Comunicazione Del Cultural Heritage*, edited by Sandra Costa, Paola Cordera, and Dominique Poulot, 221–34. Bologna: Bologna University Press.

Cordera, Paola. 2023. 'Molto più di una mostra d'arte'. In *L'Italia al Lavoro. Un Lifestyle da Esportazione*, edited by Paola Cordera and Chiara Faggella, 77–84. Bologna: Bologna University Press.

Cordera, Paola and Chiara Faggella. 2023. 'Italy at Work, un laboratorio per la modernità'. In *L'Italia al Lavoro. Un Lifestyle da Esportazione*, edited by Paola Cordera and Chiara Faggella, xvii–xxiv. Bologna: Bologna University Press.

Currie, Elizabeth. 2014. 'Knitwear'. In *The Glamour of Italian Fashion Since 1945*, edited by Sonnet Stanfill, 115–20. London: V&A Publishing.

De Buzzaccarini, Vittoria. 1985. *La Sartigianeria. L'Artigianato Dell'abbigliamento Nel Tempo*. Monza: Modart.

De Pascalis, Ilaria A. 2023. 'La Contessa Scalza e i suoi vestiti'. In *The Italian Presence in Post-War America, 1949–1972. Architecture, Design, Fashion. Volume 1, Architetture, Interni e Oggetti Nel Passaggio Attraverso l'atlantico*, edited by Marta Averna, 250–69. Transatlantic Transfers. Studi e Ricerche Interdisciplinari 1. Milan: Mimesis edizioni, 2023.

Dellapiana, Elena. 2018. 'Italy Creates. Gio Ponti, America and the Shaping of the Italian Design Image'. *Res Mobilis* 7(8): 20–48.

Di Giangirolamo, Gianluigi. 2019. *Istituzioni per La Moda. Interventi Tra Pubblico e Privato in Italia e Francia (1945–1965)*. Collana Scientifica 'Culture, Moda e Società. Milan: Pearson-Bruno Mondadori.

Dior, Christian. 1957. *Christian Dior and I*. New York: E.P. Dutton & Company.

Duffy, Ben. 1951. *Advertising Media and Markets*. Hoboken: Prentice-Hall.

Durovicová, Nataša, and Kathleen E. Newman, eds. 2009. *World Cinemas, Transnational Perspectives*. New York: Routledge.

Ellwood, David W. 1977. *L'alleato nemico. La politica dell'occupazione anglo-americana in Italia 1943/1946*. Milan: Feltrinelli.

Ellwood, David W. 1992. *Rebuilding Europe: Western Europe, America and Postwar Reconstruction*. London: Longman.

Ellwood, David W. 2021. 'Taking Soft Power Seriously: Power and Prestige in International Relations Today'. *Annals of the Fondazione Luigi Einaudi* LV (December 2021): 305–326.

Esposito, Chiarella. 1994. *America's Feeble Weapon: Funding the Marshall Plan in France and Italy, 1948–1950*. Westport: Greenwood Press.

Evans, Caroline. 2001. 'The Enchanted Spectacle'. *Fashion Theory* 5(3): 271–310.

Evans, Caroline. 2013. *The Mechanical Smile: Modernism and the First Fashion Shows in France and America, 1900–1929*. New Haven: Yale University Press.

Fadigati, Neri. 2018. 'Giovanni Battista Giorgini, La Famiglia, Il Contributo Alla Nascita Del Made in Italy, Le Fonti Archivistiche'. *ZoneModa Journal* 8(1): 1–15.

Faggella, Chiara. 2016. 'Itinerari di moda fiorentina fra il dopoguerra e la fine degli anni sessanta: dal guardaroba alla memoria storica'. In *Moda, città e immaginari*, edited by Alessandra Vaccari, 148–59. Milan: Mimesis edizioni.

Faggella, Chiara. 2019. '"Not So Simple": Reassessing 1951, G.B. Giorgini and the launch of Italian fashion' (PhD Dissertation, Stockholm University).

Faggella, Chiara. 2022. '*Nutida Italiensk konst/Italiana* (1953). Popularizing Italian Fashion Through Art'. Conference *Art Exhibitions as Intersections in Post War Europe*: Stockholm, Royal Academy of Arts and Moderna Museet, 11–12 May 2022.

Faggella, Chiara. 2023a. 'Il nuovo Rinascimento della moda italiana: Ferragamo e il dopoguerra'. In *Salvatore Ferragamo 1898–1960*, edited by Stefania Ricci, 482–89. Milan: Skira.

Faggella, Chiara. 2023b. 'Dietro Le Quinte Alla G.B. Giorgini. Le Assistant Buyers e l'esportazione Di Moda Italiana Negli Stati Uniti, 1946–1956'. In *Un Oceano Di Stile. Produzione e Consumo Di Made in Italy Negli Stati Uniti Del Dopoguerra*, edited by Simone Cinotto and Giulia Crisanti, 163–80. Milan: Mimesis edizioni.

Faggella, Chiara. 2023c. 'Prima della couture: la promozione della moda italiana in *Italy at Work*'. In *L'Italia al Lavoro. Un Lifestyle da Esportazione*, edited by Paola Cordera and Chiara Faggella, 87–96. Bologna: Bologna University Press.

Faggella, Chiara. 2024. 'Before 1951: Setting up the Network of G.B. Giorgini and the Launch of Made in Italy'. *Italian American Review* 14(1): 95–109.

Fallan, Kjetil and Grace Lees-Maffei. 2013. 'Introduction: the History of Italian Design'. In *Made in Italy: Rethinking a Century of Italian Design*, edited by Grace Lees-Maffei and Kjetil Fallan, 1–34. London: Bloomsbury Academic.

Ferragamo, Salvatore. 1957. *Shoemaker of Dreams. The autobiography of Salvatore Ferragamo*. London: George G. Harrap & Co.

Filippini, Ali. 2023. 'Paolo De Poli e l'America: 1947–1967. Gli Smalti Verso Il "Nuovo Mondo"'. In *L'Italia al Lavoro. Un Lifestyle da Esportazione*, edited by Paola Cordera and Chiara Faggella, 133–40. Bologna: Bologna University Press.

Fiorentini Capitani, Aurora. 1991. *Moda Italiana Anni Cinquanta e Sessanta*. Florence: Cantini & C.

Fiorentini Capitani, Aurora, and Stefania Ricci. 1992. 'The Winning Card of Italian Fashion'. In *The Sala Bianca: The Birth of Italian Fashion*, edited by Giannino Malossi, 91–130. Milan: Electa.

Fogu, Claudio. 2006. 'Italiani Brava Gente. The Legacy of Fascist Historical Culture on Italian Politics of Memory'. In *The Politics of Memory in Postwar Europe*, edited by Richard Ned Lebow, Wulf Kansteiner, and Claudio Fogu, 147–76. Durham: Duke University Press.

Forgacs, David, and Stephen Gundle. 2007. *Mass Culture and Italian Society from Fascism to the Cold War*. Bloomington: Indiana University Press.

Fortunati, Leopoldina and Elda Danese. 2005. *Manuale Di Comunicazione, Sociologia e Cultura Della Moda. Volume III: Il Made in Italy*. Rome: Meltemi Editore srl.

Gaddis, John Lewis. 2002. 'Causation, Contingency, and Counterfactuals'. In *Landscape of History*, 70–80. Oxford: Oxford University Press.

Gamble, Antje. 2023. *Cold War American Exhibitions of Italian Art and Design: 'Italy at Work: Her Renaissance in Design Today'*. New York: Routledge.

Gardner, Anthony, Mark Nicholls, and Anthony White. 2012. 'Cold War Cultures and Globalisation. Art and Film in Italy: 1946–1963'. *Third Text* 26(2): 205–15.

Geczy, Adam. 2013. *Fashion and Orientalism. Dress, Textiles and Culture from the 17th to the 21st Century*. London: Bloomsbury.

Genoni, Rosa. 1908. *Per Una Moda Italiana. Relazione al I° Congresso Nazionale Delle Donne Italiane in Roma*. Milan: Tipografia Ercole Balzaretti.

Giacomoni, Silvia and Alfa Castaldi. 1984. *The Italian Look Reflected*. Milan: Mazzotta.

Ginsborg, Paul. 1990. *A History of Contemporary Italy: Society and Politics, 1943–1988*. London: Penguin Books.

Giordani Aragno, Bonizza. 1985. 'The Mirror's Role in the Atelier'. In *Italian Fashion: The Origins of High Fashion and Knitwear*, edited by Gloria Bianchino, Grazietta Butazzi, Alessandra Mottola Molfino, and Arturo Carlo Quintavalle, 90–105. Milan: Electa.

Gnoli, Sofia. 2000. *La donna, l'eleganza, il fascismo: la moda italiana dalle origini all'Ente Nazionale della Moda*. Catania: Edizioni del Prisma.

Gnoli, Sofia. 2005. *Un Secolo Di Moda Italiana, 1900–2000*. Roma: Meltemi Editore srl.

Gnoli, Sofia. 2014a. *The Origins of Italian Fashion 1900–1945*. London: V&A Publishing.

Gnoli, Sofia. 2014b. 'Hollywood Sul Tevere'. In *Bellissima. L'Italia Dell'alta Moda 1945–1968*, edited by Maria Luisa Frisa, Anna Mattirolo, and Stefano Tonchi, 362–65. Milan: Electa.

Gnoli, Sofia. 2017. *Eleganza Fascista: La Moda Dagli Anni Venti Alla Fine Della Guerra*. Rome: Carocci Editore.

Gordon, Robert S.C. 2014. 'Hollywood and Italy: Industries and Fantasies'. In *The Italian Cinema Book*, edited by Peter Bondanella, 123–29. London: BFI Palgrave.

Guilbaut, Serge. 1983. *How New York Stole the Idea of Modern Art*. Chicago: University of Chicago Press.

Gundle, Stephen. 2000. 'Memory and Identity: Popular Culture in Postwar Italy'. In *Italy since 1945*, edited by Patrick McCarthy, 183–96. Oxford: Oxford University Press.

Gundle, Stephen. 2002. 'Hollywood Glamour and Mass Consumption in Postwar Italy'. *Journal of Cold War Studies* 4(3): 95–118.

Gundle, Stephen. 2008. *Glamour: A History*. Oxford: Oxford University Press.

Higson, Andrew. 1989. 'The Concept of National Cinema'. *Screen* 30(4): 36–47.

Hoyt, Eric. 2015. 'Asset or Liability? Hollywood and Tax Law'. In *Hollywood and the Law*, edited by Paul McDonald, Emily Carman, Eric Hoyt, and Philip Drake, 183–208. London: BFI Palgrave.

Inguanotto, Irina and Giuseppe Tattara. 2010. 'Innovazione, reti di comunicazione e di competenze. Elda Cecchele, Roberta di Camerino e gli artigiani della campagna veneta'. *Rivista di storia economica* 1: 93–120.

Jarvie, Ian C. 1994. 'The Postwar Economic Foreign Policy of the American Film Industry: Europe 1945–1950'. In *Hollywood in Europe: Experiences of a Cultural Hegemony*, edited by David W. Ellwood and Rob Kroes, 155–75. Amsterdam: VU University Press.

Jones, Michelle. 2022. *London Couture and the Making of a Fashion Centre*. Cambridge: MIT Press.

Lasansky, D. Medina. 2004. *The Renaissance Perfected. Architecture, Spectacle & Tourism in Fascist Italy*. University Park: The Pennsylvania State University Press.

Lombardo, Ivan Matteo. 1950. 'Prefazione', in Claudio Alhaique, *Le esportazioni dei prodotti artigiani e la Compagnia Nazionale Artigiana nel suo primo anno di attività*, 7–8. Rome: Scuola Tipografica 'Don Luigi Guanella'.

Lupano, Mario and Alessandra Vaccari. *Fashion at the Time of Fascism: Italian Modernist Lifestyle 1922–1943*. Bologna: Damiani Editore.

Malossi, Giannino, ed. 1992. *The Sala Bianca: The Birth of Italian Fashion*. Milan: Electa.

Mannes, Marya. 1971. *Out of My Time*. Garden City: Doubleday and Company.

Marcucci, Raffaella. 2004. *ANIBO e Made in Italy. Storia dei Buying Offices in Italia*. Florence: Vallecchi.

Marfella, Claudia. 2015. 'Tra Arte e Arte Applicata. Gli Artisti Alla Mostra "Italy at Work: Her Renaissance in Design Today", New York 1950'. *Annali Delle Arti e Degli Archivi* 1: 41–48.

Martin, Marcella. 2023. 'Fashion in the Art Museum: A Case Study of Salvatore Ferragamo Shoes'. In *L'Italia al Lavoro. Un Lifestyle da Esportazione*, edited by Paola Cordera and Chiara Faggella, 187–94. Bologna: Bologna University Press.

Martin, Richard and Harold Koda. 1994. *Orientalism. Visions of the East in Western Dress*. New York: The Metropolitan Museum of Art.

Martinez, Edda, and Edward A. Suchman. 1950. 'Letters From America and the 1948 Elections in Italy'. *The Public Opinion Quarterly* 14(1): 111–25.

Masuda, Minoru. 2008. *Letters from the 442nd: The World War II Correspondence of a Japanese American Medic*, edited by Hana Masuda and Dianne Bridgman. Seattle: University of Washington Press.

Merlo, Elisabetta. 2012. *Moda e Industria 1960–1980*. Biblioteca dell'economia d'azienda. Milan: EGEA.

Merlo, Elisabetta and Mario Perugini. 2015. 'The Revival of Fashion Brands between Marketing and History: The Case of the Italian Fashion Company Pucci'. *Journal of Historical Research in Marketing* 7(1): 91–112.

Merlo, Elisabetta and Mario Perugini. 2017. 'Making Italian Fashion Global: Brand Building and Management at Gruppo Finanziario Tessile (1950s–1990s)'. *Business History* 62(1): 1–28.

Merlotti, Andrea. 2013. 'I Percorsi Della Moda Made in Italy'. In *Enciclopedia Italiana Di Scienze, Lettere e Arti*, 630–40. Istituto dell'Enciclopedia italiana.

Mingardi, Lorenzo and Davide Turrini. 2021. 'Il Made in Italy come atto politico. HDI e CADMA, Max Ascoli e Carlo Ludovico Ragghianti 1945–1948'. *LUK* 27: 85–95.

Monti, Gabriele. 2014. 'Attraverso Uno Specchio Di Carta'. In *Bellissima. L'Italia Dell'alta Moda 1945–1968*, edited by Maria Luisa Frisa, Anna Mattirolo, and Stefano Tonchi, 34–39. Milan: Electa.

Monti, Gabriele. 2015. 'Are Clothes Modern? La moda secondo Bernard Rudofsky'. In *Il corpo umano sulla scena del design*, edited by Massimiliano Ciammaichella, 94–117. Padova: Il Poligrafo.

Mulassano, Adriana. 1979. *I Mass Moda: Fatti e Personaggi Dell'Italian Look*. Florence: G. Spinelli & C.

Olschki, Marcella. 1996. *Oh, America!* Palermo: Sellerio.

Pagliai, Letizia. 2007. 'Giovan Battista Giorgini: Alle Origini Del "Made in Italy". Economia e Modernizzazione Tra Fascismo e Repubblica' (PhD Dissertation, Università degli Studi di Pisa).

Pagliai, Letizia. 2011. *La Firenze Di Giovanni Battista Giorgini. Artigianato e Moda Fra Italia e Stati Uniti – Florence at the Time of Giovanni Battista Giorgini / Arts, Crafts and Fashion in Italy and the United States*. Florence: Edifir.

Palmer, Alexandra. 2001. *Couture & Commerce: The Transatlantic Fashion Trade in the 1950s*. Vancouver: UBC Press.

Palomino, Elisa. 2022. 'Indigenous Arctic Fish Skin Heritage: Sustainability, Craft and Material Innovation' (PhD Dissertation, London College of Fashion, University of the Arts London).

Paris, Ivan. 2006. *Oggetti Cuciti: L'abbigliamento Pronto in Italia Dal Primo Dopoguerra Agli Anni Settanta*. Milan: F. Angeli.

Paris, Ivan. 2010. 'Fashion as a System: Changes in Demand as the Basis for the Establishment of the Italian Fashion System (1960–1970)'. *Enterprise and Society* 11(3): 524–59.

Paris, Ivan. 2020. 'Le Istituzioni Della Moda. Uno Sguardo al Caso Italiano Nel Secondo Dopoguerra'. In *La Formazione Del Sistema Moda Italiano. Industria, Istituzioni, Innocazioni e Family Business*, edited by Cinzia Capalbo, 19–40. Collana Di Scienze Della Moda e Del Costume. Rome: Edizioni Nuova Cultura.

Paulicelli, Eugenia. 2002. 'Fashion, the Politics of Style and National Identity in Pre-Fascist and Fascist Italy'. *Gender & History* 14(3): 537–59.

Paulicelli, Eugenia. 2004. *Fashion under Fascism: Beyond the Black Shirt. Dress, Body, Culture*. Oxford: Berg.

Paulicelli, Eugenia. 2015. *Rosa Genoni, La Moda è Una Cosa Seria: Milano, Expo 1906 e La Grande Guerra*. Rome: Deleyva editore.

Pecorari, Marco. 2018. 'La Moda All'università: Una Ricostruzione Delle Prime Forme Di Studio e Ricerca in Ambito Accademico'. In *White Book. Imparare La Moda in Italia*, 76–112. Venice: Marsilio.

Pellegrino, Anna. 2012. *La Città Più Artigiana d'Italia. Firenze 1861–1929*. Studi e Ricerche Storiche. Milan: FrancoAngeli.

Pepall, Rosalind. 2006. '"Il buon design è un buon affare." La promozione del design italiano del dopoguerra in America'. In *Il Modo Italiano: Italian Design and Avant-garde in the 20th Century*, edited by Giampiero Bosoni, 78–89. Milan: Skira.

Pinchera, Valeria. 2009. *La Moda in Italia e in Toscana: Dalle Origini Alla Globalizzazione*. Venezia: Marsilio.

Pinchera, Valeria. 2011. 'I provvedimenti per la ripresa economica nel secondo dopoguerra. Promozione e sostegno della moda italiana (1945–1970)'. In *L'intervento dello Stato nell'Economia Italiana: continuità e cambiamenti (1922–1956)*, edited by Alberto Cova and Gianpiero Fumi, 485–514. Milan: FrancoAngeli.

Pisetzky, Rosita Levi. 1978. *Il Costume e La Moda Nella Società Italiana*. Torino: G. Einaudi.

Pouillard, Véronique. 2004. 'From Dressmakers to Fashion Consulting: Intermediaries in the Fashion Business (1920–1960)'. EBHA Conference, Barcelona, 16–18 September 2004.

Pouillard, Véronique. 2013. 'Keeping Designs and Brands Authentic: The Resurgence of the Post-War French Fashion Business under the Challenge of US Mass Production'. *European Review of History: Revue européenne d'histoire* 20(5): 815–35.

Pouillard, Véronique. 2015. 'Keeping Designs and Brands Authentic: The Resurgence of the Post-War French Fashion Business under the Challenge of US Mass Production'. In *Made in Europe: The Production of Popular Culture in the Twentieth Century*, edited by Klaus Nathaus, 815–35. London: Routledge.

Pouillard, Véronique. 2021. *Paris to New York. The Transatlantic Fashion Industry in the Twentieth Century*. Cambridge: Harvard University Press.

Ratti, Giuseppe. 1949. 'Esportare La Moda Italiana in America'. In *I Congresso Nazionale Della Moda: Atti Ufficiali*, edited by Camera di Commercio Industria e Agricoltura Roma, 122–27. Rome: Tipografia Ugo Pinto.

Rogers, Meyric R. 1950. *Italy at Work. Her Renaissance in Design Today*. Rome: Compagnia Nazionale Artigiana.

Rossi, Catharine. 2015. *Crafting Design in Italy: From Post-War to Postmodernism*. Manchester: Manchester University Press.

Rostagni, Cecilia. 2020. '"Bellezza" Della Vita Italiana. Moda e Costume Secondo Gio Ponti'. *La Rivista Di Engramma*, 175(September), 287–302.

Rudofsky, Bernard. 1947. *Are clothes modern? An essay on contemporary apparel*. Chicago: Paul Theobald.

Saunier, Pierre-Yves. 2013. *Transnational History*. London: Palgrave Macmillan.

Savi, Lucia. 2023. *A New History of 'Made in Italy'. Fashion and Textiles in Post-War Italy*. London: Bloomsbury Publishing.

Scarpellini, Emanuela. 2017. *La Stoffa Dell'Italia: Storia e Cultura Della Moda Dal 1945 a Oggi*. Bari: Laterza.

Scarpellini, Emanuela. 2019. *Italian Fashion since 1945: A Cultural History*. London: Palgrave Macmillan.

Schiaparelli, Elsa. 1954. *Shocking Life*. London: J.M. Dent & Sons.

Segre Reinach, Simona. 2014. 'The Italian Fashion Revolution in Milan'. In *The Glamour of Italian Fashion Since 1945*, edited by Sonnet Stanfill, 58–75. London: V&A Publishing.

Settembrini, Luigi, ed. 2001. *1951–2001 Made in Italy?* Milan: Skira.

Shandley, Robert. 2008. 'How Rome Saved Hollywood'. In *Cinematic Rome*, edited by Richard Wrigley, 53–61. Leicester: Troubadour Publishing.

Sharman, Lydia Ferrabee. 2004. 'Fashion and Refuge: The Jean Harris Salon, Montreal, 1941–1961'. In *Fashion: A Canadian Perspective*, edited by Alexandra Palmer, 270–90. Toronto: University of Toronto Press.

Soldi, Manuela. 2019. *Rosa Genoni. Moda e politica: una prospettiva femminista tra '800 e '900*. Venice: Marsilio.

Soldi, Manuela. 2021. 'Mostrare l'artigianato. L'attività espositiva dell'ENAPI'. In *Design Esposto. Mostrare La Storia / La Storia Delle Mostre. Atti Del Convegno AIS/Design 2021*, edited by Fiorella Bulegato and Maddalena Dalla Mura, 64–83. Venice: Università IUAV di Venezia.

Sparke, Penny. 1998. 'The Straw Donkey: Tourist Kitsch or Proto-Design? Craft and Design in Italy, 1945–1960'. *Design History Society* 11(1): 59–69.

Stanfill, Sonnet. 2021. 'Anonymous Tastemakers: The Role of American Buyers in Establishing an Italian Fashion Industry, 1950–55'. In *European Fashion. The Creation of a Global Industry*, edited by Regina Lee Blaszczyk and Veronique Pouillard, 146–69. Manchester: Manchester University Press.

Stanfill, Sonnet. 2021. 'G.B. Giorgini: Fashion, Florence and Diplomacy, 1950–55'. *ZoneModa Journal* 11(15): 29–40.

Stansbery Buckland, Sandra. 2020. 'The Fashion Worlds of Paris and the USA during World War Two: Competition, Contact and Business, 1939–45'. In *Paris Fashion and World War Two*, edited by Lou Taylor and Marie McLoughlin, 138–59. London: Bloomsbury Publishing.

Steele, Valerie. 1988. *Paris Fashion: A Cultural History*. Oxford: Oxford University Press.

Steele, Valerie. 1994. 'Italian Fashion and America'. In *The Italian Metamorphosis, 1943–1968*, edited by Germano Celant, 484–94. New York: Guggenheim Museum Publications.

Steinmann Curtis, Frieda. 1953. *Careers in the World of Fashion*. New York: Woman's Press.

Taiuti, Alessandra, ed. 2006. 'La "Rimessa a Foco" Dell'Italia. Il Carteggio Tra Max Ascoli e Carlo Ludovico Ragghianti (1945–1957)'. *Nuova Antologia* 141(2237): 5–45.

Taylor, Lou. 1993. 'Paris Couture, 1940–1944'. In *Chic Thrills: A Fashion Reader*, edited by Juliet Ash and Elizabeth Wilson, 127–44. Berkeley: University of California Press.

Taylor, Lou. 2002. *The Study of Dress History*. Manchester: Manchester University Press.

Taylor, Lou and Marie McLoughlin, eds. 2020. *Paris Fashion and World War Two*. London: Bloomsbury Publishing.

Taylor, Lou and Marie McLoughlin. 2020. 'The Liberation of Paris and the State of the Haute Couture Industry: Late August 1944–1946'. In *Paris Fashion and World War Two*, edited by Lou Taylor and Marie McLoughlin, 302–17. London: Bloomsbury Publishing.

Tognetti, Benedetta. 2016. 'Vittorio Giorgini Architetto (1926–2010). Un Viaggio Con La Natura: Dalla Costruzione Della Casa Esagono al Mondo Della Spaziologia' (MA Dissertation, Università degli Studi di Pisa).

Tonelli, Maria Cristina. 2023. 'Italia e Stati Uniti, 1948–1954: un percorso di opportunità'. In *L'Italia al Lavoro. Un Lifestyle da Esportazione*, edited by Paola Cordera and Chiara Faggella, 21–28. Bologna: Bologna University Press.

Tosh, John. 2013. *The Pursuit of History*. London: Routledge.

Tosi Brandi, Elisa. 2009. *Artisti Del Quotidiano: Sarti e Sartorie Storiche in Emilia-Romagna*. Bologna: CLUEB.

Tregenza, Liz. 2023. *Wholesale couture. London and beyond, 1930–1970*. London: Bloomsbury Publishing.

Troy, Nancy. 2003. *Couture Culture: A Study in Modern Art and Fashion*. Cambridge: MIT Press.

Urry, John. 2002. *The Tourist Gaze* (second edition). London: Sage Publications.

Vaccari, Alessandra. 2022. *Indossare la trasformazione. Moda e modernismo in Italia*. Venice: Marsilio.

Van Cassel, Elke. 2007. 'A Cold War Magazine of Causes: A Critical History of The Reporter, 1949–1968' (PhD Dissertation, Radboud University, Nijmegen).

Van Riper, A. Bowdoin. 2004. *Imagining Flight: Aviation and Popular Culture*. College Station: Texas A&M University Press.

Veillon, Dominique. 2020. 'The Impact of Shortages on Couture Fashion Accessories in Paris'. In *Paris Fashion and World War Two*, edited by Lou Taylor and Marie McLoughlin, 76–95. London: Bloomsbury Publishing.

Vergani, Guido. 1992. 'The Sala Bianca: The Birth of Italian Fashion'. In *The Sala Bianca: The Birth of Italian Fashion*, edited by Giannino Malossi, 23–87. Milan: Electa.

Vergani, Guido. 2001. 'February 1951. Italian Fashion Is Born. Not Even Mussolini Succeeded in Accomplishing as Much'. In *1951–2001: Made in Italy?*, edited by Luigi Settembrini, 130–41. Milan: Skira.

Votolato, Gregory. 2010. 'Nice Threads: Identity and Utility in American Fashion'. In *The Fashion History Reader*, edited by Giorgio Riello and Peter McNeil, 478–91. Abingdon: Routledge.

Wall, Wendy L. 2008. *Inventing the "American Way": The Politics of Consensus from the New Deal to the Civil Rights Movement*. Oxford: Oxford University Press.

White, Nicola. 2000. *Reconstructing Italian Fashion: America and the Development of the Italian Fashion Industry*. Oxford: Berg.

Zanon, Johanna. 2017. 'The 'Sleeping Beauties' of Haute Couture: Jean Patou, Elsa Schiaparelli, Madeleine Vionnet' (PhD Dissertation, University of Oslo).

Index

Alexander, Ramy 66, 81, 98, 100
Alfieri, Dino 189, 203
American Relief for Italy 39
aristocracy 17, 18–20, 21, 23, 24, 25,
    27–28, 29, 32, 96, 103, 142,
    183, 184
Arnold, Rebecca 176, 204
Art Institute of Chicago 100, 116, 118,
    119
Artigianato Produzione ed
    Esportazione Milano (APEM) 98,
    99
Ascoli, Marion 42, 53
Ascoli, Max 8, 26, 28, 37, 39–40, 42,
    43, 47, 48, 61, 67, 69, 70, 79, 81,
    88, 98, 118, 180, 202, 204
    The Power of Freedom 26, 41
Associazione Nazionale Produzione
    Artistica Abbigliamento 133,
    137, 157
Avedon, Richard 54, 154

Baskins, Cristelle 180
Bedarida, Raffaele 41
Belfanti, Carlo Marco 176
Bennett, Isadora 103, 108
Bergman, Ingrid 103
Biennale di Monza 83
Bissinger, Karl 103

Blaszczyk, Regina Lee 5, 9
Bloch, Marc 4, 7, 128, 200
    The Historian's Craft 4
Blow, Richard 24
Bordoni, Enrico 52
Bottinelli, Silvia 180
Boucher, François 140
Brooklyn Museum 53, 100, 103, 110
    Murphy, Michelle 115
Burckhardt, Jacob 176
buyers 11, 84, 168, 169, 173, 185,
    199, 208
    Dinsmore, Gertrude 43, 46, 47, 48,
        69, 98, 146
    Frankau, Ethel 14, 164, 168,
        170, 187
    Hanania, Stella 164
    Meison, Violet 114, 164
    Millas, John 149, 150, 152
    Roberts, Ann 45, 46, 98, 165
    Tedesco, Odette 164
    Trissell, Julia 152, 164
    Ziminsky, Gertrude 164
buying offices 40, 70, 78, 79, 88, 164
    competition with CADMA and HDI
        79, 88, 99
    Gimbels 71, 77, 79, 149
    Ricci, Mario 153, 161
    Roditi & Sons 88

Camera Nazionale della Moda 139
Capalbo, Cinzia 153
Caratozzolo, Vittoria Caterina 32, 52
Carnegie, Hattie 29, 54
Carocci Vedres, Eva 54, 101
Castaldo Lundén, Elizabeth 8, 144
Cecchele, Elda 111, 125
Centro di Firenze per la Moda Italiana
        116, 190
Centro Internazionale delle Arti e del
        Costume (CIAC) 140
Centro Italiano della Moda di Milano
        (CIMM) 6, 114, 115, 139–42,
        147, 156, 166, 171, 188, 189,
        190, 202, 206
    fashion show in Rome 141
Chambre Syndicale de la Couture
        Parisienne 11, 13, 130, 133, 178
Checchi, Vincent 44
Christian, Linda 142, 145, 147
Cialfi, Carmine 137, 140, 189, 203
Cirillo, Ornella 40, 102, 156
Clerici, Fabrizio 52
Cochrane Dunn, Cynthia 146
Coffin, Clifford 24, 25, 27, 60, 72, 145
Cole, Martin 165, 170
Collobi Ragghianti, Licia 68
Comitato Assistenza Distribuzione
        Materiali Artigianato (CADMA)
        5, 39, 42–45, 48, 53, 54–55, 61,
        62, 67, 71, 79, 98, 118, 203
    dissolution 80, 81
Comitato della Moda 137, 139
commissionaire 82, 93
Communism 38, 61
    fear of 7, 38,.42, 121, 180, 202
    Italian Communist Party (PCI) 38
Compagnia Nazionale Artigiana (CNA)
        60, 61, 70, 82, 98, 99, 117, 161
Corti, Mita 30–31
couture en gros 149, 206
Crespi, Consuelo 103
Croce, Benedetto 41

d'Harnoncourt, René 42, 100
De Gaspari, Carlo 133, 137
De Gasperi, Alcide 38
De Pascalis, Ilaria A. 145
del Corso, Gaspero 131
Dellapiana, Elena 53, 196
department stores

Au Bon Marché 197, 208
Aux Galeries Lafayette 188, 208
B. Altman 14, 88, 89, 114, 163,
        164, 205
    Keillor, James A. 14, 89, 114, 164
Bergdorf Goodman 14, 28, 29, 30,
        152, 164, 187
Bloomingdale's 98
Carson Pirie & Scott 163
fashion shows in store 114, 115,
        167, 168
Fortnum and Mason 72
Halle Brothers Co. 89
Henry Morgan's 89, 205
I. Magnin 164, 168, 175
    Carpenter, Russel 175
J.L. Hudson 149–52, 175, 206
La Rinascente 98
Lord & Taylor 164
Marshall Fields 153, 161
May's 149, 150
Neiman Marcus 12, 74, 77
Saks 164, 168
Saks Fifth Avenue 22, 72, 73
Sears, Roebuck & Co 42
The White House 109
di Frassineto, Marinetta 97
di Giardinelli, Gabriella 17, 19
Diamond, Freda 42, 43, 46, 47, 69
Dior, Christian 73, 74, 148, 192,
        206, 208
Donzé, Pierre-Yves 9
Dunn, James Clement 113, 146, 202

Economic Cooperation Administration
        (ECA) 38, 39, 45, 98, 113
Edizioni Moda Società Anonima
        (EMSA) 130, 131
Ellwood, David W. 38, 202, 211
Ente Italiano della Moda (EIM) 5, 132,
        133, 134, 137, 138, 139, 153,
        171, 188, 189, 190
    Mazzonis, Ernesto 137
Ente Nazionale Italiano per il Turismo
        (ENIT) 206
Ente Nazionale per l'Artigianato e
        le Piccole Industrie (ENAPI)
        82, 83, 87
European Recovery Program (ERP) 8,
        38, 39, 122
Evans, Caroline 167

exhibitions
  Are Clothes Modern? 21
  Esposizione Internazionale dell'Arte Tessile e dell'Abbigliamento 137, 138
  Handicraft as a Fine Art in Italy 52, 68
  Italian Artisans Exposition 119
  Kultur und Mode 148
  La casa italiana nei secoli 68, 207
  La Sala Bianca 8, 192
  Mostra Nazionale Arte Moda 133–37
  The Italian Metamorphosis 8
  Twentieth Century Italian Art 41
  Vita all'Aperto 68
Export-Import Bank 99

fabrics and fibers 136, 151, 178
  Bemberg 137
  Bevilacqua 103
  Cerruti 166
  cotton 101, 137
  De Angeli Frua 98
  DuPont 89
  fleece 176
  Gavazzi 139
  linen 47
  Marzotto 139
  organdy 47
  Rosasco 139
  Rossi 139
  silk 45–46, 47, 148, 151, 176
  Terragni 89, 91, 137, 158
    Orsi, Domenico 89, 91
  Tiziano 139
  tweed 151, 165, 176, 204
  Visconti di Modrone 148
  wool 47, 151, 154, 204
Fadigati, Giovanni Maria 89
fascism 4–5, 26, 41, 43, 57, 70, 77, 88, 132, 166, 204
  colonial past of Italy 103
  Ente Nazionale della Moda (ENM) 5, 28, 129, 130, 131, 132–33
  Italian Social Republic (RSI) 131, 132
  Ministry of Popular Culture 189
Fashion Group 13, 30, 47, 76, 115, 165
Fiorentini, Aurora 184
Foà, Bruno 42, 44, 69, 81

Fogu, Claudio 203
Fondazione Ferragamo 71, 72, 111
footwear 21
  'Bernardo sandals' 21
  Ferragamo 71, 125
    'calfskin boot' 72
    'Cortina' 73
    'Invisible' 73, 108
    'Mercury' 108
    'Moorish' 72
    'Ninfea' 73
    'Valle' 108
  Julianelli 21
  sandals 15, 17, 20, 21, 23, 25, 51
Forgacs, David 145
Fornasetti, Piero 52, 54–55, 119
Fortuny 86
Freudenthal, David 98

Genoni, Rosa 182, 207
Gerli, Paolino 42
Gimbel, Adam 47, 168
Giordani Aragno, Bonizza 167
Giordano delle Lanze, Filippo Alberto 136
Giorgini Fadigati, Graziella 89
Giorgini, Carlo 89
Giorgini, Giovanni Battista 1, 6, 10, 58, 67, 116, 137, 140, 143, 153, 162–92
  Allied Gift Shop 85, 86–88, 181, 205
  archive 82, 91, 119, 163, 185, 187, 188, 193, 200, 205, 206
  G.B. Giorgini commissionaire firm 22, 62, 82, 168, 185, 190, 197, 199, 201
    Franca (Giorgini's assistant) 89
  Le Tre Stanze 83, 84, 85, 118, 181, 205
  Paris showroom 83, 84, 85, 87
  role in *Italy at Work* 98, 113–16, 117, 118, 119, 147, 200, 206
  VeroGlacia icecream parlor 84
Giorgini, Matilde 3, 87, 200
Giorgini, Nella 84
Giorgini, Vittorio 84
Gnoli, Sofia 5, 16, 19, 170
Gordon, Robert S.C. 144
Greco, Emanuele 92
Guilbaut, Serge 39

Gundle, Stephen 27, 145, 195
Guttuso, Renato 52

Hagmayer, Albert C. 119
Handicraft Development, Inc. (HDI) 5,
    28, 37, 39, 40, 54, 61, 72, 79, 88,
    98, 118, 163, 165, 179, 203
Haus der Kunst Museum, Münich 148
Higson, Andrew 7
'Hollywood on the Tiber' 142, 144–47
Holy Year 142–44, 177, 178, 207
House of Italian Handicrafts (HIH) 5,
    14, 47, 48, 52, 54, 59, 76, 83,
    98, 99, 118, 203
  Christman Gift Exhibition 80
  fashion exhibition 53, 80
  Handicraft as a Fine Art in Italy 68
  Piazza (shop) 60
  Vita all'Aperto 68
Hubs, Ben 9

Inguanotto, Irina 111
Italian accessory makers 148
  Aloisi De Reutern, Luciana 20, 54,
    97, 101, 132
  Barra of Italy 49, 51, 65, 143
  Bruzzichelli, Aldo 21
  Cattaneo, Leli 60
  Coen, Giuliana (Giuliana Camerino)
    97, 111
  Corallo 22
  Ferragamo 25, 44, 54, 60, 70, 71,
    108–11, 148, 164, 192
  Frattegiani 54, 108
  Gucci 25, 60, 72, 97, 108
  Ivancich, Emma 101
  Paoli, Emilio 108
Italian Art Museum of Lima 68
Italian dressmakers 113, 142, 152,
    167, 208
  Aiazzi Fantechi, Adele 115
  as 'copyists' 16, 115, 166, 175
  Biki 115, 139, 143, 149
  Capucci, Roberto 1–2, 18, 129
  Caraceni 30, 137
  Carosa 114, 137, 140, 165
  Cerri, Adriana 140
  De Gaspari Zezza 133, 137
  Fabiani, Alberto 96, 197
  Fercioni 139, 141, 152

Ferrario 131
Gabriellasport 16, 19–20, 28,
    29, 167
Galitzine, Irene 20, 115, 167
Gattinoni, Fernanda 96, 115
Genoni, Rosa 57, 178, 179
La Boutique 147
Longo e Comollo 166
Marianna 115
Marucelli, Germana 140, 147, 148,
    153, 154, 166
Modelli, Rina 115
Montorsi 137
Noberasco 139, 149, 152, 153, 166,
    176
Pucci, Emilio 164, 176, 200
San Lorenzo 166
Schuberth, Emilio 114, 147, 165,
    166, 167, 204
Sorelle Chiostri 138
Sorelle Fontana 96, 114, 137, 140,
    145–47, 148, 165, 166,
    167, 170
  American clients 145, 147
Tizzoni 16, 139, 152
Vanna 115, 130, 139, 149, 152, 166
Veneziani, Jole 139, 166
Ventura 19, 139, 149
Villa 115, 164
Visconti, Simonetta 30, 34, 114, 116,
    129, 147, 148, 152, 166, 170,
    171, 174, 176, 197
Italian fashion
  'invisible exports' 83, 86, 147
  'Italian Look' 8, 22, 27, 29, 30, 96,
    97, 103, 112, 116, 140, 149, 154,
    162, 175, 176, 192, 202, 209
  as 'couture' 6, 97, 101, 112, 114,
    115, 116, 132, 134, 137, 138,
    140, 145, 147, 148, 149, 150,
    152, 153, 154, 162, 163, 166,
    167, 182, 184, 206
  as handicraft 20, 39–40, 47, 59, 74,
    122, 179, 208
  foundation myth of 2–4, 91, 122,
    128, 129, 182, 184, 186, 191,
    192, 199, 200
  independence from France 6, 16, 32,
    114, 134, 145, 163, 166, 171,
    173, 176, 202

intermediaries 4, 5, 6, 37, 48, 71, 78,
    98, 121, 128, 133, 147, 156, 166,
    169, 188, 200, 203, 206, 208
knitwear 154, 176, 204, 209
moda boutique 6, 24, 97, 102, 155,
    162, 175, 202, 204, 207
recognition 6, 16, 61, 62, 91, 97,
    101, 116, 122, 154
rivalry with Paris fashion 162, 184,
    185, 186, 192, 207, 208
transformability 104, 106, 204
under Fascism 5, 16, 106, 129, 132,
    189, 207
Italian Fashion Service 171, 172, 188,
    189, 190
Italian High Fashion Shows 153,
    162–92, 204
1st edition 1, 2, 62, 116, 147, 153,
    163, 170, 171, 174, 175, 176,
    181
2nd edition 118, 168, 171, 185, 186,
    190, 196, 208
3rd edition 172, 186, 188, 191, 197
4th edition 173, 182, 186
5th edition 183, 197
disagreements 171, 172, 173, 186,
    188, 189, 190, 191, 197, 199
fees 173, 186, 187
Sala Bianca, Palazzo Pitti 8, 168, 182
significance 67, 205, 206, 208
value for money 186–87, 191
Italian knitwear 156
Adriana 156
Aponte, Laura 155
Mirsa 154, 156, 176
Italy at Work 6, 41, 52, 53, 56, 58, 60, 68,
    70, 91, 96, 161, 181, 199, 204
failed fashion show 112, 113–16,
    163, 181, 182
publicity 108
relevance for Italian fashion 97,
    101–12, 120, 122, 140, 163

Jones, Michelle 208
journalists 170
Armani, Misia 3, 170, 172
Ballard, Bettina 17, 20, 22, 24, 25,
    59, 170, 171, 204
Bartolomei Corsi, Sandra 170
Brin, Irene 96–97, 131, 140, 172, 173

Cattaneo, Margherita 2
Giacomoni, Silvia 209, 210
Giordano, Antonio 152
Graziani, Gilbert 185, 186, 187, 188,
    190, 191, 207
Hammond, Fay 183
Hofmann, Paul 143, 144
Keene, Frances 22, 32, 166, 179,
    204
Kirkland, Sally 171
Kuster Rosselli, Emilia 182
Mannes, Marya 24–26, 28, 29, 56,
    59, 72, 166, 179, 180, 204
Massai, Elisa Vittoria 152, 170,
    171, 176
Mead, Anis 15–18, *See* Ballard,
    Bettina
Mulassano, Adriana 209
Perkins, Alice B. 115, 153
Perkins, Bertram J. 191
Ratti, Giuseppe 116, 138, 154, 158,
    163, 175
Robiola, Elsa 18, 130, 131, 140, 155,
    170, 188, 189
Rossi Lodomez, Vera 3, 148,
    170, 172
Snow, Carmel 13, 172, 192
Testa, Michelangelo 131
Vanner, Anna 135
Vergani, Guido 192
Vitti, Gemma 170
Wallis, Dorothy L. 208

Kaufmann, Arthur 149

La Guardia, Fiorello 12, 69
Langley Moore, Doris 140
Lasansky, D. Medina 57
Laver, James 140
Lombardo, Ivan Matteo 98, 100, 132,
    138, 203
Lupano, Mario 5, 20

M.H. de Young Memorial Museum 108,
    109
Marcus, Stanley 12, 13, 76
Marinotti, Franco 139, 141
Martin, Marcella 125
Masuda, Minoru 86
McNeil, Elsie 86

Mediterranean 21, 53, 102, 108, 156
Merlo, Elisabetta 9
Metropolitan Museum of Art, New York
    Costume Institute 103, 108, 111
Ministry of Finance 44
Ministry of Foreign Commerce 71,
    98, 199
Ministry of Industry and Commerce 44,
    100, 132, 138
Ministry of Industry and Foreign
    Commerce 190
Monti, Gabriele 21
Mower, Jennifer M. 12
Museo Salvatore Ferragamo 71
Museum of Modern Art, New York 21,
    22, 41, 42, 100
Myricae 101, 103

Nagel, Charles 100, 113, 114, 121
Neiman Marcus Award for
    Distinguished Service in the
    Field of Fashion 74, 115, 192
Nivola, Costantino 53
novelty textiles 54
    Bronzini, Gegia 97
    Cheti, Fede 54
    Kowaliska, Irene 101
    Marandino, Dianora 103
    Tessitura di Rovezzano 97

Occupation
    of France 11, 13, 16
    of Italy 19, 27, 97, 129, 132

Pagliai, Letizia 94, 126
Pallavicini, Federico 130, 146
Paris, Ivan 148, 170, 209
Pasqui, Ferruccio 54
Paulicelli, Eugenia 5, 16
Pavolini, Alessandro 43
Pellegrino, Anna 43
Pinchera, Valeria 190
Pitti Immagine 1, 116
Pleasant, Richard 103, 108, 113
Polese, Francesca 9
Ponti, Gio 21, 56, 99, 117, 130,
    131, 134
Ponti, Lisa 102
Pouillard, Véronique 9, 13, 114
Power, Tyrone 145, 178

Prince of Foxes (1949 film) 145, 146, 178
publications 14
    'advanced trade editions' 59
    Bellezza 2, 5, 15, 16, 25, 28, 111,
        130–32, 134, 140, 141, 174, 176,
        182, 203, 204
    Chicago Tribune 119
    Christian Science Monitor 118
    Cinémonde 103
    Commercio d'Italia, Il 139
    Detroit Free Press 151
    Domus 21, 102
    Flair 103
    Harper's Bazaar 13, 22, 27, 54, 59,
        96, 103, 132, 155, 168, 204
    House & Garden 56
    I Tessili Nuovi 166
    Interiors 119
    Life 85, 145, 171
    Los Angeles Times 183
    New York Times 53, 60, 99, 107,
        142, 192
    New Yorker 51
    Nuova Stampa, La 134, 137
    Paris Match 185, 186, 190, 191
    Vogue 15, 16, 17, 20, 27, 29, 30, 54,
        59, 72, 145, 152, 170, 171, 204
    Vogue (British) 24, 72
    Women's Wear Daily 3, 14, 16, 22,
        39, 40, 45, 54, 60, 79, 84, 88,
        113, 115, 118, 135, 138, 139,
        140, 147, 148, 149, 152, 153,
        164, 171, 173, 176, 177, 187,
        189, 190, 191, 199, 208

quality 47, 48, 61, 80, 187
    of Italian exports 46, 47, 83
Quintavalle, Arturo Carlo 2, 205

Radkai, Karen 96–97
Ragghianti, Carlo Ludovico 43, 47, 60,
    61, 67, 68, 70, 180, 203
Renaissance 5, 41, 57, 113, 140,
    176, 206
Ricci, Stefania 71, 184
Rich, Daniel C. 100
Rogers, Meyric R. 100, 108, 111, 113,
    114, 117, 119, 122, 205
Rosenberg, Anna 42, 47, 53
Rossi, Catharine 60

Rossini, Vladimiro 132, 148, 153, 189, 190, 203
Rudofsky, Bernard 20, 21

Saunier, Pierre-Yves 7, 201
Savi, Lucia 46, 115, 124, 133, 209
Scarpellini, Emanuela 148
Schiaparelli, Elsa 86, 168, 192, 208
Schloss commissionaire firm 83, 84, 164, 167
Schloss, Lucien 84
Segre Reinach, Simona 48
Semmelhack, Elizabeth 20, 22
Sforza, Carlo 22, 203
Shaver, Dorothy 14, 47, 204
Simonetto, Marzio 166
simplicity 12, 15, 17, 22, 23, 32, 97, 138, 154, 155, 186, 204
   lack of 173–75
Simpson, Adele 89, 90, 205
Simpson, Wesley 89
Sindacato Italiano Alta Moda 199
Skillen, Sara 33–34
SNIA Viscosa 28, 139, 141, 166
   fiocco 16
   rayon 140
Snow, Carmel 171
Soldi, Manuela 83
Spalletti, Sandra 29–30
Sparke, Penny 97, 121
specialty shops 164
Stanfill, Sonnet 168, 202
Steele, Valerie 8, 11, 61, 122

Taiuti, Alessandra 68
Tamagna, Frank M. 42
taste 69, 81
   of American consumers 11, 22, 37, 53, 61, 71, 80, 96, 112, 115, 121,
138, 140, 147, 150, 174, 175, 176, 187, 204
   of Italian women 24, 29, 30, 32
   tastemakers 5, 42, 45, 70, 80, 81, 154, 164, 168, 175, 185, 204
Taylor, Lou 40
Taylor, Myron C. 39
Teague, Walter Dorwin 100, 181
Tessitrice dell'Isola 97, 103, 107, 176
Textile Color Card Association 84
Tonelli, Maria Cristina 119
tourist gaze 53, 205, 209
transnational history 4, 7, 9
Triennale di Milano 83, 100
Troy, Hannah 165, 174

United Nations Relief and Rehabilitation Administration (UNRRA) 44

Vaccari, Alessandra 5, 20, 105
Vacirca, Silvia 130
Valstar 172
Vannini Parenti, Mario 43, 44, 45, 46, 48, 61, 62, 68–71, 81, 88, 190, 203, 204
   relationship with Ferragamo 71, 72
Veillon, Dominique 11
Venice Film Festival 114, 140
   fashion show 140, 202, 206

Walker, Hélène 42
Watson & Boaler 118, 119
Westinghouse Electric Corporation, import division 44, 45–46

Zuffi, Piero 140

Printed in the USA
CPSIA information can be obtained
at www.ICGtesting.com
JSHW051954251024
72425JS00005B/52

9 781526 155245